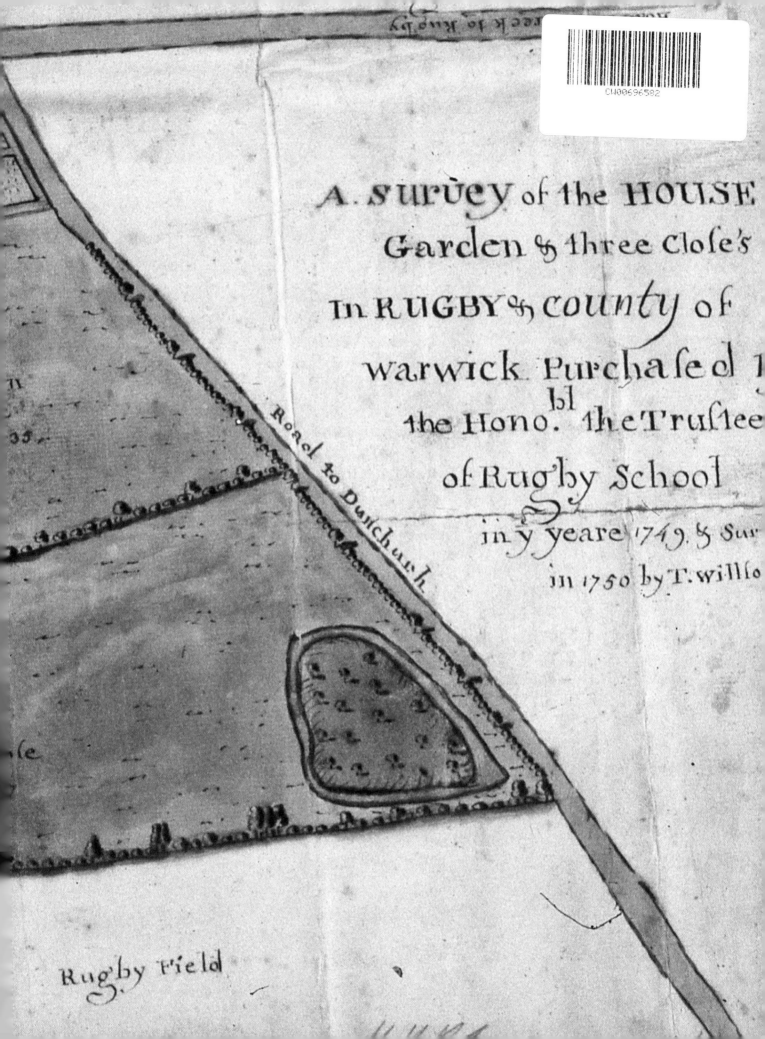

A. Survey of the HOUSE

Garden & three Close's

In RUGBY & county of

warwick. Purchased 1

by

the Hono. the Trustee

of Rugby School

in y yeare 1749. & Sur

in 1750 by T. willſo

Road to Dunchurch

Rugby Field

from
ELIZABETH
to
ELIZABETH

EDITED BY ROBIN FLETCHER

First published in 2016 by Mercer Books

www.mercerbooks.co.uk

ISBN 978-0-9935733-1-6

Copyright © Rugby School 2016

Creative Director – Tim Mercer
Design – Reuben Wakeman
Picture research – Katie Morriss

Printed in the UK by Emtone Printing Services Limited, Bath

Image credits
Tim Mercer, Getty Images, iStock by Getty Image, Shutterstock, National Portrait Gallery, Alamy,
Look & Learn History Picture Library and the Arthur Ransome Literary Estate. Rugby building illustrations by Samantha Cope

CONTENTS

EDITOR'S NOTE

from Elizabeth to Elizabeth is not a definitive or comprehensive history of Rugby School or of significant world events since 1567. Judgements of what to include or exclude have therefore had to be made, some of which may spark debate or raise eyebrows. Satisfying every reader is clearly an impossible task, but on balance it is hoped those with an interest in the School and the wider world over the past four and a half centuries will find the book interesting and informative.

Given Rugby's historic contribution to team sport, it is appropriate the book has involved a wide range of contributors. Readers will find pieces written by guest contributors shown by their initials at the end of articles, with all other pieces written by the editor.

A wide range of print and digital sources have been used to help research this book. In particular we have naturally referenced previous books on the School including GD Rowse's *A History of Rugby School*, JD Hope Simpson's *Rugby Since Arnold* and Catherine Walston's *With A Fine Disregard*.

Profound gratitude goes to all who have contributed to *from Elizabeth to Elizabeth* in whatever way. Inevitably there will be those whose individual contribution has been inadvertently overlooked, for which sincere apologies. In alphabetical order, however, heartfelt thanks to those listed below for playing their part.

Finally, while every effort has been made to ensure accuracy (particularly the dates of Rugbeians who attended the School) some error is unavoidable. We apologise, therefore, for any mistakes that have crept into this book and hope they do not detract from the enjoyment of readers.

Robin Fletcher (K 79-84), Editor, November 2016

Lizzie Beesley, staff, English department, on playwright Polly Stenham
Peter Berners-Price (St 56-61), former President of the Rugbeian Society
Angus Crichton-Miller (SF 53-58), on Sir Ralph Abercromby
Michael Fowle (St 53-58), former Chairman of Governors, on the School's foundation and governance, and Frederick Temple
Peter Green, Head Master, for an article on the current ethos and the future vision of the School
David Hempsall, former Head of History, for around 40 world history articles
Lucinda Holmes, Chair of Governors, for the 'At the Forefront'
David Howe, Vice Chairman of Governors at Lawrence Sheriff School, on that school and the Percival Guildhouse
Rusty Maclean, School archivist, on the School's buildings
Ian Newton, on Crescent House and Geoff Foxcroft
Denise Osborne, for research and distribution
David Ray, staff (1978-09), on William Webb Ellis and Rugbeians in the two world wars
Roger Ringrose (SH 79-85), actor, on William Macready, David Croft and Anthony Quayle
Sir Hew Strachan, (K 63-37), former Governor, historian, for the Foreword
Rt Revd. David Urquhart (K 65-70), Governor, Bishop of Birmingham, on Frederick and William Temple
Kerry Wilson, School's Director of Development, on the Arnold Foundation.

FOREWORD

Schools – and especially boarding schools – are self-contained communities. It requires a major event to punctuate the rhythms of their daily routines. When I was at Rugby, with no access even to a telephone let alone the internet, newspapers and transistor radios were the principal means to link school life to the wider world. In 1963 the news of J.F. Kennedy's assassination broke during prep, when all radios should have been switched off. Otherwise the even tenor of our existences was broken only by rugby internationals (the moment when televisions were wheeled over from the private side of the house) or by another crisis in the Rolling Stones' relationship with the law.

from Elizabeth to Elizabeth portrays two parallel universes: the life of a great British public school and the epoch-making events of a wider world which in the short term barely impinged on it. The separation is remarkable because Rugby had become a 'national' school by the late eighteenth century. Ralph Abercromby, to die a hero in 1801 on the battlefield of Alexandria, travelled to Warwickshire from Clackmannanshire, and parents, dubbed 'sojourners', had begun to move to Rugby specifically to exploit Lawrence Sheriff's benefaction for their sons' education. The town's advantageous position from the mid-nineteenth century, in the centre of a country linked by a national railway network, consolidated a reputation rather than enabled it.

Schools naturally take pride in their former pupils who go on to achieve great things. The evidence of this book shows that Rugby has produced many stars such as the poets Walter Savage Landor and Arthur Hugh Clough. The latter bore the influence of Thomas Arnold throughout his life. The former was so at odds with his Head Master that he was expelled. Not all Rugby's successes have been as enamoured of the school as it is now proud of them.

This is to miss the point, both of the book and of the School itself. Many luminaries who have exercised the privilege of walking across The Close, Heads of School or Captains of the XV, have never hit the national headlines, however worthy their subsequent lives. For a school of its standing, size and longevity, Rugby has in some respects under-performed: only one Prime Minister in 450 years, and his reputation was savaged by an Old Harrovian. The test of a good school is less how it teaches its best pupils, or how many national or international leaders it produces, but what it does for its middle, for the bulk of its output.

This is where Rugby can stand tall, in its contributions to business, industry and the professions, to the clergy, to medicine, to accountancy, to teaching itself. In George Eliot's greatest novel, *Middlemarch*, its heroine, Dorothea, finally finds happiness by marrying Will Ladislaw. Will has been working for a Midlands newspaper: he is free of class, a man of honour, decency and humanity. In a fiction full of fundamental truths so acutely observed, it is striking that he is also a Rugbeian.

Sir Hew Strachan (K 63-67)

SYMBOLS THROUGHOUT THE BOOK

RUGBY SCHOOL EVENT HEADINGS IN BLUE

DENOTES RUGBY SCHOOL HEAD MASTER
DENOTES RUGBEIAN

WORLD EVENT HEADINGS IN RED

DENOTES A UK MONARCH
DENOTES A UK PRIME MINISTER
DENOTES A US PRESIDENT

1567

FROM THIS POINT,
THE WHOLE PERSON,
IS THE WHOLE POINT

1567-1640
THE GROCER'S DREAM

1567 LAWRENCE SHERIFF DIES,
RUGBY SCHOOL FOUNDED
THE FIRST 'SCHOOL HOUSE'

1567 MARY, QUEEN OF SCOTS,
ELIZABETH I AND JAMES VI
ALL THE WORLD'S A STAGE

1574 FIRST HEADS
EDWARD ROLSTON BECOMES HEAD

1580 RICHARD SEALE BECOMES HEAD

1581 TRUSTEES
NICHOLAS GREENHILL BECOMES HEAD

1588 SPANISH ARMADA

1600 CHARLES I BORN

1602 AUGUSTINE ROLFE BECOMES HEAD

1605 GUY FAWKES

1625 WILGENT GREENE BECOMES HEAD

1630 CHARLES II BORN

MARY, QUEEN OF SCOTS, ELIZABETH I AND JAMES VI

While Lawrence Sheriff's legacy was founding a new school, 350 miles north in the heart of Scotland a one-year-old boy was busy becoming a king.

The boy was called James, son of Mary, Queen of Scots.

Mary, who ascended her throne in 1542 at an even earlier age (six days) than her son, was raised across the Channel and married the man who in 1559 became King Francis II of France for just one year before his death.

Widowed Mary returned to rule Scotland and in 1565 married her English cousin Lord Darnley to press her claim to succeed Elizabeth I, her first cousin once removed, as ruler south of Hadrian's Wall.

When Darnley died mysteriously in an accident two years later, fingers pointed at Mary's lover, the Earl of Bothwell.

Bothwell was cleared of culpability but, following an uprising against the couple, he and Mary were imprisoned at Loch Leven Castle on a tiny island north of the Forth in Scotland and she was forced to abdicate her throne in favour of their son, James.

Three years later Mary escaped from the castle and managed to raise an army of 6,000 men, but was defeated and fled to England.

Elizabeth was at first cordial to her cousin, but after rumours of plots against her, the former queen was placed under house arrest.

Suspicion reared its head again, however, in 1586 with news of a major plot to murder Elizabeth, and Mary was charged with treason.

At her trial, Mary tried vainly to save herself with the words:

"Look to your consciences and remember that the theatre of the whole world is wider than the kingdom of England."

As she prepared to be beheaded, her executioners knelt before her and asked forgiveness.

On his mother's death James became King of Scotland, and when Elizabeth died in 1603 he added England and Ireland to his realm.

Elizabeth I triumphed over her cousin and rival Mary, Queen of Scots

ALL THE WORLD'S A STAGE

Just three years before the founding of the School, England's greatest playwright William Shakespeare was born a few miles down the road in Stratford-upon-Avon. Creator of some of the most memorable and enduring characters ever to strut the stage, Shakespeare's works are still performed around the world today. The man who gave us *Hamlet*, *Macbeth* and *Romeo and Juliet*, died on April 23, 1616, his 52nd birthday.

1567.

Rugby was born under
the House of Tudor,

ITS HEALTH,
SINCE THEN,
BECOMING
EVER RUDER...

LAWRENCE SHERIFF AND THE FOUNDING OF THE SCHOOLS

Born in Rugby around 1515, Lawrence Sheriff came from a family sufficiently well off to be able to apprentice him to William Walcott, a London grocer. Sheriff learnt and succeeded enough to be admitted as a Freeman of the Grocers' Company in 1541. He prospered further and 10 years later was supplying 'grocery and spicery' to the household of the young Princess Elizabeth at Hatfield. In 1554, still prospering, Lawrence Sheriff was promoted to Liveryman of the Grocers' Company – and briefly entered national history in *Foxe's Book of Martyrs*, not always a reliable source.

Sir Thomas Wyatt's rebellion against Catholic Mary had failed, London having risen for the Queen. Protestant Elizabeth had been imprisoned and interrogated, before grudgingly being reinstated at Court. Grocer Sheriff objected forcibly to the gossip of his Newgate neighbour and erstwhile friend, Robert Farrer, a haberdasher. Farrer insulted the name of the Princess, accusing her of being *"one of the chief doers of the rebellion ... Some hope that she will have the crown, but she and they (I trust) that so hope, shall hop headless, or be fried with faggots before she come to it."*

Sheriff protested *"I defie thee, and tell thee, I am her Graces sworne servant, and she is a Princess and daughter of a Noble king."* Sheriff, bravely in Mary's England, swore a complaint against Farrer before a Commission headed by the Bishop of London. The Bishop made light of the matter but Farrer was formally rebuked.

Four years later Elizabeth was Queen – and her grocer's success was assured. Lawrence Sheriff was granted a coat of arms, the arms upon which the School's arms are based, with the griffins of the Grocers' Company and

the bunch of grapes to symbolise his trade. By 1562 we find the Queen and her grocer exchanging New Year's gifts, from him *'a suger loaf, a box of ginger, a box of nutmegs, and a pound of cynomon'*, receiving in exchange *'one gilt salt with a cover'* weighing seven ounces. What a treasure that salt would be if we could find it today!

Prosperity brought land purchases. First in 1560, jointly with his wife Elizabeth, Sheriff purchased for £320 a 24-acre field in Holborn called Conduit Close. Then he bought property in many counties, including land in Brownsover and Rugby. On his Rugby property, near the parish church, he started to build a house. In 1562 Sheriff became a Grocers' Company Court Assistant, and in 1566 was elected the Company's Second Warden.

But only a year later, aged around 52, he made his will on July 22, 1567, *"being sicke of Bodie but of good and perfitt remembrance."* Lawrence and Elizabeth had no children, so after providing for Elizabeth, leaving funds for Rugby parish church, for the poor of Rugby and of London, funds to repair Rugby market cross and Rugby bridge, to the Grocers' Company and to relatives, apprentices and friends, he left Conduit Close to Elizabeth for life and then, divided into three parts, to his sister Brigett Howkins and members of her family. Crucially he left £50 to his friends George Harrison and Bernard Field as Trustees *"towards the building of a schole house and Almes howse in Rugby aforesaid according to the tenor of certain writings bearing date the daye of the date hereof conteyninge myne intent in that behalf."* The same day he conveyed his land in Brownsover and Rugby to Harrison and Field, as Trustees for the same purpose. His will left a further

£100 *"to purchase therewith somme other lands ... assured to the purposes and intents expressed in the said writings conteyninge myne intente ... as I do thinke that the same Landes ...will not be sufficient for the purposes thereof."*

Lawrence Sheriff's *'certain writings'* of July 22, 1567 are his *'Intente'* – the trust for his new school, requiring the Trustees to build near his house in Rugby a *"fayre and Convenyent Schoole-howse ... and distinct Lodgeings for four poore men ... [and to] Cause an honeste and discreete and Learned man being a Master of Artes to bee Reteyned to teach a free Grammar Schoole in the said Schoole."*

A month after writing his Will and Intent, Sheriff travelled to Rugby. There, by codicil executed on August 31, 1567 he revoked the bequest of £100 to the School's Trustees, instead leaving the Trustees one third of Conduit Close (much the same value) – the other two thirds remaining with the Howkins family. Three weeks later he was dead, being buried in September at Greyfriars' Church, Newgate Street. The eight acres in Holborn have stood Rugby School and Lawrence Sheriff School in good stead.

Lawrence Sheriff's Intent acknowledged his sister Brigett and her husband Nicholas Howkins as occupants of the Brownsover land, paying rent to the School. But soon there was confusion as to the Howkins family's rights and the School's. Similarly, after the death of two original Trustees, the family of the second Trustee, Bernard Field, claimed the School's eight Holborn acres as their own. In 1598 Field's heir refused to pay sums due to the School Master and the Almsmen, causing Head Master Nicholas Greenhill to commence a Chancery action – the beginning of 70 years of litigation. Greenhill's action

1567.

THE FIRST 'SCHOOL HOUSE'

was soon overtaken by a Chancery Commission appointed in 1602 under the Statute for Charitable Uses. The Commission held an Inquisition at Rugby in 1603 and apparently appointed twelve gentlemen of Warwickshire as the School's Trustees (with provisions for appointment of future new Trustees). The Commission confirmed the School's ownership of the land at Brownsover and Conduit Close, and confirmed Greenhill as Master and dealt with the condition of the buildings.

Stained glass window in the School Chapel showing Lawrence Sheriff with a model of the School he founded

Under the terms of Lawrence Sheriff's will, a property in the town was given to provide the first schoolhouse. This 'mansion house' stood across the road from the parish church of St Andrew.

The mansion house, the Founder's house, was built on the site of earlier cottages, and retained cottage rights over common land in Rugby. The land comprised an area of one rood and thirty perches, or less than half an acre, and had been inherited from his father.

Whilst the existing mansion house was for the residence of the schoolmaster, and lodgings for four almsmen, the School was built to teach the boys of Rugby, Brownsover and adjoining parishes. It is thought the School itself was completed by around 1574. The arrangement was that the schoolmaster and his successors should live in the mansion house without charge and a salary of £12 each year. The four almsmen, also provided for in Sheriff's will, would each have 7d per week, in addition to their lodgings. The upkeep of the School, including the buildings, would be funded out of any profits from the properties included in the will.

The first School was a long and high-ceilinged timber room, probably similar in nature to Old Big School, which would eventually replace it. One old Rugbeian described being called into one of the rooms to be heard by the master:

''I have said many a lesson in a small room, into which the Doctor occasionally called some boys, and in which he smoked many a pipe, the fragrance of which was abundantly retained in the blue cloth hangings.''

By the 1650s, legal proceedings on the administration of the endowments of the charity gave a depressing picture of the the School, stating:

"That the mansion house, school, and almshouses, are so ruined that…they will take at least £63. 1os. od., to be put in repair."

Sadly, little was to change until almost a century later.

When the architect, a Mr Hiorn, was employed to survey the old buildings in 1748, he reported they were almost a ruin. The roof could not be repaired, but if it was removed, the entire structure would collapse. This would necessitate the building of completely new premises but the existing ones were already proving to be too cramped and there was no space to extend. There was also no adequate space for the boys to play, and their use of the churchyard at Holy Trinity was not welcomed by the local curate.

It was for these reasons that by late 1749 the decision was made to move.

FIRST HEADS

Edward Rolston did not have the influence of Arnold, he did not become Archbishop of Canterbury like Temple, or Chairman of the BBC like fforde. But he was the first recorded 'Master' of Rugby School. When the School was founded it was laid down that 'an honest, discreet and learned' man should be appointed to lead it, preferably a Master of Arts.

The 'Master' would live for free in the School building, the Mansion House, and receive a salary of £12 a year.

Rolston was appointed in 1574. He graduated from Christ's College, Cambridge in 1567 and gained his MA in 1572.

Apart from being Rugby's first Head, history does not record any particular contribution he made to the School during his six-year tenure. Rolston was followed in around 1580 by **Richard Seale**, a Warwickshire man and a graduate of Trinity College, Oxford.

Seale was not destined to last long and around 18 months after his appointment was effectively ejected for reasons which may have involved his relationship with a powerful local family deemed to threaten the Trust overseeing the School.

The School's third Master, in 1581, was **Nicholas Greenhill** who was appointed on three years' probation *"after which he was to be and continue to be schoolmaster there during his life, if there should be no just cause given to him to the contrary"*.

Little is known about the academic credentials of Greenhill (who was allowed £4 a year out of the rent of Conduit Close, over and above his salary), but he does appear to have been a man of some means.

While running the School he invested his own money in a range of material improvements, including adding some new rooms (later destroyed by fire in 1654), adding wainscot to the hall and making some cupboards.

But not all was rosy. A change of ownership of Conduit Close led to Greenhill instituting a suit in Chancery when his £4 share of rent was stopped. These legal proceedings, which started around 1598, dragged on until 1602.

Next in line was **Augustine Rolfe** (or Rolph) who took his Master's degree at Queen's College, Cambridge in 1595. He can be credited with the first record of a Rugby boy going on to university. His name was George Isham, and he went to Sussex College, Cambridge.

The unusually named **Wilgent Greene** followed Rolfe, sometime before 1633, probably no later than 1625. Greene took his BA at Oriel College, Oxford in 1616 but there is no record of him later adding a Master's degree.

Again during Greene's time in charge, boys from the School started to go on to university, including a certain Knightley Harrison who went to Cambridge and later came back to Rugby as Master, the first boy to do so.

1574.

TRUSTEES

Lawrence Sheriff's Executors and the first Trustees of his School were his London friends George Harrison and Bernard Field. Their Trusts were properly discharged, with Field taking the lead – the first Master was not appointed until the building was ready, seven years in, but the House was built well and lasted for 200. While the first two Masters were not successful, the third, Nicholas Greenhill, was a strong man who ran the School successfully from 1581 until his death in 1604. Soon after, the Chancery Commission appointed twelve Warwickshire gentlemen as new Trustees to recover the London property from Field's family and the Rugby property from Sheriff's family.

The Commission made rules for appointing new Trustees to fill vacancies but made no other rules for the Trustees – who did little beyond unsuccessful short-term efforts to resolve the property issues, not even filling up vacancies in their number. A second Commission in 1612 confirmed the first. Yet the Trustees' neglect continued, and by the 1650s the School was in a parlous state. There was only one living Trustee, the premises were dilapidated, and all the Brownsover and London properties were in Howkins' hands. They were not paying proper rentals and Raphael Pearce, the Master, died of privation.

Finally the third Chancery

Commission in 1653 and the Lord Keeper's 1667 judgement resolved the Trust – the Lord Keeper awarding costs against the Howkins family. At last a full group of Trustees, again twelve Warwickshire gentlemen, appointed a Clerk, bought a chest for their documents, collected their arrears (having to imprison a Howkins as part of the process), started on their quarterly meetings, repaired the buildings and paid arrears of income to the widows of former Masters. From 1667 new Trustees were appointed to fill vacancies. At last, the Trust and hence the School were being governed by the Trustees. **MF**

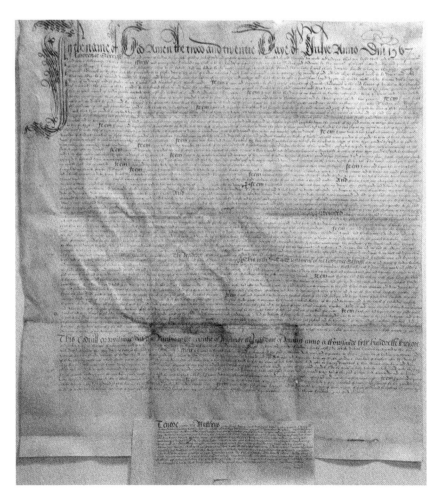

1581

Lawrence Sheriff's final will

THE SPANISH ARMADA

On Plymouth Hoe stands the famous bronze statue of Sir Francis Drake, who according to legend elected to finish the game of bowls he had started before getting down to the more serious business of defeating the Spanish Armada.

Sir Francis was called into service when a Spanish fleet of 130 ships, 2,500 guns, 8,000 seamen and almost 20,000 soldiers sailed for Flanders in May 1588. The fleet, commanded by the Duke of Medina Sidonia, had a simple mission: to overthrow Queen Elizabeth I and Protestantism in England, so reducing English interference in the Spanish Netherlands.

Famously, the Spanish quest became instead the defining moment of a queen who declared that, while she had the body of a woman, she had the 'heart of a king'.

The Armada, which reached England in July, lost a ship in the Channel to Drake after choosing not to attack the English fleet in Plymouth, and then failed to make anchor in the Solent.

Dropping back to Calais to await orders, it was then dispersed following an attack by eight English fireships at midnight on July 29 and later damaged in the fierce eight-hour Battle of Gravelines.

Retreating north chased by the English, Sidonia then ordered a return to Spain during which the Armada was damaged by severe storms, with boats wrecked on the shores of Scotland and Ireland.

A third to a half of the original Spanish fleet failed to return home, along with an estimated 15,000 men. **DH**

The Spanish Armada was defeated by the English fleet, led by dashing SIr Francis Drake

1588.

CHARLES I BORN

Charles I was born in Scotland in 1600. A sickly child, he overcame his physical limitations to become an accomplished horseman, marksman and fencer.

His elder brother having died in 1612, Charles ascended the English, Irish and Scottish thrones in 1625. That year, he married the Catholic Henrietta Maria of France, causing suspicion about his commitment to Protestantism throughout his reign. The marriage was eventually a happy one and two sons – Charles II and James II – succeeded their father.

Believing in the Divine Right of Kings, Charles' autocratic tendencies led to conflict with Parliament, principally over finance. Early in his reign, England was involved in expensive and ultimately unsuccessful wars against Spain and France. Charles came to realise that he could reign without Parliament if he avoided the expense of war. He dissolved Parliament in 1629, made peace with Spain and France and then ruled without Parliament till 1640.

In 1637, an attempt to reform the Church of Scotland led to the Bishops' War. This forced Charles I to recall Parliament in 1640. In return for its help, Parliament ensured it could not be dissolved without its own consent, no more than three years could elapse between Parliaments, and Ship Money and other levies were abolished.

Parliament was now dominated by opponents of Charles I. An Irish uprising in 1641 increased hostility. To silence opposition, Charles and armed accomplices entered Parliament to arrest five of its members. Forewarned, the five escaped, and, thwarted by the Speaker, Charles left London in January 1642 to raise an army to regain control by force. This led to the English Civil War. **DH**

1603 James I and VI of Scotland

1600

1605

GUY FAWKES

Guy Fawkes was born in 1570 in York. His parents were Protestants. When Guy was eight, his father died. His mother married a Catholic and Guy himself converted, possibly influenced by masters he encountered at St Peter's School in his home city. At the age of 21 and by now a committed Catholic, Fawkes sold the estate bequeathed him by his father and left for the continent as a soldier of fortune, fighting for Spain against the Protestant Dutch. It was there that he adopted the Italian variant of his name, Guido.

In 1604, following his return to England, he joined the 13-man provincial conspiracy master-minded by Robert Catesby, a charismatic Catholic who planned to assassinate King James I and restore Catholicism. The plotters leased a cellar beneath the House of Lords where they stockpiled 36 barrels of gunpowder. Prompted by a tip-off, the authorities searched the Palace of Westminster in the early morning of November 5, 1605 where they caught Fawkes, guarding the barrels.

At first, he gave his name as John Johnson. After two days of torture, he finally admitted his involvement in the plot. Asked about motive, he replied that it had been his intention *"to blow you Scotch beggars back to your native mountains"*. He signed his confession "Guido". Conducted to Old Palace Yard at Westminster with three other conspirators for execution, Fawkes escaped the traditional fate meted out to traitors – hanging, drawing and quartering – by leaping from the scaffold, breaking his neck. **DH**

Guy Fawkes and fellow conspirators nearly succeeded in destroying Parliament in 1605

CHARLES II BORN

Charles was born in 1630, the eldest surviving son of Charles I. Parliamentary victory in the Civil War drove him into exile and he was in the Netherlands when his father was executed in 1649.

Allying with the Scots, Charles was defeated by Cromwell at the Battle of Worcester in 1651 and returned to exile. Charles was restored to the thrones of England, Scotland and Ireland in 1660, ending the short-lived experiment in republican rule in England.

Punishing those who had signed Charles I's death warrant, the new king appeared to favour both political and religious tolerance and power-sharing. He inclined towards Catholicism and his efforts to extend toleration to Catholics and non-conformists were thwarted by a hostile Parliament.

Charles' early years were marked by the Great Plague of 1665 and the Great Fire of 1666 which led to the rebuilding of much of London. War with the Dutch ended in defeat in 1667 which drove Charles into the arms of Louis XIV of France with whom he signed a secret treaty in 1670. The terms included an alliance and renewed war against the Dutch and to Charles' promising to convert to Catholicism. In return, Charles received French money which gave him some room for manoeuvre in his dealings with Parliament.

Charles and his ministers were masters of 17th-century spin. To this day, the myth of "The Merrie Monarch" persists. Charles was an opportunist with absolutist intentions. In 1677, he married his niece Mary to William of Orange to try to establish his own Protestant credentials. He had no legitimate children by his wife, Catherine of Braganza, but several by his mistresses. His brother James, a known Catholic, was his heir and this, together with knowledge of Charles' conspiring with France, caused conflict with Parliament which he dissolved in 1681. Charles ruled alone until his death in 1685.

What was his legacy? Charles' reign saw the rise of colonisation and trade in the Far East and North America. The Navigation Acts led to Britain becoming the predominant European sea power. Most lasting of all, Charles founded the Royal Society in 1660. **DH**

Charles II was the monarch later restored to the thrones of England, Scotland and Ireland

1625 Charles I

1630.

1641-1787
TAKING SHAPE

1641 HENRY HOLYOAKE BECOMES HEAD

1649 CHARLES I EXECUTED

1666 THE GREAT FIRE OF LONDON

1686 THE LONDON ESTATE

1688 GLORIOUS REVOLUTION

1740 A NEW SCHOOL BUILDING

1748 THE RUGBY SCHOOL ACT

1776 AMERICAN INDEPENDENCE

1777 RICHARD BLOXHAM
RALPH ABERCROMBY

1778 THOMAS JAMES BECOMES HEAD

HENRY HOLYOAKE

In the four decades or so after Wilgent Green's death in 1641, the School went through seven more 'Masters', the most durable being **John Allen** who was in charge for a decade from 1660.

All have their place in the School's history, but it was **Henry Holyoake** in 1688 who was the first really to make his mark.

Holyoake, who was probably born in Warwickshire in 1657 and came from a scholastic family, led Rugby for 43 years and over this time helped the School to build its reputation.

He joined Rugby from Magdalen College, Oxford, where he graduated in 1674, and proceeded to MA in 1681.

For his first two years at Rugby, Holyoake held both posts of Master and Chaplain, but this did not stop the School beginning to progress under his leadership.

Numbers grew, including boys from Cheshire, Kent and Somerset, and with it the quality of pupils.

Among these were Thomas Carte, a respected 18th-century historian, academic Charles Holt, and the unfortunate Reverend William Paul, who was hanged, drawn and quartered for his part in the Jacobite Rebellion of 1715.

Another luminary was Edward Cave, who despite leaving Rugby after some sort of fall-out with Holyoake, went on to found *The Gentleman's Magazine* and later wrote the first historical sketch featuring the School.

The quality of Holyoake's tenure at Rugby was recognised by his holding (with permission) two 'livings' as an incumbent while running the School – and the Trustees specifically recording their appreciation of his efforts on two separate occasions.

The first of these reveals that despite Holyoake appearing in a continuing list of 'Masters', his predecessors evidently had not done their job quite so well and the Trustees praised him for *"recovering the Creditt and reputation of the Schoole"*.

Numbers in Holyoake's time appear to have increased to around 100 pupils and in an early example of managing what are now called 'pupil-teacher' ratios, he began to bring in assistant masters to share the load.

An investment was also made to add another storey to the schoolroom to accommodate more boarders, but it is unclear whether this was

sufficient to cater for them all.

When Holyoake died in 1731 he had built up wealth of £1,600, which was not bad given his annual salary on joining Rugby was only £56 a year.

Having never married, he left his cousin Judith, who kept house for him, a legacy and praised her for *"having been very serviceable in my house and seemingly kind."*

More important for the School, however, was the bequest of his personal library of books, in an age when books were not cheap.

Commenting on Holyoake's time at the School, the *History of the County of Warwick (Vol 6)*, although geographically biased, described him as *"the first Head Master of Rugby School to raise it above the level of purely local importance"*.

This was echoed in the pages of *Northamptonshire Past and Present* in the words:

"Of the Head Masters of Rugby School in the first two centuries of its existence, only one has any claim to eminence… the Reverend Henry Holyoake."

1641.

CHARLES I EXECUTED

By 1647 the Parliamentarians had scattered the Royalist armies and held Charles I a prisoner on the Isle of Wight. Exasperated by the King's deviousness which made negotiation impossible, Oliver Cromwell and his allies determined to charge him with treason.

In December 1648, the army prevented 130 MPs from entering Parliament. The remaining 70, supporters of Cromwell, formed the Rump Parliament which passed a bill charging Charles with high treason. Declaring itself the supreme authority in the land, the Rump passed the bill into law but only by a vote of 29:26. Fearing the outcome, many of Cromwell's allies baulked at putting a king on trial.

Proceedings began on January 20, 1649 in Westminster Hall before a crowd of 5,000. Charles was kept in an area sectioned off from the crowd and was allowed no legal representation. He assumed an air of indifference and, when charged, declined to offer a plea and challenged the legality of the proceedings. A two-day adjournment failed to shake Charles' resolve. He was returned to gaol and the trial continued without him.

On January 27, Charles was brought back to hear his sentence which ended:

"For all which Treasons and Crimes this court doth adjudge that he, the said Charles Stuart, as a Tyrant, Traitor, Murderer and public Enemy to the good people of this Nation shall be put to Death."

January 30, 1649, was bitterly cold. Charles donned three shirts to avoid his shivering being misinterpreted as fear. After a delay of four hours, Charles was marched to the scaffold. His head was severed by a single stroke but when the executioner held it up, the only response from the crowd was a low groan. **DH**

On the freezing day of his execution Charles I wore three shirts to avoid any shivering being misinterpreted as fear

1649

A cigar, a spud and Lear's fool

A HEADLESS QUEEN AND RUGBY SCHOOL

THE GREAT FIRE OF LONDON

The Great Fire of September 1666 was the second tragedy to hit the city in the space of a year. Just as London was recovering from the Great Plague, residents had to flee once again.

The fire started in Pudding Lane at the premises of the King's baker, Thomas Farriner, when the ovens were not properly put out. Sparks set Farriner's home alight and because buildings were largely constructed of wood which was dry after the summer, the fire rapidly took hold, fanned by strong northerly winds and burning for almost five days.

Those who could get out of the city did so and viewed the destruction from the relative safety of nearby heathland. King Charles II remained in London and supervised attempts to save the city by creating firebreaks. This involved knocking down existing buildings and met with some success. The greatest fear was that the fire would spread south of the Thames. On this occasion, the wind veered and, with little remaining to burn in the devastated northern area, the fire died out.

The Great Fire destroyed 84 churches, including old St Paul's where the heat melted the lead on the roof. Samuel Pepys recorded:

"I saw a fire as one entire arch of fire above a mile long: it made me weep to see it."

The fire claimed only five lives. One unforeseen benefit was the destruction of the filth associated with the Great Plague. Slums were reduced to ash and the Fleet – an open sewer – was effectively sterilised by the heat of the fire. **DH**

1625 Charles II   **1653** Oliver Cromwell   **1658** Richard Cromwell   **1666**

The 1666 Great Fire of London was caused by stray sparks in a baker's oven in Pudding Lane

THE LONDON ESTATE

From the late 1660s the School prospered under successive Masters, the Trustees feeling confident enough to seek and obtain from Knightley Harrison (Master 1670-75) a surety of £500, to be forfeited if the Master refused to obey the Trustees' orders or to quit the School on three months' notice. Harrison's successor Robert Ashridge (1675-1681) started the School Register. The first entries in the Register show that Rugby was no longer chiefly a free school for the neighbourhood – half of the 1675 entries obviously boarded, one from as far away as Cumberland. The School seemed to prosper under Ashridge, but his successor Robert Jeacock (1681-88) was less successful.

The successive bands of 'twelve Warwickshire gentlemen' who to 1667 did so badly for the School, did it well thereafter. It is interesting how families frequently provided Trustees. Amongst the nearly 80 Trustees from 1602 to 1750, we find eight Feildings, seven Leighs, seven Caves, five and three each of the Boughtons, Bromleys, Dixwells, Greens and Shuckburghs. Many of these names occur again after 1750, the record holders being the Leighs of Stoneleigh who contributed twelve Trustees between 1602 and 1938.

A key event of Jeacock's time was the Trustees' decision in 1686 to lease the London property for 51 years at £50 a year to Nicholas Barbon MP. Nicholas If-Jesus-Christ-Had-Not-Died-For-Thee-Thou-Hadst-Been-Damned Barbon owed his immense second name to his father, the preacher and Fifth Adventist Praise-god Barbon. Barbon was London's leading (and most disreputable) late 17th-century property developer. His lease was the beginning of the London Estate's commercial development and some of his houses survive.

More important even than the lease to Barbon was the Trustees' 1688 appointment of Henry Holyoake as Master, to reign for 43 years. Numbers soon built up – 26 boys entered in Holyoake's first year compared with none during the two previous years. 630 boys joined the School in Holyoake's time, nearly four-fifths of the pupils being boarders, many the sons of old Warwickshire and Northamptonshire families and others from further afield. Some of the Trustees sent their own sons – who became Trustees in their turn,

so building tradition. The School's reputation stood higher than ever before.

In London, Barbon had died in 1698 and the Estate was having difficulty collecting the rent, but by 1705 the arrears were paid up and a new lease at £60 pa was granted to William Milman who continued the Estate's development. The Brownsover lands were bringing in £28 pa. But maintenance of the now ancient School premises was a heavy cost. **MF**

70. LAMBS CONDUIT STREET.

Lambs Conduit Street in the heart of London is part of the property left to the School by its founder Lawrence Sheriff, now known as the 'Rugby Estate'

1686.

1685 James II and VII of Scotland 👑

In 1688 William of Orange arrived in England with his fleet to take over the throne in a bloodless revolution

GLORIOUS REVOLUTION

The United Kingdom in the 17th century enjoyed the leadership of eight rulers, including five kings and one queen.

One, a Puritan commoner, cut off the head of his royal predecessor and led a civil war and another tried to turn back the clock on the Reformation.

But such domestic drama was arguably nothing compared to a king and queen called William and Mary, who sailed from the Netherlands to take over the throne in the 'Glorious Revolution' of 1688.

The revolution had its roots in the religious tolerance of James II, who succeeded his brother Charles II in 1685.

Under James, England began a Catholic revival which threatened to reverse the country's abandonment of papal supremacy.

Concerned Tory and Whig politicians decided to act and invited William and Mary of Orange in the Netherlands to take over the throne.

Mary, William's wife, had been in line to the English throne as a Protestant daughter of James II, until the birth of his son (also called James) which sparked fear of the country firmly reverting to Catholicism.

In a largely bloodless revolution, the Dutch visitors, accompanied by a sizeable fleet, managed to remove James, establish themselves as joint monarchs and, through the introduction of the Bill of Rights a year later, formally prescribe the authority of Parliament.

For William and Mary the takeover of the English monarchy was not as smooth as it looks, with military resistance continuing for several years in Ireland and Scotland.

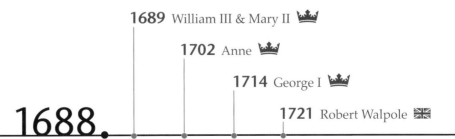

1689 William III & Mary II

1702 Anne

1714 George I

1721 Robert Walpole

1688.

A NEW SCHOOL BUILDING

When the School decided to move from its cramped position by the parish church, the search for suitable premises began. A nearby property, a 'large and convenient house', belonging to the Clerk to the Trust might have proved suitable, but with hindsight, the falling through of the purchase was to prove much more beneficial.

The Manor House, sited to the southern edge of the town, had been advertised to let in 1740 together with 'good outhouses, and large gardens, with one or more closes thereto adjoining'. A brick house, 'four rooms on a floor, with a kitchen, and four large vaults under it, all new built and sashed' came with barns, stables, another farmhouse, and outbuildings, and another close. The house which stood where School House now stands, consisted of a central core with two wings which were joined by a long corridor.

Although substantial, the property needed considerable alterations, although most of these were to fixtures and fittings.

A new schoolroom was built, which stood where the current School House Old Hall sits, and seems to have been a close copy of the original School.

The tall room had two rooms above it where the boys who boarded would sleep. One alteration to the original plan was the addition of a semi-circular apse to the south-facing end, a raised area from which the Master would keep his eye on the various classes below him. This was the original of Old Big School and this was the new School to which the boys moved in 1750. **RM**

1754 Thomas Pelham-Holles 🇬🇧
1756 William Cavendish 🇬🇧
1757 Thomas Pelham-Holles 🇬🇧
1762 John Stuart 🇬🇧
1763 George Grenville 🇬🇧
1765 Charles Watson-Wentworth 🇬🇧
1766 William Pitt the Elder 🇬🇧
1767 Augustus Fitzroy 🇬🇧
1770 Frederick North 🇬🇧

1748

A new school building in 1740 was the start of the School's early expansion

1727 George II 👑

1740

1742 Spencer Compton 🇬🇧

1743 Henry Pelham 🇬🇧

THE RUGBY SCHOOL ACT

Holyoake died in office in 1731, a wealthy man, leaving his library to the School. He was succeeded by John Plomer whose eleven years were not successful – though this was no reason for the Trustees to lose interest as they did, leaving almost everything to one of their number, the Rector of Rugby, Mr Towers. Plomer's successor, Thomas Crossfield, was a young man of brilliant achievement and potential, attracting 53 new boys in his first year, all but two being boarders. But within two years, Crossfield was dead. His successor, William Knail, continued Crossfield's success, so the School's premises, already almost beyond repair, were obviously too small.

The solution was the London Estate. The effective leader of the Trustees, Sir Thomas Cave MP, shepherded the first Rugby School Act (1748) through Parliament. The Act authorised raising £1,800 on mortgage of two-thirds of the London Estate, making provision for the application of the proceeds, enabling the Trustees to acquire new School premises. £1,000 acquired the old Mansion House of Rugby (standing where Old Quad now stands), the balance being used to build a new Big School Room. In 1751 the School moved from its historic site near Rugby parish church to the head of High Street.

Knail resigned in 1751 and his two successors, Joseph Richmond (1751-1755) and Stanley Burroughs (1755-1778), did little more than keep the place going. The School's income seems rarely to have exceeded its expenses, let alone to have permitted repayment of the mortgage. Milman's lease on the London Estate was coming to an end in 1780 but the School's debts in 1776 were £6,600. Again, the solution lay in the London Estate. The leader of the 1770s Trustees, Sir John Eardley Wilmot, Lord Chief Justice of the Common Pleas, drafted a bill which became the 1777 Rugby School Act.

As with the 1748 Act, but in broader terms, the 1777 Act enabled the Trustees to raise money (£10,000) by mortgaging, selling or letting all or parts of the Estate, being allowed to acquire land and invest. Importantly, the Trustees were formed as a corporate Trustee with a common seal – thus bringing limited liability and governance as we know it today.

An 18th-century map defining the School's land in Rugby

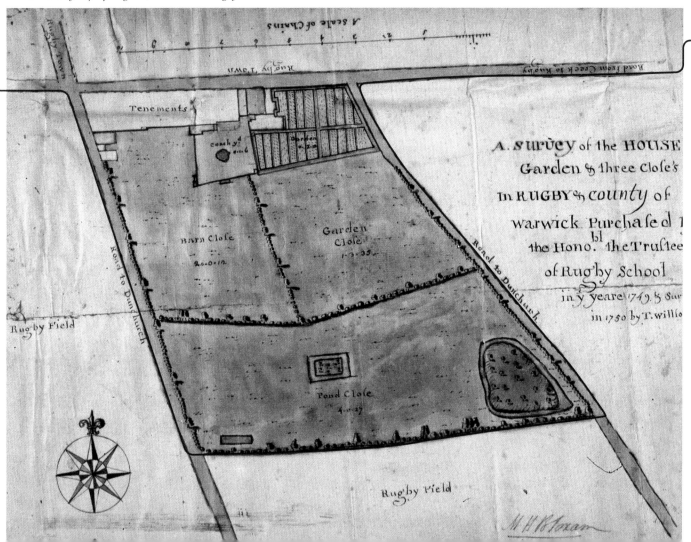

America declared itself free of colonial rule from the British in 1776

1760 George III 👑

1776

AMERICAN INDEPENDENCE

"We hold these truths to be self-evident: that all men are created equal; that they are endowed by their Creator with certain inalienable rights; that among these are life, liberty, and the pursuit of happiness."

The words which many people remember amount to a tiny fraction of a document which includes some decidedly illiberal attitudes towards black slaves and Native Americans. Over half the Declaration lists grievances which the colonists felt against the British government.

The colonies had been set up with little clear economic expectation but provided a haven for refugees from Europe. After Virginia was founded in 1607, the British government took

very little interest for the next century and a half and the colonists took full advantage of their liberty.

In the mid-18th-century, however, Britain developed a new imperial policy, waging expensive wars against France in Europe, India and North America. Having defended the settlers against the French, the British government expected the colonists to contribute to the costs. From 1763, they tried repeatedly to tax the Americans and for twelve years the colonists resisted until the War of Independence broke out in 1775.

Fifteen months after war began, the Declaration of Independence was issued. It is only at the very end that the document states that the colonies were now independent, beholden to no-one and free to act accordingly.

Why had it taken so long? Many

colonists had no wish to sever links with Britain. Too radical an approach carried with it the risk that some states would declare independence whilst others did not.

After more than a year of debate, independence won a majority in all the colonies. In June 1776, a committee was established which, on July 4, approved and published the Declaration. **DH**

1776

The School's first science lessons were delivered by visiting lecturer Adam Walker in 1776. The subject was then taught by a parent called Dr Sharp in 1849 before a regular science curriculum was introduced in 1851 by Edward Goulburn.

1777.

RICHARD BLOXHAM

Just over two centuries after the School's foundation, **Richard Bloxham** joined Rugby as a pupil. He later took holy orders, worked as an assistant master and was father to the antiquary Matthew Bloxham, the man who first wrote of William Webb Ellis' fine disregard for the rules of the game of football.

Despite his obvious later affection for Rugby, Richard was not a happy boy at the outset, believing he was underfed – and he had to provide his own towels, knife, fork and drinking horn.

Deciding on drastic action, young Bloxham elected to escape home from School to Market Harborough.

The journey meant passing a brook and when he got there the prospect of crossing it persuaded him to change his mind and he returned, thankfully, to the School.

RALPH ABERCROMBY

Rugby's greatest fighting hero, **General Sir Ralph Abercromby**, was an 18th-century man.

Born in 1734 into a high-achieving Scottish family from Clackmannanshire (a brother and son also became Generals) he enjoyed a highly successful military career until retiring in 1783 to become an MP. However, the French threat following the 1789 Revolution brought him back into service (he was Pitt's favourite general) and produced his finest hour.

First, Abercromby led the British force in the Caribbean that wrested much territory from the French, including Trinidad. Then he commanded the attempt to drive the French out of Egypt, which they controlled.

In 1801, after a brilliantly executed disembarkation at Aboukir Bay, Abercromby confronted the much bigger French army (20,000 strong) at the Battle of Alexandria. Superior tactics won the day which led to the French abandoning Egypt and their Middle East ambitions.

Tragically, Abercromby was wounded and died a week later, a grateful country made his widow a Baroness and awarded her a pension of £2,000 a year.

From 1777, Abercromby attended Rugby, despite the long and slow journey from Scotland and only returning home once a year for the summer holidays. He is remembered at the School through a stained glass window in Chapel and a portrait in the Temple Speech Room, while a famous painting of him at Alexandria hangs in Edinburgh's National Portrait Gallery.
AC-M

1778

THOMAS JAMES

The appointment of **Thomas James** as Rugby's nineteenth Head in 209 years introduced the School to stronger scholarship and firmer leadership.

James' reign began after a near half century of five Heads… **John Plomer** from 1731 until 1742, **Thomas Crossfield** until 1744, **William Knail** until 1751 **Joseph Richmond** until 1755, and finally **Stanley Burroughs** until 1758.

Under Plomer numbers fell but they flourished again under Crossfield, although he sadly died after just two years in charge.

Under Knail, the School moved to new premises and Rugby continued to produce some pupils who went on to greater things, including Sir Ralph Abercromby who became Commander-in-Chief of the British army in Egypt.

Knail's successor, Richmond, made little mark, but under Burroughs *"we find the first attempt to unite the School for religious services on Sunday".*

And again some notable alumni emerged including William and John Sleath, who went on to be Heads themselves at Repton and St Paul's.

James was Rugby's Head Master for just six years and was the first formally to hold the title. But compared to some earlier Heads his time was productive.

After boarding at Eton, James, a classical scholar with a strong bent for maths, won academic prizes at Cambridge and become a Fellow and Tutor of King's College.

Two of James' main impacts as Head Master were in teaching and organising the School.

The teaching timetable revolved around five lessons, the first at 7am, the last at 5pm. There were half holidays on Tuesday and Saturday and harder-working fifth and sixth formers could also earn an extra Thursday half holiday (to be used for play, learning,

dance lessons, drawing, fencing or 'other accomplishments').

Dividing the School into six forms, James taught the top two. Classics, scripture and history were the core subjects, plus mathematics, which James himself taught.

James described the effort of teaching maths *"not only kept my mind upon the full stretch during the delivery, and so was sometimes painful, but even wearied my body to excess, and made it hot, or at any rate perspire too much".*

Administrative innovations included 'tradesmen's notes', which meant that local traders could not sell supplies to boys without getting signed authority from their boarding house-keeper.

Any boy who lost his books, or left them about carelessly, faced a fine, and a system of pocket money, rising in value as boys progressed through the School, was also brought in.

On discipline, James had a reputation for firmness. But he also believed in the 'principles of justice', using the 'rod' where necessary but not ruling by it.

He did not favour gaining information on miscreants from pupils, writing that expecting boys to be 'traitors to their fellows' was a 'high crime and against the Virtue and Honour of the School'.

But it seemed anonymous informants kept him aware of what was going in the School through *"good-natured hints thrown in at my study window"* and notes even hung *"on the knocker of my street door".*

Yet despite bringing a focus on greater discipline than previous Heads, boys still pushed the boundaries.

The second of two unsuccessful rebellions, in late 1786 (just three years before a larger event over the Channel and thirteen years before the School's Great Rebellion), brought a

note of censure from the Trustees.

This solemnly declared that they: *"…entirely and earnestly disapprove of the late Riotous and Rebellious Behaviour of the Scholars…and are unanimously determined to support the Authority and Discipline of the Master".*

The note added that they hoped James *"would not hesitate to remove every Boy from the School who shall presume to Dispute his Authority".*

Writing in 1895, School historian WHD Rouse praised James' abilities to put in place a good team around him.

"James clearly had one mark of genius, the power of attracting exceptional men, and of inspiring even ordinary men to carry out his ideas. What makes the quality of these men the more remarkable (and consequently the attraction of James) is the small salary which they were paid."

While Rugby clearly benefited from James' efforts as Head Master, the job was a strain and after sixteen years he retired to become a country clergyman in Worcestershire.

The change did him good and he described *"no longer seeing anything in a gloomy light…after a long absence".*

Today James is remembered, although probably unnoticed by most, in a tablet in the School chapel, wearing his wig and gown.

Thomas James: Head Master from 1778 to 1784

1788-1827
REBELLION AND RUGBY

1788 WALTER SAVAGE LANDOR

1789 FRENCH REVOLUTION

1791 THE OLD QUAD AND 'SOJOURNERS'

1797 THE GREAT REBELLION

1797 ADMIRAL LORD NELSON

1800 THE DAVY ELECTRIC LAMP

1801 THE UNION JACK

1803 MACREADY AND FELLOW ACTORS

1805 THE BATTLE OF TRAFALGAR

1807 DR JOHN WOOLL BECOMES HEAD

1808 BEETHOVEN'S FIFTH

1811 WHITELAW

1814 MILES JOSEPH BERKELEY

1815 SCHOOL HOUSE

1815 THE BATTLE OF WATERLOO

1816 EMMA AND KUBLAI KHAN PUBLISHED

1818 THE CHAPEL

1823 RUGBY FOOTBALL EARLY YEARS

WALTER SAVAGE LANDOR

Born in 1775, **Walter Savage Landor** entered the School in 1788. He became a controversial writer of poetry and prose. A fiery character, he sometimes wrote in Latin when attacking his enemies, a ploy which backfired when his targets proved equally adept in the language. Expelled from Rugby and rusticated from Oxford, he penned moving and often tender poetry, such as the well-known *Rose Aylmer*, dedicated to one of his several Muses. His *Imaginary Conversations*, prose pieces produced between 1824 and 1853, received great critical acclaim.

A rumbustious polemicist, his life was characterised by adventure and some mishap. He was a known sympathiser with the republic in France and yet in his thirties decided to fight for the Spanish against Napoleon in the Peninsular War, but never saw action. Amongst his political pieces were tracts in which he inveighed with gusto against the 'drunken democracy of Mr William Pitt' whom he saw as threatening liberal values. His love affairs were legion, some resulting in lyrical poetry of considerable delicacy.

Headstrong and rebellious, he attracted supporters and opponents in equal measure. Falling foul of the authorities both at home and abroad, he seemed often to be on the verge of prosecution. Among his friends and admirers were Browning, Dickens and Southey. Amongst his fiercest critics were members of his own family. He travelled extensively in France, Spain and Italy. Aged 89, he died and was buried in Florence. **DH**

1788.

1789 George Washington

1789

THE FRENCH REVOLUTION

In 1789, France's economic and intellectual development was not matched by social and political change. King Louis XVI ruled autocratically while the country was governed by privileged groups, the nobility and the clergy. The productive middle classes were taxed heavily to pay for foreign wars, court extravagance and a rapidly escalating national debt. The nominally free peasantry were still subject to a range of feudal dues.

The immediate cause of revolution was finance. Involvement in the American Revolution had brought the French government to near bankruptcy. Called in an attempt to get the privileged classes to share in the financial burden, the Assembly of Notables of 1787 refused to co-operate, so Louis was compelled to call the Estates General. Elections were held in 1788 and the Estates met in 1789 for the first time since 1610.

Instead of considering fiscal reform, each of the three Estates - clergy, nobility and the *tiers état* (Third Estate or commons) - presented its grievances to the crown. Further grievances poured in from the provinces. What was required was sweeping reform far beyond the proposed fiscal measures. The three estates deliberated: should they meet separately or jointly?

As the king too vacillated, the Third Estate seized the initiative, declaring themselves to be the National Assembly. They were joined by some clergy and a few nobles. The King's attempt at suppression backfired and he retreated to Versailles, surrounding himself with troops and sacking his finance minister in whom the Third Estate – including the bourgeoisie - had had some confidence.

Suspecting the king of duplicity, Paris rose up. A mob stormed the Bastille, a fortress housing political prisoners (of whom reportedly there were only five). This marked the beginning of the French Revolution. **DH**

THE OLD QUAD AND 'SOJOURNERS'

The 1777 Act coincided with the appointment of **Dr Thomas James** ('James the first') as Master. Trustees found that they had too much business at their August meetings to allow for Speeches, so from 1791 the Speeches with Trustees attending were moved to the second Tuesday in June, just before the summer holidays.

The late 18th-century was a time of general revolt and Rugby School was no exception. We know James put down two rebellions, without having to resort to the Riot Act like his successor Dr Ingles.

Sixteen years of hard work led Dr James to retire in 1794 from a School with 200 pupils and six assistant masters. To succeed him the Trustees appointed 'the Black Tiger', **Henry Ingles**.

Under Ingles the numbers fell away, but the School and its London Estate generally prospered. It is sad that all that is remembered of Ingles is the great Rebellion of 1797, when the Militia were called out and the Riot Act was read to the boys barricaded on the Island. But to the Trustees, this revolution was clearly trivial compared with that put down by James in 1786 – their minutes do not mention it.

In 1807 Ingles in turn retired and from stiff competition the Trustees selected **Dr John Wooll** to be Head Master. Wooll's long tenure was a time of building. By the turn of the century the premises had already become inadequate – and the Trustees were accumulating cash. So plans were made for new buildings. The construction of Old Quad, School House, the Head Master's house and the Chapel took twelve years, from 1809 to 1820 – and took more money even than the £40,000 that the Trustees had accumulated.

The Rugby School Act 1814 shows pupil numbers had increased from 200 to 320 (including 35 Foundationers). The Trustees were authorised to raise £14,000, to purchase new land and buildings nearby to enlarge the School, to build a chapel and increase the number of Exhibitioners.

In 1818 the Charity Commissioners were set up by Act of Parliament. The Act was explicit that its provisions did not extend to six named schools: Westminster, Eton, Winchester, Charterhouse, Harrow and Rugby. It was not until the 1970s that these schools came within the Commission's net.

During the 1820s upper-class migrants - sojourners they were called - first became a major feature of the town of Rugby: well-off people who moved to Rugby in order to get ten years of Rugby School education for their boys, funded by Lawrence Sheriff's foundation. Sojourners were an important contribution to the town's prosperity for fifty years or more. **MF**

The court of Louis XVI was overthrown in bloody fashion in 1789 in the French Revolution

"
1791.
"

THE GREAT REBELLION

To generations of Rugbeians, visitors and the passing public it probably looks like a small grass hill. Historically, however, 'The Island' (now called The Mound) means more than just a good place to stand and watch the first XV on The Close.

This nondescript slope would probably be significant enough as simply a Bronze Age burial mound.

But it was what happened there in the 'age of revolution' that gives it its real claim to fame.

The last quarter of the 18th-century was a time of rebellion and revolution, particularly in America and France. Compared with guillotining the French aristocracy, events at Rugby were small beer but in the context of the School they were dramatic enough.

The excitement started when a boy called Astley was hauled up by Head Master Dr Henry Ingles for firing corks at windows with his gun. Ingles demanded to know where Astley had acquired his gunpowder and was informed it had come from a grocer in the town.

The shopkeeper, who had entered the sale falsely in his book, denied the offence, so Astley was duly publicly flogged by Ingles.

A schoolboy being beaten by a teacher in an 18th-century public school would not be unusual. Yet on this occasion, the punishment was not viewed by Astley's peers as befitting the crime and dissent soon spread like wildfire across the school.

The boys vented their indignation by stoning the grocer's windows and in response Ingles decided to charge the cost of replacing the glass to the fifth and sixth form.

This provoked the boys to go one step further and to use a petard bomb to blow Ingles' study doors off their hinges, fly flags of rebellion from boarding houses and ring the School bell.

Next they barricaded corridors, stripped Ingles' study of its books and threw them, along with wainscotting and furniture, on a bonfire.

Ingles would have normally called on his assistant masters for support but as most of them were away on country pursuits, he took advantage of an army recruitment unit visiting the town and requested assistance. At this the ringleaders of the mob crossed the moat that used to surround The Island where they stood their ground while the Riot Act was read to them.

As the boys faced the front and listened, the militia crept round the back of The Island bringing the drama to a swift conclusion.

Punishment was inevitably severe with the worst culprits expelled or disciplined, and order was restored. Inevitably, the ending of the Great Rebellion and the ejection of the rebel leaders was not the end of the story.

While Ingles resigned as Head in 1807, some members of the rebel cast list managed to restore their reputations and achieve success in public service.

With true irony one became a bishop, while another, Willoughby Cotton, became a Lieutenant General in the Army.

School rebels in 1797 retreated to The Mound before surrendering to soldiers from the local militia

ADMIRAL LORD NELSON

1797, eight years before Trafalgar, was a year of professional and personal pain for Horatio Nelson.

On July 22 Nelson, then a Rear-Admiral, launched an amphibious assault on the Spanish port city of Santa Cruz de Tenerife.

The action, which cost the lives of several hundred men, was defeated and on July 25, Nelson's forces retreated under a truce.

Nelson lost part of his arm in the battle, a blow which along with the loss of an eye in another encounter, ironically contributed to his fame.

Despite some initial difficulties and aerial bombardment from the Spanish, Nelson managed to land a force of 1,000 soldiers on Valle Seco beach.

After heavy fighting the next day, Nelson called the troops back to his ships and decided to lead a new force into the harbour.

But the Spanish, led by Lieutenant General Gutierrez, foiled this assault and Nelson was wounded in the arm in the process.

Nelson instructed his surgeon: *"Doctor, I want to get rid of this useless piece of flesh here."*

On the morning of July 25 Nelson sent a message to his opposite number asking for an honourable withdrawal with full military honours in exchange for abandoning the assault.

This was granted and Nelson's exchange of letters with Gutierrez, now on display at the new Spanish Army Museum in Toledo, includes the offer of a cheese as a token of gratitude.

Naval hero Lord Nelson lost to the Spanish in 1797 and presented his opposite number with a cheese

THE DAVY ELECTRIC LAMP

Every motorist knows, or should, that the car engine moves because electricity crossing a spark plug gap combusts, causing camshafts to rotate.

In 1800 this principle of physics also enabled Sir Humphry Davy to invent carbon-arc lighting, or the first electric light.

Davy gave the world electrically powered light by using charcoal sticks and a 2,000-cell battery to create an arc across a 4-inch (100 mm) gap. Placing electrodes horizontally he found the strong air flow convection formed an arch-shaped arc. He called this an 'arch lamp', which was later contracted to 'arc lamp'.

Born in Cornwall in 1778, Davy also discovered several alkali and alkaline earth metals and contributed to the discoveries of the elemental nature of chlorine and iodine.

By the time he died in 1829 Davy had been President of the Royal Society, Member of the Royal Irish Academy and Fellow of the Geological Society (FGS).

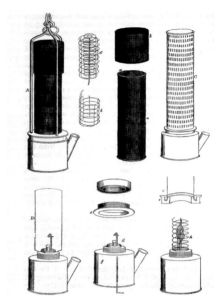

Davy pioneered the electric lamp

1800

1801

THE UNION JACK

The origins of the Union Jack lay in 1606. James VI of Scotland, having ascended the English throne on the death of Elizabeth I, commanded ships to fly a flag combining the red cross of St George and the saltire of St Andrew.

There was argument over which cross should overlay the other. This was settled in 1707 by Queen Anne who selected red over white from various designs. In the same year, the Acts of Union unified the two crowns and two parliaments in one United Kingdom. A further Act of Union – that with Ireland – added the red cross of St Patrick in 1801, providing today's Union Jack flag.

The lack of a distinct Welsh element in the flag is because Edward I annexed Wales in 1282, so the principality is represented by the cross of St George. The most recent attempt to introduce a Welsh element to the flag failed in 2007.

Debate over whether the design is a flag or jack continues today. The flag has no legal status and both terms are equally applicable. However, only the Royal Navy may fly it at sea. **DH**

1801 Henry Addington

1801 Thomas Jefferson

The Union Jack symbolised the joining together of England and Scotland

MACREADY AND FELLOW ACTORS

William Charles Macready was the first of a distinguished cast of Rugbeian actors.

Born on March 3, 1793 in London, William was the fifth of eight children. The first three died in infancy and the fourth, a daughter, survived until the age of seven. She remained in her younger brother's eyes a constant 'angelic influence'.

In 1803, after a first term of rude awakenings into the boarding school world, the young Macready returned home to learn the news *"…that mother, whom I had so longed to see, so dear, so precious, was gone"*.

Back at School his progress moved on apace. Having shone as a young boy in English grammar, reading and recitation, transition to the classics came relatively easily. Also his father's profession (Theatre Manager) secured him favour with senior boys performing plays in Over School Hall, School House. In return for props and dresses the junior boy soon found himself grappling with larger and larger (predominantly female) roles.

When, in 1807 the Head Master, Dr Ingles ('a grave, dignified and awe-inspiring man') was succeeded by Dr Wooll ('agreeable, good-natured and pompous') the latter introduced English verse and speaking prizes. Macready was noted as having performed the

closet scene in Hamlet *"surprisingly well indeed"*.

His return home that Christmas was again greeted with life-changing news. His father had fallen into financial difficulty. Life at Rugby would have to come to an end, as would all thoughts of going to the Bar.

At the age of sixteen the loyal son decided to join forces with his father and become an actor/manager. After a period of learning the ropes and then indeed unlearning some of the performance advice handed down during his apprenticeship, William Macready quickly became one of the most sought-after actors of his generation – renowned for his pathos and tenderness as well as great artistic and intellectual perception.

In 1819 Macready played *Richard III* at Covent Garden, a venue he later managed for two years from 1837. From 1826 to 1828 he made successful tours to the US and Paris and a decade later returned *King Lear* to the original Shakespeare, not Tate's happy-ending adaptation.

After Macready's final performance of *Macbeth* at Drury Lane, Alfred, Lord Tennyson wrote him a valedictory sonnet, which included the lines:

Farewell Macready, since tonight we part:
Full-hearted thunders often have contest
Thy power well used to move the
public breast.
We thank thee with one voice, and from
the heart.

Macready died in 1873 and in the early 1980s the School's theatre was permanently renamed in his honour.
RR

1803

In an unorthodox tactic, Nelson with 27 British ships took on 33 enemy vessels in a single line before dividing into two columns to secure victory

THE BATTLE OF TRAFALGAR

Vice Admiral Lord Nelson demonstrated exactly what it meant to 'go out at the top' when he led the Royal Navy against the French and Spanish at the Battle of Trafalgar on October 21, 1805.

Although no British ships were lost in the encounter, the nation did lose its heroic naval commander when Nelson was mortally wounded by a French sniper.

Nelson was walking on the deck of his flagship *Victory* when at 1.15pm he was hit by a 0.69 inch diameter musket ball which severed an artery in his lung and lodged in his spine.

Taken below deck, he was kept informed about the progress of the battle by his close associate, Hardy. Nelson succumbed at around 4.30pm, two hours after his opposite number, Villeneuve, had surrendered, and after repeating the phrase: *"Thank God I have done my duty."*

Success at Trafalgar, which saw 27 British ships take on 33 enemy vessels, was due to unorthodox naval tactics, including engaging the French and Spanish in a single line and then dividing into two columns.

The price of victory was 1,700 British casualties, while Nelson's opponents lost 6,000 and surrendered 20,000 prisoners.

Villeneuve, while on parole as a prisoner, was given permission to attend Nelson's public funeral. On his later return to France he was murdered by Napoleon.

1804 William Pitt the Younger 🇬🇧

1805.

1806 William Grenville 🇬🇧

DR JOHN WOOLL

The spiritual and moral renewal of Rugby under Arnold suggests he inherited a rotten school.

But this overlooks the improving work of two of Arnold's predecessors, Thomas James, and James' successor but one, **Dr John Wooll**.

Wooll took the reins in 1807 after the headship of Henry Ingles, best known for presiding over the Great Rebellion of 1797.

The trustees chose Wooll over former pupil and perhaps more obvious candidate Samuel Butler, who went on instead to great things at Shrewsbury School.

Wooll holds the distinction of being Head Master during the creation, albeit accidentally, of a new sport now played across the world, thanks to the fine disregard of one of his pupils, William Webb Ellis, in 1823.

A Winchester and Balliol man, Wooll came to Rugby via a Somerset rectorship and seven years as Head of Midhurst Free Grammar School.

Like James he was a reformer, introducing prizes for Latin, Greek and English and overseeing significant building expansion.

The School roll rose to its highest ever at 381 (though not sustained) and with it the number of assistant masters, who also enjoyed improved pension arrangements.

Under Wooll, Rugby's standing as a major public school rose and the School continued to produce boys who would go on to achieve eminence in later life, including the great actor of the day, William Macready.

For all his popularity, Wooll, like Ingles and James before him, had to keep an eye on discipline at the School and take action when required.

When 38 boys in the Lower Fourth decided to leave their class mid lesson (except for one standing next to the master's desk) Wooll 'flogged the whole of them from first to last, including the innocent boy who did not go out with the rest'.

In the last decade of Wooll's headship numbers at the School fell considerably, a fact that may have contributed perhaps to his resignation in 1828.

Wooll headed for Worthing in Sussex and passed away five years later.

Dr John Wooll: Head Master from 1807 to 1828

Wooll's memorial in the School Chapel

BEETHOVEN'S FIFTH

Beethoven's Symphony No. 5 in C minor, first performed in Vienna in 1808, is best known for its 'dit dit dit dah' dramatic opening notes. These were borrowed by the Allies during the Second World War and played on the drums by British percussionist James Blades at the start of BBC broadcasts. Blades also provided the famous 'gong' sound at the start of Rank films.

Symphony No. 5 was written between 1804 and 1812 in a rich creative phase for Beethoven during which he composed an opera, six symphonies, four solo concerti, five string quartets, six string sonatas, seven piano sonatas, five sets of piano variations, four overtures, four trios, two sextets and 72 songs.

Beethoven was born on or about December 16, 1770 in the city of Bonn in the Electorate of Cologne, a principality of the Holy Roman Empire.

Plagued by ill health throughout his life, including near complete deafness for his final decade (during which he composed some of his most important works), Beethoven caught a cold in 1826 after arguing with his brother. He died on March 26, 1827, just as a storm broke out.

1808.

Ludwig van Beethoven: 1770-1827

1809

The oldest known drainpipe at the School, in the Old Quad, shows the date 1809, six years before School House was built. Next to it is the drinking trough where Tom Brown was ducked in *Tom Brown's Schooldays*.

1811.

1809 Spencer Perceval 🇬🇧
1809 James Madison 🇺🇸

WHITELAW ⭐

Whitelaw is the oldest house in continuous use for boarding boys, as it was one the dame's houses before the creation of the boarding house system by Thomas Arnold. The current House was built for James Hoare Christopher Moor and the house officially moved to its current location in 1811.

His father the Rev. Christopher Moor, who became an Assistant Master in 1757, made enough money from taking boys in that he was able to purchase land between Hillmorton Road and the south side of Horton Crescent.

At Easter 1867 the Housemaster J M Wilson gave up part of his front garden for the boys. It was converted into a gymnasium and known by the boys as 'The Bear Garden'. During the Christmas holidays in 1869, the Bear Garden was altered, and three fives courts built. The old fives courts to the front of the house, replaced 'The Bear Garden' which was an area used for ball games until Dr Sharpe complained about the balls coming over to his garden (6 Horton Crescent).

As with other boarding houses, which were privately owned, their names changed with their Housemasters. Between 1879 and 1913, the house was owned by Robert Whitelaw, an outstanding teacher and classics master. After a dispute with the Head Master about the need to speak about him at Speech Day, on his retirement Whitelaw refused to sell his house (for £8,800) to the school in 1913, stating *"You may take my boys, but the house is my own."*

JM Hardwick bought it from Whitelaw for £10,000, on the understanding that the Governing Body would buy it for £8,800, and be responsible for all necessary alterations, and would guarantee a lump sum of £600 to him, if he left the house within six years. The house was permanently named Whitelaw in 1936.

In 1939 a major rebuilding of study and library blocks took place, and during the Second World War, boys from Stanley and Cotton moved in (Stanley had been taken over by the Government as a reception hostel for women). The current kitchens were built in 1954, replacing a number of studies.

The most recent major physical change, with a generous gift from Rugbeian Roger Pilkington, was the expansion into 6 Horton Crescent (now the Assistant Housemaster's accommodation), and 6A became study bedrooms and common rooms.

In 2002 the last remaining boys from Tudor House moved in, when Tudor became a girls' house.

Notable Whitelaw Rugbeians:
Donald Michie – one of the leading Enigma code-breakers at Bletchley
Arthur Ransome – Author, and journalist.
Pelham Warner ('Plum') – Cricketer
Frederick Courtney Selous – hunter and early conservationist
Harry Riccardo – Developed the two-stroke engine
RH Tawney – Economic historian, social critic, Socialist.

MILES JOSEPH BERKELEY

As a vicar **Miles Joseph Berkeley** (Robert Stanley 1817-1821) knew God created the Earth. He also knew a great deal about what happened below its surface.

Born in 1803, Berkeley left Rugby for Cambridge University, after which he became a priest and vicar of Sibbertoft, near Market Harborough.

Along the way, he developed a deep knowledge of lichens, fungi, mosses, algae and plant pathology.

His mid-19th century work on diseases afflicting fruit and vegetables significantly advanced the field of study in this area and he was widely acknowledged as the expert of his time.

Berkeley's collection of over 9,000 specimens, plus notes and sketches, is kept for posterity at the Royal Botanic Gardens in Kew.

Before his death in 1889, Berkeley was made a Fellow of the Royal Society, won its Royal Medal and was made a Fellow of his old Cambridge college.

1814
1815

1812 Robert Jenkinson

Waterloo: The end of Napoleon's military and political career

THE BATTLE OF WATERLOO

After escaping from exile on Elba and returning to France in 1815, Napoleon embarked on what became known as the Hundred Days Campaign against a coalition of Austria, Britain, Prussia, the Netherlands and Russia. Napoleon's strategy was to pick off the allies one by one before they could mount a concerted attack.

In June 1815, Napoleon's forces marched into Belgium where, at the Battle of Ligny, Napoleon defeated, but was unable totally to destroy, a Prussian army commanded by Blücher. Two days later, on 18 June,

Napoleon pitched his army of 72,000 against 68,000 troops commanded by Wellington at Waterloo, south of Brussels.

Napoleon made an uncharacteristic error. Heavy rain having fallen during the previous night, he waited until midday to allow the ground to dry out before he ordered the attack. Napoleon's troops mounted a fierce assault against the British lines but the timely arrival of Blücher with his remaining 30,000 troops swung the battle decisively against the French. Now heavily outnumbered,

Napoleon's forces retreated in chaos, suffering over 30,000 dead, wounded and captured against the allies' losses of 22,000.

The battle marked the end of Napoleon's military and political career. He had made tactical mistakes and was poorly supported by his commanders. Ill and exhausted, he reportedly abandoned the battlefield in tears. He abdicated for a second time four days later and was exiled to the remote island of St Helena where, six years later, he died aged 51, almost certainly from stomach cancer. **DH**

SCHOOL HOUSE

As the School grew in numbers, more of the outbuildings were used for teaching and one of the barns was used as the chapel. By the end of the 18th century, plans were being drawn up to build a new house for the Head Master, a chapel, classrooms and other necessary buildings. The original architect, one Samuel Wyatt, designed a range of buildings, with a small chapel on Lawrence Sheriff Street and high walls hiding the school from the town. With Wyatt's sudden death, the Trustees appointed Henry Hakewill in 1808 to take over the project.

The result was a late Georgian building in Tudor style, an example of Gothic Revival. It was one of the first in the country to combine classrooms, boarding for the boys, and accommodation for staff.

Building work began in 1809 and would continue, in this first phase, until 1815. School continued during the building and boys would often leave their lessons in the outbuildings, to be greeted by the workmen and their pickaxes as they prepared to demolish the structures.

The Head Master's house replaced the original manor, with Old Quad on the site of the stable yard. A single storey enclosed this space, with cloisters to the east and south. Dormitories would be built above these two wings in 1815.

To the north side lay the main gates and the Writing School. On the east and south sides, above classrooms and storerooms, was accommodation for the boys. The range of classrooms on the south side was completed by the Great School, the classroom for the lower school. It was here that up to five classes would congregate at the same time for their lessons and it was here, too, that prayers were held until the building of the first chapel in 1820.

The first addition to Old Quad was the building of the library in 1827. This became the Sixth School, and was used by Thomas Arnold as his classroom. Better known as Upper Bench, it was extended in 1846 as a memorial to Arnold, and became the Arnold Library. The extension also includes Lower Bench. The remainder of the extensions to Old Quad would be to School House. **RM**

School House: Combining classrooms, boarding for boys and accommodation for staff

EMMA AND KUBLAI KHAN PUBLISHED

Jane Austen's *Emma* was published in December 1815, though publisher John Murray's title page shows the date as 1816. Written between January 21, 1814 and March 29, 1815, *Emma* has Austen at the height of her powers. It's the story of a young woman blessed with good looks, wealth, intelligence and an adoring father. The plot revolves around Emma's attempts to make matches among her friends and her own mild flirtation with a good-looking charmer. It ends with her marriage.

Austen tells us on the book's first page, that Emma is in danger of *"having her own way rather too much and a disposition to think too well of herself"*. Austen presents the world from Emma's point of view with all her errors of perception. Considered by many to be Austen's finest work, it is at the end of the novel that Austen springs her trap, showing the reader's own vulnerability to error and misconception.

Samuel Taylor Coleridge's reputation as a major literary figure rests primarily on three works written between 1797 and 1800, one of which - *Kublai Khan* - was published in 1816. Coleridge subtitled the poem "A Vision in a Dream: A Fragment". In a preface, Coleridge described how, after taking opium, he had grown drowsy while reading about the court of the 13th-century ruler of the Mongol Empire in China. Coleridge said that having fallen into a deep sleep, he had composed between 200 and 300 lines of verse based on vivid images in a dream. When he woke, he remembered the entire poem and immediately began to write it down. Distracted by a visitor for an hour, Coleridge returned to his writing only to find that he had been left with only vague recollections and the 54 lines of this poetic fragment. Many challenge the truthfulness of Coleridge's account, believing that the poem is complete. **DH**

Jane Austen

Samuel Taylor Coleridge

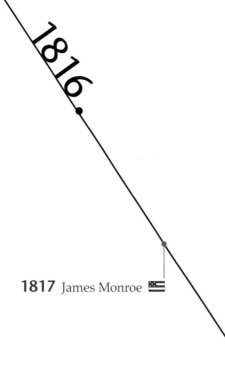

Kublai Khan

1816.

1817 James Monroe

Window in the North transept of the Chapel designed by Butterfield and installed in 1882

THE CHAPEL

After the range of buildings comprising Old Quad and School House were completed, Henry Hakewill moved on to design the first Chapel. In earlier days, one of the old barns of the manor house had been used, and the boys had also walked in pairs down to St Andrew's in the centre of town for their services. In 1818 the foundation stone was laid for the first Chapel, a squat rectangular building of white brick, some 30 feet wide and 90 feet long. It was opened in 1820, but by the late 1840s was struggling to cope with a growing school. Narrow transepts were added in 1848 (north), and 1851 (south) and the Narthex was added in 1856, under the guidance of Assistant Master Edward White Benson who would later become Archbishop of Canterbury. The gallery at the west end was removed in 1855, and the organ moved from here to the north-east corner.

As part of the Tercentenary celebrations, £7,000 was raised to enlarge the building, and William Butterfield was employed as architect. The building was lengthened by some 40 feet, which involved the removal of an elm tree which was taller than the School House. The tree was replanted in The Close and survived until 1895, when it was destroyed in the Great Storm. The transepts were enlarged and the west end widened and the roof raised. Although Frederick Temple had left the school by 1870, the organ chamber in the north-east corner was erected as a memorial to him.

The west end was left untouched, and so the building presented an incongruous appearance. The low west end was raised and the stone exterior replaced by the polychromatic brickwork in the style of Butterfield's east end. The architect was Thomas Jackson, under guidance from Butterfield, who was too old to take on the task. The bell tower, known as the Pepperpot, was completed in 1883, and the unified building was finally finished and opened by Archbishop Frederick Temple in October 1898. The original pews and wainscoting were re-used, as were many of the stained glass windows. These included 16th-century Flemish and German glass.

The transept windows were designed by Butterfield, and later additions include windows by Burne Jones and the west window, from the William Morris workshops.

Major refurbishment work was carried out in the 1960s, supervised by Dykes Bower, the Master of Fabric at St Paul's. The work included a rebuilding of the organ, replacement of the lighting, and relocation of some of the memorial tablets. It was at this time that the famous carved figure of the footballer was installed. The piece was by Thomas Faulkner, who had been a pupil at Rugby in the late 1920s and was placed on the last surviving pillar which had held up the old organ. In 2003 work was completed on a new organ, designed by Kenneth Jones. Ceiling restoration in 2011 was followed in 2012 by a new computerised lighting system, which complements this starred Grade 1 listed building. **RM**

The School Chapel in 1856

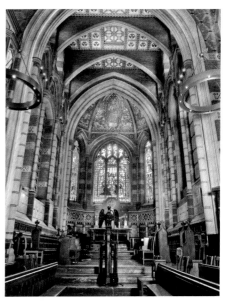

Butterfield's Chapel today, beautifully refurbished in the 1960s

1820 George IV

1818.

1823.

RUGBY FOOTBALL

The Early Years

"Few and simple were the rules of the game: touch on the sides of the ground was marked out, and no one was allowed to run with the ball in his grasp towards the opposite goal. It was Football, and not handball; plenty of hacking, but little struggling."

(Matthew Bloxam (Bloxam 1813-1822) reminiscing in 1880).

By the mid-18th-century Rugby School had outgrown its mid-town position. In 1749 an old manor house on the edge of town was selected as the new site for the School. Along with the building, came *"some old enclosures annexed to it, which were capable of offering every accommodation that could be required for the exercise of young gentlemen"*. A plot of eight acres, *"within a few perches"*, became known as The Close after fences were eventually removed and ditches filled in.

As in many schools a type of football evolved. There were no written rules and no staff involvement. Reflecting the fluid and casual nature of football in those early days, Head Master Henry Ingles called William Charles Macready (Birch 1803-1809) out of a game on The Close. He bid the youngster to keep his cap on and walk with him around The Close to talk about his future.

The original playing area was in the north-west corner of The Close but once the chapel foundations were laid down the players moved to the area south of what became the Doctor's Wall. A couple of the best players selected the first 20 on each side, then split the rest up to keep goal. When the game got stuck at one end the youths under the goal posts at the other end often started their own puntabout game. No special kit was worn, no records of the early games survive, there was lots of kicking and what, today, might be described as an enormous 'rolling maul' involving up to 60 players. The chief movement came from hacking the ball along the ground in the general direction of the opposition goal. If the ball got airborne a fair catch or mark was allowed. The opposition could advance up to that mark but no further. The catcher had three options. He could punt it ahead [today's up-and-under], attempt a drop kick at goal or place the ball for another player to kick.

One autumn afternoon in 1823 **William Webb Ellis** (Town 1816-1825) did none of those things. He legally caught the ball but then ran forward with it through a surprised and increasingly irate opposition, thus originating one of the distinctive features of the game.

Certainly Bloxam was writing long after the incident. Nevertheless Bloxam was universally believed to be an honest historian. He didn't take to Ellis and he preferred the old game, *"Football and not handball"*. He was not a creator of myths.

1824
When the King and Queen of Hawaii died from measles on a visit to England, Rugbeian **Andrew Bloxham** was the naturalist on board on the ship which returned their bodies home. On the voyage he recorded observations about Hawaii's native birds.

1825 John Quincy Adams

Thomas Harris entered Rugby in 1819 and recalls Ellis as *"an admirable cricketer but one who was inclined to take unfair advantage at Football"*. Did Ellis have form? The questions that doubters have about the origins of football at Rugby come largely from the decisions made by an Old Rugbeian Committee set up at the end of the 19th-century and the ensuing plaque that remains in pride of place right by Old Bigside. *".......with a fine disregard for the rules of the game as played in his time....."*; the rules changed almost every time the boys turned out to play. *"....first took the ball in his arms and ran with it......"*.

It took time for Webb Ellis's action to be accepted. Running with the ball gradually gained respectability. However, even in 1834 it was observed that *"running with the ball to get a try by touching down was not absolutely forbidden, but a jury of Rugby boys of that day would almost certainly have found a verdict of justifiable homicide if someone had been killed running in."* On a similar theme, Head Master Frederick Temple, when questioned by a visitor disturbed by the rough nature of the game, was asked if he ever stopped play. He replied, *"Never.......short of manslaughter."*

On August 28th, 1845 the first codified rules of the game were submitted by three senior boys and were immediately approved and printed. There were 37 of them and it had taken them three days. Not bad for a trio of sixteen and seventeen year olds. These rules were for the initiated at the School and really just tried to clarify a number of disputes and details. The true breakthrough came with the revised version of 1862. Critically, this edition had a major impact on the spread of the game beyond the confines of The Close.

A remarkable number of terms and instructions remain today. Off side remains a fundamental element of the game as is its early version of obstruction. No player may be held unless he is himself holding the ball. Scrummage, drop kick, place kick, touch, knock on and try at goal are all there. Readers may be interested to know that originally a try did not secure any points. Someone had to convert the touch down as it was merely a try or attempt to kick the goal. With the goalmouth packed and players permitted to charge the attempted kick at goal, no wonder the conversion was forced to go over the crossbar

The first evidence of staff involvement came in 1858 when Frederick Temple abolished standing in goal as a waste of the younger boy's time. There was an outcry from Old Rugbeians and so the Head Master compromised by allowing them out for the three major matches of the year.

The new rules recommended an oblong pitch rather than a square one and touch judges were introduced to decide who first handled the ball beyond the line of touch and therefore had the right to throw it back into play. There were still no referees. Arthur Astley Pearson (Arnold 1861-1866) wrote, *"......and yet we got on very well without them."* Most players were forwards but three or four of the swiftest runners and drop kick experts started to keep to the rear and someone clever at "dodging" acted as the link between the two groups. The game as we know it today was slowly taking shape.

Hacking and hacking over proved highly contentious matters as the game spread to other schools and universities. The former, kicking the ball carrier in a maul below the knee to encourage him to release it, slowly died out and heeling in scrummages took over.

By 1852 Marlborough was playing the Rugby game and the first recorded inter-school match was Merchiston Castle versus Edinburgh Royal High School in 1857. This was the year Richard Sykes (Shairp 1853-1857) brought a Lindon Bigside ball from Rugby to the north west. He also proved an invaluable source of advice before a match between Liverpool and The World. Some of the World team came from as far afield as Yorkshire and Cheshire.

When he left Rugby, Sykes founded the Manchester Club in 1860 so Liverpool now had regular, local opponents. He was also responsible for taking the game to the west coast of the USA – Rugby only played its first "foreign" match in 1867. This encounter between the School XX and AC Harrison, Esq.'s is worthy of note. The Head Master, Dr Temple, insisted the opposition should be either Old Rugbeians or residents of or near Rugby. After some 40 minutes the teams changed over so that each might have an equal share of the strong wind.

1827 George Canning 🇬🇧

1827 Frederick Robinson 🇬🇧

Some have suggested this was the origin of half time. The School held out against playing another school until 1896. They lost that match and the next three until 1899 when they managed to defeat both Cheltenham and Uppingham.

The first International was played in Edinburgh in 1871. England's XX arrived to find a pitch 120 yards long and 55 yards wide. This was much narrower than any pitch south of the border. Mutterings of skulduggery were heard to come from some of the visitors. England lost by a converted push-over try which England declared to be an illegal act.

In 1876 Rugby reduced its numbers to XV for foreign matches. One wit commented that they used to win most of their matches before this. The Rugby Football union took another twelve months to follow the School's lead on numbers.

In the England versus Scotland match at The Oval in 1874 Rugby School had representatives in both teams. This was a first, as was a rare event in 1878 when Rugby provided both half backs in the Irish team at Lansdowne Road against visitors England. What remains remarkable is that scrum half Thomas Gisborne Gordon (Hutchinson 1866-1868) only had one hand; the other had been lost in a shooting accident. John Douglas Boswell (School 1881-1882), described as "florid and stout almost to rotundity" played fifteen times for Scotland, captaining them four times, in the late 1880s and early 1890s. He was the first forward to kick a drop goal in an International.

By 1884 Rugby School had produced English, Scottish, Irish and Welsh Internationals. Finally

mention must be made of Herbert Hayton Castens (Bowden Smith 1878-1883) who was the first Springbok captain. Great Britain toured South Africa in 1891. Castens captained the Springboks in the opening Test, was dropped for the second and refereed the third.

The game of 'Rugby' football may have changed out of all recognition since those 'primitive' days nearly 200 years ago. Nevertheless, the name remains and the School was fully recognised by the World Cup authorities in 2015 at the opening match and at the Final, when the School choir sang on the Twickenham pitch. The School can be justly proud of this wonderful heritage – let's hope we can do young Webb Ellis proud in 2023. DR

As the ball first between
the posts curled,

A GAME WAS INVENTED THAT COVERED THE WORLD

1823.

1828-1841
THE DOCTOR WILL SEE YOU NOW

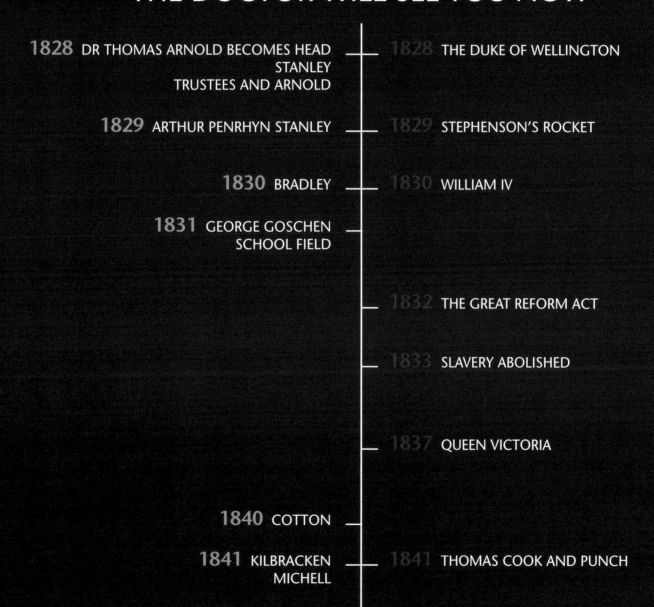

1828 DR THOMAS ARNOLD BECOMES HEAD STANLEY TRUSTEES AND ARNOLD	**1828** THE DUKE OF WELLINGTON
1829 ARTHUR PENRHYN STANLEY	**1829** STEPHENSON'S ROCKET
1830 BRADLEY	**1830** WILLIAM IV
1831 GEORGE GOSCHEN SCHOOL FIELD	
	1832 THE GREAT REFORM ACT
	1833 SLAVERY ABOLISHED
	1837 QUEEN VICTORIA
1840 COTTON	
1841 KILBRACKEN MICHELL	**1841** THOMAS COOK AND PUNCH

DR THOMAS ARNOLD

The hero of *Tom Brown's Schooldays* was fishing when he heard **Thomas Arnold** had died. The news hit him hard.

"He felt completely carried off his moral and intellectual legs, as if he had lost his standing-point in the invisible world, besides which, the deeply loving loyalty which he felt for his old leader made the shock intensely painful."

It is difficult to imagine many people being so affected by the death of a former head teacher. But Arnold was no ordinary Head Master.

Born one of six children in 1795 on the Isle of Wight, Arnold excelled in classics at Oxford, after which he started up his own school at Laleham, tutoring students for university and later took holy orders.

Appointed to Rugby in 1828 at just 33, he inherited a school with a reputation for poor behaviour and an undistinguished academic standing. While lesser men might have flinched, Arnold was a leader with a clear vision for his school:

"First religious and moral principle, second gentlemanly conduct, third academic ability."

Against a backdrop of bullying and sexual immorality among pupils, Arnold took on the role of school chaplain to drive home a theme of turning Rugby into a home for Christian gentlemen.

Stirring sermons from the pulpit were accompanied by practical action.

Prefects, or praeposters, were given responsibility to help keep discipline and improve the running of boarding houses, and former dame houses were closed.

In the classroom, Arnold introduced a form system and alongside a core curriculum of classics added mathematics, modern history and modern languages.

Although not a sporting evangelist, Arnold did allow games, as an alternative to poaching or fighting, a stance that certainly did enough to convince Baron de Coubertin (later founder of the modern Olympic Games) to describe him as 'one of the founders of athletics chivalry'.

Arnold died from a heart attack aged 47 in 1842 after thirteen years at the Rugby helm, during which he transformed and restored the School's reputation.

His methods were also soon adopted as the template for Victorian boarding schools, aided in no small measure by many of his assistant masters going on to become heads themselves.

Arnold and Arnoldian are still used today as shorthand for excellence in education, and of course the name has enjoyed greater prominence since the creation of the Arnold Foundation in 2004.

There is little doubt that Arnold would have achieved enduring fame through his work at Rugby, or as an educator, alone.
However, consistent with the polymath spirit of the age, the Doctor was active on many different fronts. As a cleric, his sermons were favoured by no less an admirer than Queen Victoria herself.

When not urging his pupils to higher moral standards, he found time to speak out on wider religious matters.

A believer in state over Church, he strongly opposed the High Church movement, supported Catholic emancipation and in just his fifth year at Rugby published *Principles of Church Reform.*

A year before his death, Arnold was appointed Regius Professor of Modern History at Oxford. He also published a short-lived newspaper calling for social reform, based on strong sympathy and support for the poor.

Arnold's reputation was burnished through the successful biography *Life of Arnold*, written by one of his former pupils, Arthur Penrhyn Stanley (later Dean of Westminster) two years after his death.

While Stanley praised Arnold, he was also not afraid to cover more difficult moments, including a motion of censure brought against him in 1836, which was duly lost.

For all Arnold's success and influence, he was not without critics and was one of Lytton Strachey's (whose younger brother James was a friend of Rupert Brooke) targets in his best-seller *Eminent Victorians.*

In particular Strachey mocked Arnold's Old Testament certainty, use of prefects to run his school and sometimes forbidding leadership style.

"...Arnold hoped to turn Rugby into a place of 'really Christian education'. The boys were to work out their own salvation, like the human race. He himself, involved in awful grandeur, ruled remotely, through his chosen instruments, from an inaccessible heaven."

So like all leaders Arnold was not perfect and it is no surprise his particular brand of faith-led, strong discipline, high ideals and morally certain approach to education did not win universal acclaim.

What cannot be doubted, however, is that, while Lawrence Sheriff was the founder of the School, Arnold was the man who saved it and put it on the map of great public schools.

1828

Dr Thomas Arnold: Head Master from 1828 to 1842

THE DUKE OF WELLINGTON

In 1828, the Duke of Wellington took on his other great leadership role as Prime Minister.

After a military career, the democratic nature of his new post was a shock to the 'Iron Duke's' constitution.

Following his first Cabinet meeting he wrote: *"An extraordinary affair. I gave them their orders and they wanted to stay and discuss them."*

Wellington's boldness in battle was not matched on all fronts in politics and he was a conservative on electoral reform.

He did however fight for, and win, Catholic emancipation and the granting of almost full civil rights for Catholics.

This brought him into conflict with Lord Winchilsea who railed against Wellington's *"treacherous destruction of the Protestant constitution"*.

The two men faced up to each other in a duel in Battersea Park but both fired to miss and honour was satisfied.

In 1834 Wellington refused a second invitation to lead the nation, becoming instead Foreign Secretary under Sir Robert Peel. He later led the House of Lords and retired from politics in 1846. He died in 1852.

Wellington: Boldness in battle not matched in politics

1828.

STANLEY

Stanley was built around 1828 for Anstey, the first House Master, who was also the school Chaplain. He was a pupil from 1811 to 1815 and a master from 1819 to 1864. There was a Stanley House in the late 18th century, belonging to Robert Stanley, which was sited in the north-east corner of New Quad. It became extinct in 1847. The building was purchased by the School in 1913 for £9,000 and named Stanley in 1931 after Arnold's biographer, Dean Stanley. Towards the end of 1941, Stanley was used as a reception hostel for women. In the 1950s, the architect KG Kellett's designs for the new building at Stanley, were awarded a Civic Trust Award. The house crest comes from Viscount Cross (Richard Assheton Cross).

Stanley alumni include **Adrian Dura Stoop** (England Rugby international 1905-1912 after whom The Stoop at Harlequins' ground is named)…
Christopher Lloyd (garden designer, plantsman and garden writer)…
and more recently, **Polly Stenham** (playwright). **RM**

A copy of the bust of Arnold that is in the Temple Speech Room

TRUSTEES AND ARNOLD

Though the School's popularity and numbers slipped at the end of Wooll's tenure, 1828 brought Thomas Arnold to Rugby. From the beginning, Arnold was clear that it was his task to lead and manage the School and its staff, saying the Trustees must support him or sack him. The Trustees did support him, though not without occasional strong misgivings, and on one occasion Arnold only survived a vote of censure due to a four-four vote by Trustees.

Arnold persuaded the Trustees to limit the benefits of the Foundation to boys whose parents had lived in Rugby for two years or more, thus stymieing the most bare-faced sojourners. At the same time he got the Trustees to agree to limit the number of non-Foundationers to 260 boys, holding the School's size to not much over 300. Arnold also disliked taking boys under twelve into the School, whether on the Foundation or not, because he felt it was not suited to them.

Under Arnold the School became immensely popular and the limitation on size was abandoned. While Arnold (and later Tom Brown) deserve most of the credit for Rugby's success, the London and Birmingham Railway shares the laurels. Originally the line was to go south of the School, near to The Close, but in late 1830 the School's Trustees employed a leading local solicitor, William Wratislaw, to protest. A survey committee having visited Rugby, Robert Stephenson advised the Company to redraw the line to its present position north of the town.

This change had a fundamental impact on the growth of Rugby from a small town of 2,500 people to its later prosperity. The new line encouraged industrial expansion in the flat lands north of the town and influenced the routes of other lines, thus making Rugby a junction town. London and Birmingham were now in easy range. Sojourners were still buying large houses in the town and Arnold's endeavours to keep small boys out of the School meant prep schools opened… and girls' schools opened for sisters.

The evidence in 1839 Chancery proceedings on a petition from Wratislaw tells us a little about how the Trustees exercised their duties and much about how Arnold ran the School.

Wratislaw's 1839 cause of action was a claim that the Trustees were in breach of trust in accepting Arnold's actions to the prejudice of Rugby people with boys under twelve The Master of the Rolls found partly for the Trustees and partly for the petitioners, the charity to bear the costs.

The Wratislaw case tells us that Sir Gray Skipwith of Newbold Hall, leading Trustee in the 1820s and 1830s, had put two sons through the School. He had been a Trustee since 1804, since when he had taken an active part in the management of the Trust and had, with only five exceptions, attended every annual meeting of the Trustees. George Harris, a Rugby solicitor, had been the Trustees' clerk for 37 years. Mr Harris explained that *"besides their annual meeting, at which the Trustees devote two days at their sole cost, they assemble at special meetings, when any emergency or business relative to the affairs of the school and charity require their attendance"*.

Arnold was succeeded by **Dr Tait** (1842-50) and then **Dr Goulburn** (1850-58). Tait's was a period of consolidation but perhaps Rugby was gaining an undeserved reputation for ecclesiastical innovation. When Tait, overtaken by illness, moved to the Deanery of Carlisle, the Trustees chose as his successor the deeply conservative Goulburn. Goulburn loved Rugby. He gave the School the field called New Bigside, built School Field House at his own expense and wrote the School's history. Even so, during his time the School's fame faded and numbers fell away. **MF**

The Rocket became the template for engine design across the world

STEPHENSON'S ROCKET

Rainhill village in Merseyside is the perhaps unlikely setting for the first truly successful run by arguably the world's most famous steam train.

The *Rocket*, built by George Stephenson, beat off competition from ten other engines in trials at Rainhill in 1829. He was aided in his victory by the fact that five failed to make the race and two broke down.

Watched by 15,000 people, the *Rocket* (which travelled only horizontally, despite its name) achieved an average speed of 24 miles per hour over the course's 20 laps and a top speed of 36 mph. The competition was held by the Liverpool and Manchester Railway Company which wanted to find the best locomotive to serve the needs of both cities.

Built at Stephen's Forth Street works in Newcastle-upon-Tyne, the *Rocket* was the first locomotive to have a multi-tube boiler - with 25 copper tubes rather than a single flue or twin flue – and became the template for engine design across the world over the next century and a half.

Finished in mustard yellow, the *Rocket* featured a distinctively tall black chimney. Inside, its blast pipe also increased the draught to the fire by concentrating exhaust steam at the base of the chimney. This meant the boiler generated more steam power so the *Rocket* was able to go faster than its rivals.

The *Rocket* can be seen at the Science Museum in London.

1829.

ARTHUR PENRHYN STANLEY

Religion, academia and Rugby School were central to the life of the eminent Victorian **Arthur Penrhyn Stanley**.

Stanley arrived at Rugby in 1829, a year after Arnold, before heading off to Oxford, where he scooped up a host of academic prizes.

Taking a fellowship and holy orders, he stayed in Oxford for ten years as a tutor, and wrote his best-selling *Life of Arnold*.

The book cemented Arnold as the leading Head Master of his day and helped market Rugby to the world.

As a broad churchman, Stanley supported Arnold against Newman's controversial and divisive Tract 90 and as an academic devoted time to university reform and modernisation.

In 1856 he became Regius Professor of Ecclesisastical History at Oxford and canon of Christ Church and, seven years later, was appointed Dean of Westminster.

Stanley excelled in many fields, was a strong and admired preacher, published widely on church history and devoted himself to preserving the fabric of Westminster Abbey.

He explored and wrote about Egypt and Palestine, helped to improve water supplies in Jerusalem and also helped found the Palestine Exploration Fund.

Alongside these accomplishments, he also built strong connections, including with Benjamin Jowett, Queen Victoria, and later with Rugby Heads Temple and Tait.

For all his talents, Stanley was said to be *'incapable of distinguishing one tune from another'* and wrote some unremembered hymns.

Despite these shortcomings, his funeral service at Westminster Abbey in July 1881 was attended by the Prince of Wales (later King Edward VII), cabinet ministers, representatives from literature, arts and science and working men of Westminster. He was buried next to his adored wife Lady Augusta Bruce, who had been an attendant to Queen Victoria.

Said to be Thomas Hughes' inspiration for George Arthur in *Tom Brown's Schooldays*, Stanley is to today remembered by the tourists and office workers in Dean Stanley Street in the heart of Westminster and by the boarders and staff at Stanley House.

1830 Charles Grey   **1830** William IV

1830

William IV fathered twelve children

WILLIAM IV

William Henry was born in 1765. The third son of King George III, he never expected to become King. At the age of thirteen, he embarked on a career in the navy, joining as a midshipman. He worked his way up the ranks, eventually commanding *HMS Pegasus*. He served under Nelson in the West Indies, the two becoming good friends. Promoted Rear-Admiral in 1789, he left active service the following year.

After retiring from the navy, William lived with his mistress Dorothea Jordan, with whom he fathered ten children. Faced with huge debts, William was forced to leave her to marry Princess Adelaide of Saxe-Meiningen in 1818. The marriage proved to be a happy one but Adelaide was unable to provide William with an heir: two daughters died in infancy.

Clarence House was built for William between 1825 and 1827 at a modest cost of about £22,000. The frugally minded William continued to live there rather than at Buckingham Palace after he became King in 1830 at the age of 64 on the death of his brother George IV.

William died at Windsor in 1837 without surviving legitimate children, and so he was succeeded by his niece, Victoria. **DH**

1830

BRADLEY

Bradley is one of the School's oldest Houses in school, dating back to at least 1830, when Bonamy Price took in boys.

It was purchased by the School in 1910, when BB Dickinson took over. Although one of the earliest boarding houses, it was the last to receive its permanent name.

The House was named Bradley in September 1945 (it had been agreed to do so on the retirement of the Housemaster Mr Harris) after George Granville Bradley, who entered Rugby in 1837 (1837-1840), and who went on to become Head Master at Marlborough, Master of University College, Oxford, and Dean of Westminster (1881-1902).

During the discussions on the name, it had been suggested that Holyoake (one of the early Head Masters) might fit the bill. In 1992, 5 Barby Road became a girls' boarding house, under Claire Moreland.

Bradley alumni include **Thomas Wentworth Wills**, a pioneer of cricket in Australia (and the father of Aussie Rules Football)… **Sir Salman Rushdie**, acclaimed author… **William Bateson**, pioneering geneticist (who coined the use of the word genetics, and created words such as zygot)… **Reid Railton**, an automotive engineer who designed the record-breaking Bluebird vehicles for Malcolm and Donald Campbell. **RM**

1831

GEORGE GOSCHEN

Neville Chamberlain may be blamed for declaring war on Germany, but it is fellow Rugbeian **George Goschen** (1831-1907) whom we can point to for the vehicle tax we all know and love to this day. This was introduced during Goschen's six-year rule at the Treasury from 1886 to 1892 which followed the impetuous resignation of Lord Randolph Churchill (father to Winston) who believed he was irreplaceable. Realising belatedly he wasn't, Churchill senior famously remarked that he had 'forgotten Goschen', a phrase forever attached to his successor. Goschen's other political roles included President of the Poor Law Board and First Lord of the Admiralty, while outside interests involved Presidency of the Royal Statistical Society and penning *The Theory of the Foreign Exchanges*.

SCHOOL FIELD

The earliest record of what was to become School Field is in 1831, when JP Lee took in boys at his home in Hillmorton Road. By the early 1850s, the Head Master, Edward Meyrick Goulburn, realised the need for a more permanent solution. Prior to building the house in 1852, the land in The Close had been a dairy farm. Once the house was built, the farm buildings were removed to the site of the current gymnasium. Designed by George Gilbert Scott, and opened in 1852, it was paid for by Goulburn. The Governing Body had refused to build the house but leased an acre of the school field to Goulburn at £5 per annum. Goulburn still owned the house almost 20 years after he left Rugby. He offered to sell it to the school for £7,500 but was beaten down to £6,000 in 1872. It thus became the first house, apart from School House, to be owned by the school. The first Housemaster was Charles T Arnold. In 1892, the house was taken over by William Parker Brooke, the father of Rupert Brooke. When William died, Rupert took over the house for one term, although he was not a member of staff. The house was permanently named in 1932. In August 1920, Winston Churchill stayed at School Field whilst up at Rugby to play polo. During the Second World War, three-decker bunks were made for the corridors, to be used in the event of an air raid. The imposing chimneys from the north side of School Field facing the old Town Room were removed by the end of 1947. New extensions were added from 1954, and in 1997 the building became the first to be converted completely to single study-bedrooms.

School Field alumni include **Rupert Brooke** and author **Anthony Horowitz**. **RM**

THE BALANCE of POWER in 1831.

The balance of power is moved towards the people

THE GREAT REFORM ACT

As memories of the French Revolution faded, there was a growing call for parliamentary reform to reflect social changes wrought by industrialism. Particular inequities included the uneven distribution of seats, the narrowness of the property franchise and the continued survival of so-called 'rotten boroughs'.

Prime Minister Wellington was increasingly out of line with his own Tory party's growing support for some limited change to reflect the increasing wealth and influence of a growing middle class. When he and his government were ousted and the incoming Whig Prime Minister, Earl Grey, promised reform. At the third attempt, a reform bill was passed after Grey had persuaded the King, William IV, to use his prerogative to create sufficient new Whig peers to guarantee the bill safe passage. On hearing this, the Tories abstained en bloc to prevent what they saw as dilution of the upper house.

The Representation of the People Act 1832 later became known as the Great Reform Act. 56 boroughs in England and Wales were disenfranchised and a further 31 had their representation cut from two to only one MP. 67 new constituencies were created. The property qualification for voting was broadened to include small landowners, tenant farmers and shopkeepers. In boroughs, all householders paying a yearly rent of £10 or more and some lodgers were enfranchised. While the majority of working men and all women remained disenfranchised, the Act proved change was possible.

1832.

1833

The Abolition of Slavery Act was the precursor of the Human Rights Act

SLAVERY ABOLISHED

It is fitting that the Slavery Abolition Act 1833 had its third reading in the House of Commons just three days before the death of the man most associated with it, William Wilberforce.

Born in 1759 in Yorkshire, Wilberforce was a politician, philanthropist and a reforming Evangelical Christian.

In the late 1780s, he was persuaded to take up the slavery cause by abolitionist campaigners.

For two decades he led the parliamentary campaign, resulting in the Slave Trade Act of 1807 (which stopped slave trading) and full abolition in 1833.

The Slavery Abolition Act 1833 ended slavery throughout the British Empire, except for territories belonging to the East India Company, Ceylon and St Helena, which had to wait another decade.

Coming into force in August 1834, the Act freed slaves under

the age of six, with the remainder redesignated apprentices, whose slavery was phased out more gradually.

It also compensated slave-owners who had lost their trade, to the tune of £20m at the time, or more than £70bn in today's terms.

Wilberforce is buried in Westminster Abbey, close to William Pitt the Elder, who was a close friend.

1837

1834 William Lamb (Lord Melbourne) 🇬🇧
1834 Arthur Wellesley 🇬🇧
1834 Robert Peel 🇬🇧
1835 William Lamb (Lord Melbourne) 🇬🇧

1837 Martin Van Buren 🇺🇸

QUEEN VICTORIA

Victoria became queen in 1837 on the death of her uncle, William IV. She was also Empress of India from 1876 until her death in 1901.

She was born at Kensington Palace in 1819, the only child of Prince Edward, Duke of Kent, who died only eight months after she was born. Her mother was Princess Victoria Mary Louisa of Saxe-Coburg-Saalfeld. Accordingly, Victoria's first language was German. Aged three, she learned to speak English and French and, much later, Hindustani. Victoria was home-schooled. As well as languages, she studied history, geography and the Bible. She played the piano and painted, a hobby that she enjoyed well into her 60s.

Victoria was only eighteen when she came to the throne. In 1840, aged 21, Victoria married her cousin, Albert of Saxe-Coburg and Gotha. The marriage was a happy one and produced nine children, 40 grand-children and 37 great-grandchildren who were eventually scattered all over the continent, most marrying into other royal families.

Victoria was greatly influenced by her husband Albert's modern outlook. So, for example, she embraced 'new' technology, proving to be a keen and proficient photographer. Albert died in 1861 at the tragically young age of 42. Victoria mourned for almost ten years and wore black for the rest of her life.

DH

Queen Victoria reigned from 1837 until her death in 1901

COTTON

1838
First running of the Crick,
the oldest school run in
the UK.

The first Housemaster of what would eventually be known as Cotton House was Rev. Percy William Powlett from 1836 to 1840. He had been a School House pupil who entered Rugby in 1810 at the age of seven. Edward Lynch Cotton took over the house in 1840. He went on to be Headmaster at Marlborough and later became Bishop of Calcutta in 1858.

A disastrous fire completely destroyed the house in 1860, and the Housemaster, R B Smythies, was so distraught that the rebuilt house was taken over by Charles Alleyne Anstey for a short time. Anstey had worked under five Head Masters, from Wooll to Temple, and built his house, which became Stanley House. During the fire a pupil, HEC Beaver, climbed onto the roof trying to direct water onto the flames.

Henry Lee Warner, Housemaster from 1875 to 1884, had been Head of School, and had written to the Trustees asking for the first Rackets court to be built. The house was finally bought by the School in 1919, at a cost of £8,750. In 1941 the house was requisitioned by the Ministry of Labour as a hostel, and the then Housemaster, Rev. Richard Broxton, took the Cotton boys over to Tudor.

After the war, RW Stott took over the house and following a very generous donation from an old Cottonite in the 1950s, major rebuilding and improvement work was carried out.

Cotton alumni include **TW Jex-Blake** (Head Master from 1874 to 1887)… philosopher and historian **RG Collingwood**… Prime Minister **Neville Chamberlain**… composer **Sir Arthur Bliss**… and BBC Chairman **Marmaduke Hussey**. **RM**

1840.

1841

THOMAS COOK AND PUNCH

On June 9, 1841, a 32-year-old cabinet maker called Thomas Cook was walking from his home in Market Harborough to Leicester to go to a temperance meeting. A former Baptist preacher, Cook believed many social problems were alcohol-related. He later recalled that as he was walking, *"the thought suddenly flashed across my mind as to the practicability of employing the great powers of railways and locomotion for the furtherance of social reform"*.

Cook set about starting his travel business. On July 5, 1841, he took 570 temperance campaigners from Leicester to Loughborough, eleven miles by train, to attend a rally, charging people a shilling each.

The trip was a success and Cook branched out, arranging tours to Scotland in the 1840s and to the Great Exhibition in 1851. Continental tours began in 1856 when parties visited Belgium and the Rhineland, en route to the Paris Exhibition.

Founded in 1841, the same year as Cook's first tour, the magazine *Punch* took to lampooning "Cook's circus" in the 1870s and 1880s ridiculing what it took to be the tourists' ignorance and vulgarity.

Cook published some of the earliest guidebooks. That covering Syria and Palestine appeared in 1891, and by the turn of the century over 12,000 tourists had visited the Holy Land with the company.

The business thrived. Profits stood at £20,000 in the 1880s, £86,000 in the 1900s, rising to £139,268 when, in 1919, Thomas Cook undertook the first Battlefield Tours of what had been the Western Front. **DH**

Thomas Cook's first tour to a Temperance Society meeting in 1841 was lampooned by Punch, founded in the same year

1841 Robert Peel 🇬🇧
1841 William Harrison 🇺🇸
1841 John Taylor 🇺🇸

KILBRACKEN ⚓

Kilbracken is named after JA Godley who became Lord Kilbracken and was also a member of the Trustees/Governing Body. The house was created in 1841 by Thomas Arnold, with J Penrose as its first Housemaster. In 1848 it moved to 1, Hillmorton Road under George Granville Bradley, a Rugbeian who would become Dean of Westminster. Bradley was succeeded by Rugbeian Thomas William Jex-Blake, who returned as Head Master of Rugby. In 1867 a major fire broke out in the building which destroyed many of the studies, and damaged the entire house. The house was bought from the then Housemaster, John Collins, in 1907 for £7,500. In 1941 Kilbracken moved to its present site. With the purchase of Hillbrow School in 1919 (the prep school attended by Rupert Brooke before he entered Rugby), it became staff accommodation for AH Peppin and two masters. It also had four music rooms and a workshop for science. The old school was demolished early in 1939, and the boarding side was being built by May. Due to the then fear of war, a gas-proof shelter was included in the plans for the building, with the total cost of the project reaching £30,000. The house was requisitioned by the Government in April 1941 but released before September when the boys moved in. The house was permanently named Kilbracken in 1932.

Kilbracken alumni include **Prince Simyen Alamayu** (the only legitimate son of King Theodore of Abyssinia), buried at Windsor Castle… **Wynne Alexander Hugh Godley** (economist and model for the statue of St Michael at Coventry Cathedral)… **Henry Greg Melly**, early aviator and the first person to fly non-stop between Liverpool and Manchester on July 7, 1911… **David Urquhart** and **Jeremy Hanley**. **RM**

MICHELL

The earliest record of Michell House is in 1841, when Henry Highton took in boys. Highton was, in addition to being a schoolmaster, a scientist. He produced important work in the development of the electric telegraph, and even invented an artificial stone, which was used in paving. By the 1870s WC Green was in charge of the grand white stone mansion opposite School House. WG Michell took over Green's House in 1883 and almost immediately started the building of the present house. It opened in Lent 1884. The house was built on the site of a property owned by a MR Joy, and the *Vive La* of the time stated that 'his first act was to drive away Joy'. The old mansion was demolished to make way for New Big School, now the Macready Theatre. The House was purchased by the School in 1913, for £10,300, and permanently named Michell in 1936.

Michell alumni include **Alec Ogilvie** (early aviator, who flew gliders with the Wright Brothers, and invented and patented the world's first airspeed indicator)… **John Stanley Hawkesworth**, award-winning producer of television programmes such as *Upstairs Downstairs*… **Robert Hardy**, actor and leading expert on the English longbow… and **AN Wilson**, renowned writer and columnist. **RM**

1841

1842-1873
THREE HUNDRED NOT OUT

1842 ARCHIBALD CAMPBELL TAIT
BECOMES HEAD

1846 LEWIS CARROLL
1847 THE OLD SAN

1848 COMMUNIST MANIFESTO
"WUTHERING HEIGHTS"

1849 TUNELESS PUNISHMENT!
1850 EDWARD MEYRICK GOULBURN
BECOMES HEAD
1851 THE CRICKET PAVILIONS

1856 VICTORIA CROSS

1857 THOMAS HUGHES &
TOM BROWN'S SCHOOLDAYS

1857 ISAMBARD KINGDOM BRUNEL
THE INDIAN MUTINY

1858 FREDERICK TEMPLE BECOMES HEAD
THE SCIENCE SCHOOLS
HENRY WILMOT

1859 CHARLES DARWIN

1860 BEER
RACKETS COURTS

1860 BRITAIN'S FIRST IRON-CLAD WARSHIP

1861 THE DEATH OF PRINCE ALBERT

1863 GETTYSBURG

1867 CRICKET
COCK HOUSE

1868 WILLIAM GLADSTONE

1870 HENRY HAYMAN BECOMES HEAD

1870 THE DEATH OF DICKENS

ARCHIBALD CAMPBELL TAIT

Archibald Campbell Tait had the unenviable task of succeeding Thomas Arnold in 1842.

Although not front-runner for the post, Tait was a distinguished candidate. Born in Edinburgh, he was a scholar at Balliol College, Oxford, where he was a lecturer and junior dean.

He, along with Arnold, was also known for his protest against Tract 90, a controversial theological pamphlet written by John Henry Newman.

Despite winning the race to take over from Arnold, Tait realised the scale of the work ahead.

"The responsibility of such a situation seems to me every day more awful; but all situations are responsible just in proportion to their usefulness, and if it were in my power to keep up that system which Dr Arnold had begun, I should certainly think my life well spent."

Tait's personal doubts about the challenge were shared by Arthur Stanley, Arnold's biographer and later the well-known Dean Stanley of Westminster.

On July 29, 1842, less than a month after Arnold's death, Stanley wrote: *"Mr dear Tait – the awful intelligence of your election has just reached me. At any time it would have been a most serious responsibility…Read Arnold's sermons. At whatever expense of orthodoxy (so called) for the time, throw yourself thoroughly into his spirit. Alter nothing at first. See all that is good and nothing that is bad in the masters and the Rugby character."*

Tait and Stanley were perhaps justified in their worries about Tait being the Head Master to follow Arnold.

For although conscientious and hardworking, Tait found the responsibility hard, and perhaps his character suffered as a result. School historian WHD Rouse acknowledged this but added: *"… whatever may be the opinion held on this point, Tait's pupils entertained for him a deep and sincere regard."*

Tait was aided at Rugby by the support of his wife, Catherine, daughter of William Spooner (who gives us the word spoonerism today). *"His beautiful and gracious wife was ever happy to talk or read to those in Schoolhouse. To her husband Mrs Tait was a help indeed, keeping her accounts for him and relieving him of many of those minor matters which a Head Master has to attend to."*

During Tait's time at Rugby numbers rose to 493, but this made the School overcrowded and difficult to manage.

As the School grew both in size and eminence there were also more boys entering who later made their mark on the world stage.

One of these was Charles Lutwidge Dodgson, a brilliant young mathematician best known for writing *Alice in Wonderland* under the name Lewis Carroll (a variation of his real Christian names).

Although not anticipating Dodgson's writing career, Tait at least recognised his abilities in a letter to his father in December 1849: *"I must not allow your son to leave School without expressing to you the very high opinion I entertain of him… His mathematical knowledge is great for his age, and I doubt not he will do himself credit in Classics…During the whole time of his being in my house his conduct has been excellent."*

After severe rheumatic fever in early 1848 completely prostrated him, on convalescence Tait accepted the less demanding post

of Dean of Carlisle, leaving Rugby in summer 1850.

When appointed to Carlisle, the Trustees wrote that he had *"fully maintained the character of the School obtained under the distinguished man who preceded him"*.

Reviewing Tait's time in charge, School historian JB Hope Simpson reflected on the difficulty Tait faced in succeeding Arnold…

"Tait, as Head Master, has had rather a poor press; there has been little positive attack on this, but he has been damned with faint praise by more than one pen….With the faintness of the praise it is a little difficult, on the evidence, to agree. There were bound to be difficulties in the early days of any successor to Arnold's post. The assistant masters were individually brilliant…It would be natural for such men to be suspicious of any new-comer and to find difficulty in accepting any deviation from Arnold's principles and methods; and it is a measure of Tait's success that in certain respects he did so deviate."

If the move to Carlisle was in some ways a physical and emotional release from the burden of leading Rugby, returning to the Church did Tait's career no harm, as in 1868 he became the first of the School's Heads to be appointed Archbishop of Canterbury.

A year later, while Tait presided over a meeting at Westminster Abbey, in the presence of Dean Stanley, word came through that workmen had successfully discovered the coffin of King James I in one of the vaults. Hurrying to view the find, Dean Stanley paused to say: *"It is fitting that our first Scottish Archbishop should lead the way into the tomb of our first Scottish king."*

Archibald Campbell Tait:
Head Master from 1842 to 1850

1842.

Writers, poets,
artists and,

THE MAN
WHO GAVE US
WONDERLAND

1846

LEWIS CARROLL

It is fitting that Lewis Carroll, the most popular and famous writer to attend Rugby, created fantasy worlds full of amazing characters.

Behind the originator of make-believe Alice, the Looking Glass, Wonderland, the Mad Hatter and the Cheshire Cat, was a highly talented mathematician and photographer called **Charles Lutwidge Dodgson**.

Dodgson was born, appropriately, in Cheshire in 1832. He was a Rugby pupil for three years from his fourteenth birthday on January 17, 1846.

As a shy stammerer he endured inevitable bullying. He also caught whooping cough, which troubled him in later life, and mumps which affected his hearing.

Recalling his time at the School, Dodgson wrote:

"During my stay I made I suppose some progress in learning of various kinds, but none of it was done with love, and I spent an incalculable time in writing out impositions – this last I consider one of the chief faults of Rugby School. I made some friends there ... but I cannot say that I look back upon my life at a Public School with any sensations of pleasure, or that any earthly considerations would induce me to go through my three years again."

Although Dodgson disliked Rugby, despite doing well and winning prizes in maths and divinity, his talents were noted, with maths teacher RB Mayor declaring that he was the 'most promising boy' he had taught at the School.

Progressing to Oxford, Dodgson stayed at the University as a tutor and later administrator until 1892, passing away six years later.

During his time in Oxford, Dodgson took holy orders as a deacon. He also took a boat trip on the river with Rev. Robinson Duckworth in 1862 with the three young daughters of the Dean of Christ Church, Henry Liddell.

After he entertained Alice Liddell with a story about the adventures of a girl, she urged him to write it down. Three years later, in 1865, *Alice's Adventures in Wonderland* were published under the pseudonym Lewis Carroll.

Dodgson's Alice books endure today as some of the most popular books in English literature and continue to be adapted in print, on stage and on film.

Like JK Rowling's reinvention as a writer for adults, Dodgson ventured beyond Alice into other areas, including nonsense verse such as *Hunting of the Snark* and *Jaberwocky*. He was also highly accomplished in the new Victorian craze of photography.

One negative by-product of Carroll's work was the interpretation of it by critics, some of whom speculated about his moral conduct, characterising him as a suspected paedophile with an unhealthy interest in young girls. Psychoanalyst writers also suggested several examples of sexual symbolism in *Wonderland*.

This interpretation has not prevented the ongoing success of Alice, who could even include Oscar Wilde and Queen Victoria among her early fans.

Victorian writer and mathematician Sir Walter Besant described *Alice's Adventures in Wonderland* as an example of *"that extremely rare kind which will belong to all the generations to come until the language becomes obsolete"*.

Alice's Adventures in Wonderland has never been out of print and has been translated into at least 174 languages. A statue of Alice can be found in Central Park in New York.

THE OLD SAN

Concerns over the health of the boys had led to the provision of sick rooms in the houses by the early 1840s, but this was felt to be inadequate. A central 'hospital' was deemed necessary and by 1847 the Trustees had agreed on the provision of the first Sanatorium. The building, which was designed by Charles Penrose, was completed by the early 1850s. An isolation ward, the Fever Cottage, was added in 1876. By this time William Butterfield was the architect favoured by the School, and the building was constructed at a cost of some £984 by John Parnell & Sons in Rugby who worked for Butterfield. During the First World War, the building was used as a hospital for Belgian war wounded and by the end of October 1914, the first war wounded had arrived with the Geneva Cross 'dangling from the Sanatorium garden wall'. The Fever Cottage was demolished in 1935. In this year, the Art Museum was moved from the Temple Reading Room to occupy one of the old wards. As a hospital, the building was now redundant as the New San had been opened in 1934 but during the Second World War it was used for producing diamond dies which were essential for making wires for precision instruments.

The first IT Schools were opened in the Old San in 1989 when the building was converted into Geography Schools and an IT Department. **RM**

The Old San in Horton Crescent

1847.

Emily Brontë

COMMUNIST MANIFESTO

On February 21, 1848, *The Communist Manifesto*, written by Karl Marx and Friedrich Engels, was published in London. The pamphlet declared that *"the history of all hitherto existing society is the history of class struggle"*. It predicted victory by the proletariat.

Karl Marx was born in Prussia in 1818. After studying law and philosophy, Marx became editor of a liberal newspaper in Cologne in 1842 which was soon suppressed by the Prussian authorities. This prompted Marx to move to Paris, at that time a centre for radical thinkers, in 1843.

Marx embraced an extreme version of socialism – communism – which called for working-class revolution. Marx and his collaborator Friedrich Engels were expelled from France in 1845 and moved to Brussels, becoming intellectual leaders of the working-class movement.

In 1847, a secret society of revolutionary German workers living in London asked Marx and Engels to join them. They did, re-naming the group the Communist League.

Back in Brussels Marx produced *The Communist Manifesto*. Delivered to London in February 1848, the tract became the group's political credo.

Marx forecast imminent revolution in Europe. Only days after the manifesto had been delivered in London, revolution did break out in France prompted by a ban imposed on political meetings and this forced the King, Louis-Philippe, to abdicate.

Revolution spread across the continent, only to be crushed by the bourgeoisie. Marx went to London where he and Engels continued their collaboration, founding the First International. In 1867, Marx published the first volume of his *magnum opus, Das Kapital*.

Marx died in 1884 and is buried in Highgate Cemetery, London.

"WUTHERING HEIGHTS"

Wuthering Heights is Emily Brontë's only book. Written at Haworth Parsonage, the story of Catherine and Heathcliff was published in 1848 under the pseudonym 'Ellis Bell' before tuberculosis claimed Emily, aged only 30, later the same year.

The book divided opinions very sharply. Its frankness conflicted with prevailing Victorian attitudes. Its explicit depiction of mental and physical cruelty outraged many. So too did Emily's discomfiting approach to religious, moral, class and gender issues.

In the *North British Review* James Lorimer wrote: *"Here all the faults of Jane Eyre (by Charlotte Brontë) are magnified a thousand fold, and the only consolation which we have in reflecting upon it is that it will never be generally read."*

American sensibilities were also outraged.

"How a human being could have attempted such a book as the present without committing suicide before he had finished a dozen chapters, is a mystery. It is a compound of vulgar depravity and unnatural horrors," was the opinion of one anonymous reviewer in the aptly named *Graham's Lady's Magazine*. Another anonymous critic, writing in *Peterson's Magazine*, was even more scathing: *"Read Jane Eyre is our advice, but burn Wuthering Heights"*.

DH

1848.

1849

TUNELESS PUNISHMENT!

Tom Brown-style 'bullying' took a variety of forms at Rugby in the mid-19th century, including punishments for poor performance in House activities. Writing in 1849 James Lee Warner recalled the reward for his below-par efforts in a School House singing competition.

"My turn came; I ascended the table and began some song which I had learnt an hour previous. 'Tune' was reechoed, but to no effect. I, alas, doomed, descended. When all had done, those who had to drink came up to the table when a brimmer was presented, muddy water crammed with salt just liquid. Taking the potion, I drank it to the dregs, and then speech was gone for an hour, my throat was as it had been skinned, and I could not drink the tea which is always given after. I was dreadfully sick and then drank 8 cups of tea, 4 mugs of milk and water and as many of water. After this they were afraid to give me any more, and then I went to bed dreadfully weak. One fellow is now staying out from the effect, and I am far from well."

1849 Zachary Taylor

Edward Goulburn: Head Master from 1850 to 1857 led the introduction of Science into Rugby School

EDWARD MEYRICK GOULBURN

Edward Goulburn may have avoided the immediate challenge of following Arnold, but was still sandwiched between two Head Masters who trod a path from Rugby to Lambeth Palace.

A Balliol scholar, former chaplain to Bishop Wilberforce and a popular preacher as vicar of Holywell, Goulburn arrived at Rugby in April 1850.

Goulburn was a strongly conservative churchman, a position which cost the School financially as parents who preferred Arnoldian liberalism sent their sons elsewhere. A roll of 466 in 1851 fell by 150 in just one year, although academic standards were maintained, with Rugby boys winning all the Open awards to Oxford and Cambridge in 1857.

After resigning from Rugby in 1857, in response to the decline, Goulburn became Dean of Norwich in 1866 via posts as prebendary St Paul's in the City and vicar of St John's, Paddington.

As Dean his conservative views continued to influence the church until he retired in 1889 and died eight years later in Tunbridge Wells.

Although not earning a strong place in the pantheon of Rugby Heads, primarily because of the shrinkage in the School roll, some progress and development were still achieved under Goulburn.

Shortly after his arrival, a teacher of natural science was appointed and in 1856 the Trustees agreed to fund a dedicated room for science teaching.

The appointment of Edward White Benson in 1852 also strengthened the common room, even though he left after just six years to become the first Master of Wellington College.

Benson, following in the footsteps of Goulburn's predecessor and successor, also went on to become Archbishop of Canterbury, reinforcing the increasingly umbilical link between school mastering at Rugby and

leading the Church of England.

On the boys' side of the equation the School, despite its contraction under Goulburn, still managed to punch its weight on the stage of public eminence.

High-achieving alumni from the Tait-Goulburn reign included three boys who took part in the charge of the Light Brigade during the conflict in Crimea, two Indian Mutiny Victoria Cross winners, First Lord of the Admiralty GJ Goschen, and more than half a dozen headmasters (including the School's own TW Jex-Blake).

Overall, however, Goulburn's period of Head Master cannot be regarded in the same light as some of the School's noted and more famous leaders.

In his words he had perhaps strived for *'too much advance in holiness from the schoolboys'*.

1851

THE CRICKET PAVILIONS

The Green Pavilion, was erected in 1851 at a cost of £152.10s., paid for by the subscriptions of the 160 members of Bigside, the senior boys who ran the games. The Island moat was still being filled early in 1850, and an illustration dating from 1854 clearly shows the pavilion. It was designed and built by Mr Haddon, a local carpenter. The Green Pavilion became a listed building in 2000, it was conserved and refurbished in 2005 and the newly restored building was opened by Michael Fowle, the then Chairman of Governors, on May 8, 2005. Its restoration was funded by the generous support of Old Rugbeians, the Rugby School Lodge and the many friends of Rugby School.

With the addition of New Bigside in 1854, as a cricket ground, the Green Pavilion was not suitable for both grounds and so another building was required. The second, the Butterfield pavilion, was opened in 1869. It was the last of three designs, the others having been considered too expensive. The veranda has long since disappeared and the building has been used successively as the School Bookshop (until 1975), and a music practice room. The authorities possibly felt it was better to keep the sound as far away from the rest of the School as they could. Most recently it has been refurbished as a classroom, for the youngest members of the school, in Marshall House.

The School's third cricket pavilion was named after the Head Master Herbert Armitage James. It was designed by Rugbeian A Russell and was constructed by Parnell & Sons. Approval for the building had been agreed in 1935 and a suitable site found on the west side of The Close, between Pontines and New Bigside. It was completed by early 1937, although not used until the 1937 cricket season, and was paid for entirely by subscription. It was officially opened on Speech Day, by Kenneth R. Swan, who was President of the Old Rugbeian Society. Sir Pelham 'Plum' Warner, the renowned cricketer, was also present at the ceremony. **RM**

The Green Pavilion, now fully restored, provides a warm retreat for parents and visitors on cold match days!

1852 Edward Smith-Stanley, 14th Earl of Derby 🇬🇧
1852 George Hamilton-Gordon, 4th Earl of Aberdeen 🇬🇧

1853 Franklin Pierce 🇺🇸

1855 Viscount Palmerston 🇬🇧

VICTORIA CROSS

Seven Rugbeians have been awarded the VC

In 1854, Britain found itself fighting a major war against Russia in Crimea, one of the earliest conflicts reported by newspaper journalists. Dispatches from William Howard Russell of *The Times* drew attention to the many instances of unrewarded bravery by British servicemen.

At the time, there was no systematised recognition of gallantry within British forces, in contrast to other European countries, such as France's *Légion d'honneur*.

Russell's dispatches created a public debate. The House of Commons took up the issue and on December 19, 1854, MPs decided Queen Victoria should create 'an order of merit for distinguished and prominent personal gallantry to which every grade and individual from the highest to the lowest may be admissible'.

There was opposition from some senior figures in the military who feared that, in an attempt to win the medal, individuals might disobey orders given by officers. Their objections, however, were trumped as the idea had one very important supporter: Prince Albert, the Queen's husband.

In 1855, Victoria issued the warrant which created the new award. Influenced by Albert, she rejected the suggestion that the medal be styled The Military Order of Victoria, preferring instead the much simpler Victoria Cross. The design too was simple, winning few plaudits in the media, *The Times* describing it as *"poor looking and mean in the extreme"*.

An order for the first 106 VCs was placed, the medals being made from bronze retrieved from Chinese-made cannon captured from the Russians at Sebastopol. Awards were backdated to 1854 and the first investiture for 62 veterans of the Crimea was held on June 26, 1857. Since its inception the Victoria Cross has been awarded 1,358 times to 1,355 individuals.

To date seven Rugbeians have received the VC and a memorial is to be unveiled in the Temple Speech Room in 2017 to commemorate their bravery. DH

1856.

THOMAS HUGHES & TOM BROWN'S SCHOOLDAYS

Each generation has its favourite boarding school books but there is only one that can reasonably claim to be the 'godfather' of the genre: *Tom Brown's Schooldays*.

Many writers depicted boarding school life in the late 18th and early 19th centuries and Dickens covered the ground well through Dotheboys Hall in *Nicholas Nickleby*.

It was Tom Brown's adventures though that really caught the mood and, since appearing in 1857, it has never been out of print.

In her 1974 introduction Naomi Lewis wrote: *"Of course to readers today Tom Brown's Rugby must seem a very odd place indeed. Apart from Latin and Greek, whatever did they learn? Apart from fishing, bird nesting, destroying small animals, and taking part in some extremely vigorous sports, how did they entertain themselves?"*

Hughes went to Rugby himself in 1833, five years after the arrival of Dr Arnold. It was while thinking how to advise his own son Maurice about boarding school that he had the idea of writing a book.

Although meant for his family, Hughes was encouraged by a friend to publish for a wider audience and Tom Brown was introduced to the world on April 24, 1857.

Tom Brown's Schooldays (which within five years had sold nearly 30,000 copies) vividly describes life at the School in the 1830s, including boarding house blanket tossing, mass rugby matches, hare and hounds runs, evening singing, fights behind chapel, writing out lines and afternoon snacks.

Most importantly it presents a portrait of powerful characters, not least Tom himself, his friend Harry East, head boy Brooke and the villainous bully Flashman.

The book is full of vivid episodes

relevant as much to students of Victorian education as to today's parents and children.

The essence is captured at the start of the fifth chapter as Tom finally arrives at the School.

"Tom's heart beat quick as he passed the great school field or close, with its noble elms, in which several games at football were going on, and tried to take in at once the long line of grey buildings, beginning with the chapel, and ending with the school-house, the residence of the headmaster, where the great flag was lazily waving from the highest round tower. And he began already to be proud of being a Rugby boy...as he passed through the school gates."

Hughes' achievements spanned law, politics and social reform. After Oxford he worked as a barrister and later a judge, alongside which he became involved in the Christian Socialist and co-operative movements. Between 1868 and 1874 he sat for Lambeth and then Frome as an MP and focused on trade union legislation.

On leaving Parliament, he wrote *The Manual for Co-operatives* and helped to establish another Rugby in

Tennessee. Hughes also continued to be active on the writing front, producing two more, but less well remembered, Tom Brown books and more than a dozen works of non-fiction.

He died from heart failure (like Tom Brown's hero Dr Arnold) at the age of 73 in 1896, just sixteen years before his daughter Lilian perished on the *Titanic* and three years before a statue in his honour was put up outside the Temple Reading Room.

The white granite depiction features Hughes in a coat showing, curiously, buttons on one side but no buttonholes on the other.

The statue was unveiled on June 24, 1899 before a large crowd in elegant hats, toppers and boaters, at a ceremony led by Frederick Temple, former Head Master of the School and by then Archbishop of Canterbury.

Meanwhile, Tom Brown and his schooldays have maintained their popularity more than a century and half after publication.

The story first appeared on the silver screen in 1916 and again in 1940 and 1951, was a television mini-series and musical in 1971, and a TV film starring Stephen Fry as Dr Arnold in 2005.

1857

ISAMBARD KINGDOM BRUNEL

Victorian titan Isambard Kingdom Brunel is rightly regarded as Britain's greatest engineer. Born in 1806, a year after Nelson's victory at Trafalgar, Brunel lived for only 53 years and in that time accomplished more than a dozen of his rivals put together. The span of Brunel's work was staggering, from tunnels to bridges to ships. Perhaps his greatest and most enduring claim to fame was the design and completion of the Great Western Rail, a route which connected London with Bristol, the capital of the south west. From the arched splendour of Paddington Station via the engineering feat of

Box Tunnel through the Wiltshire hillside near Bath, the Great Western line was a triumph of imagination, precision, toil, sweat and endeavour. Today, many of Brunel's achievements are still highly visible and remain well used by travellers, not least Temple Mead Station and the Clifton Suspension Bridge in Bristol and the 1859 Royal Albert Bridge. As a mark of his enduring legacy and place in British history, Brunel appeared in Danny Boyle's spectacular opening ceremony for the London 2012 Olympic Games, played by a bewhiskered and stove piped Sir Kenneth Branagh.

Brunel, Britain's greatest engineer

THE INDIAN MUTINY

1857 saw the start of the Indian Mutiny, a brutal episode which led to the British taking formal control in India.

Before India became part of the empire, the British East India Company, which had its own army under the command of British officers, ruled India.

In January 1857 sepoys (infantry privates) in the Company's presidency army of Bengal, reacted to rumours over which animal fat had been used to grease rifle ammunition.

Muslim sepoys believed paper cartridges had been greased with pig fat and Hindu soldiers believed they had been greased with cow fat, both of which offended their religious beliefs.

British commander Colonel Richard Birch ordered a stop to pre-greasing cartridges, but this only increased suspicion.

Events came to a head when sepoy Mangal Pandey attacked a British

sergeant and wounded an adjutant in Barrackpore. Mangal and another soldier were arrested and hanged, prompting troops of the 3rd Bengal Light Cavalry in Meerut to break ranks on May 10, 1857.

Rebellion spread across north India, with Bahadur Shah II, the Mughal Emperor, being persuaded to lead the revolt and other prominent Indian royal leaders joining in to fight the British.

In response, the British brought in regiments from the Crimean War and China, and surrounded the City of Delhi in July and August, 1857. Brevet Major William Stephen Raikes Hodson was a British leader of irregular light cavalry. He was known as "Hodson of Hodson's Horse", and his most celebrated action was to apprehend the King of Delhi, also referred to as Emperor of India. The following day he rode to the enemy camp, heavily outnumbered by the rebels, and demanded the surrender of the Mughal princes who were

leading the rebellion around Delhi and killed them.

Over the next two years, rebels fought across India, with key moments including the Kanpur massacre in July 1857, the siege of Lucknow in the second half of the year and a battle at Gwalior in June 1858. The conflict eventually came to an end when rebel leader Tantia Tope was captured and executed in April 1859.

Following the mutiny, in November 1858 the UK Parliament withdrew the right of the British East India Company to rule India.

The Mutiny was a brutal episode which lead to Britain taking formal control in India

1857 James Buchanan 🏳

FREDERICK TEMPLE

Frederick Temple saw rapid social and economic change during his lifetime from 1821 to 1902. Born in the Ionian Islands and raised in a poor Cornish farmhouse by his widowed mother, he died in Lambeth Palace as Archbishop of Canterbury.

A forthright speaker and austere moral force he made a distinguished contribution to undergraduate and adult education before becoming Head Master of Rugby in 1857, from where after twelve years he moved on to senior episcopal leadership in the Church of England.

Temple went up to Oxford in 1839, where he became a Fellow of Balliol in 1842, lecturing in Mathematics and Logic. Here he also made lifelong friends including AC Tait and Benjamin Jowett. He also developed his Christian commitments, not least in Church and Doctrine, in the Tractarian debates. This was the Oxford Movement of High Church members who argued for the reinstatement of some older Christian traditions of faith, and their inclusion into Anglican liturgy and theology.

Resisting Tait's attempts to lure him to Rugby first as an assistant master (1843) and then as candidate for Head Master (1849), Temple chose to join the Privy Council Committee for Education, and then became Principal of Kneller Hall, training work-house teachers.

He was involved fully in all the essential 19th-century debates on schools and universities.

As one biographer writes, Temple was motivated by the need to raise the condition of the working classes by helping them to help themselves. In an age of increasing secular boundaries he was *'convinced that neither education nor temperance would be effective without religion'*.

Yet Temple's Broad Church sympathies, in the Arnold tradition, were not without controversy.

Just after arriving at Rugby, his contribution of a recycled sermon to a highly contested volume *Essays and Reviews* put him in danger of being sidelined by the traditional establishment. Temple's character in dealing with the crisis was described nicely: *'he was courageous in refusing to withdraw his name when it was clamorously demanded, and not less courageous in withdrawing it when the withdrawal would expose him to the criticism of his advanced friends'*.

By this time with *'enthusiasm, physical energy and sheer hard work'* he had won the hearts and minds of staff and pupils at the School. A loyal pupil wrote home to an anxious parent *"Temple's all right, but if he turns Mahomedan, the whole school will turn Mahomedan too"*.

Doing away with pomp and ceremony, walking from the railway station on his first day and with the legend of his climbing all the old elm trees in The Close firmly rooted, Temple developed all aspects of the School's life and work. He increased the staff (of whom at least eight went on to be Headmasters), put History and English Language and Literature into the mainstream curriculum, and introduced natural science, drawing and music. Football was made 'less barbarous' during his time, including the abolition of intentional hacking.

The 300th anniversary of the School was celebrated in 1867, the year in which the first edition of *The Meteor* was published and the Natural History Society founded. Temple's was a period of great success and expansion. Numbers climbed quickly. New Quad was built at the expense of Temple and the assistant masters, Temple brushing aside the Trustees' understandable concern about the clash of Butterfield's multicoloured and striped brick with Hakewill's sober grey.

But the greatest influence on governance in Temple's time was the Clarendon Commission, set up in 1861 to investigate nine large and leading schools. 170 years later it is difficult to understand the time and energy expended on what now seems a narrow task. Each of the schools had to respond in great detail to a written questionnaire and many witnesses were examined at great length. The result was a huge quantity of detailed and fascinating information about those nine schools and clear recommendations. Temple wrote or edited Rugby's responses and some see Temple's strong influence in the Commission's 1864 recommendations. The Commission did not approve of everything at Rugby but did approve of several of Arnold's innovations which Temple followed, such as regular meetings of all teaching staff chaired by the Head.

For Rugby, the main change imposed, after considerable parliamentary debate, by the Public Schools Act 1868 and the successor Public Schools Act 1872, was to replace the incorporated body of twelve Warwickshire gentlemen Trustees with a new incorporated Governing Body

1857

of Trustees, now to include the Lord Lieutenant plus five members explicitly appointed 'for their eminence in literature and science' by the Universities of Oxford, Cambridge and London, by the Royal Society and by the Lord Chancellor. Temple vigorously objected to this proposal on the grounds that such Governors would be bound to interfere with the School's management. Temple's objections were ignored and it is ironic that the worst instance of such interference and possibly the only instance, was Temple's own conduct as Governor when appointed by London University, when Hayman was Head Master.

In truth, the Clarendon Commission changes made little impact on Rugby's governance. Ever since 1602 the Trustees of Rugby had been people of standing giving their time as pro bono, acting as disinterested Trustees looking after the School and the assets left to it by Lawrence Sheriff.

Above all Temple was *'a great teacher and a great school master'*, whose hearers *'stood on the threshold of life and were made to feel that life was worth living'*. In a telling summary one historian writes *'In a real sense Temple regarded The Close and the Chapel as working together.'*

Appointed Bishop of Exeter in 1869, then London in 1885 and Archbishop of Canterbury in 1896, Temple spent the remaining 33 years of his life throwing himself *'with his accustomed vigour into the work of the dioceses and all the great ecclesiastical and social questions of the day'*. He chaired the fourth Lambeth Conference of Anglican bishops in 1896, and crowned Edward VII in 1902, dying before Christmas that year a few days after collapsing while speaking on education in the House of Lords.

Frederick Temple retained his connections with Rugby, as a parent of two boys in School House, member of the Governing Body, and as Chair from 1892 to 1902. He is the Temple of the Reading Room and Speech Room whose choice of William Butterfield as architect of the New Quad influences Rugby's visual appearance to this day.

It is asserted that Frederick Temple was 'the greatest schoolmaster of his day'. Perhaps his most impressive legacy was in using those talents in nurturing the development of his most able younger son, William, who uniquely was to follow him on to the throne of St Augustine of Canterbury. **DU / MF**

Frederick Temple: Head Master from 1857 to 1869

THE SCIENCE SCHOOLS

Although science had been taught a decade earlier, the first building for the subject was not erected until 1858, in the north-east corner of New Quad. As the Butterfield classrooms of the Quad were completed, science extended to use some of the rooms.

A decision was made in 1901 to build a Science School in the south-east corner of The Close. The site was chosen as it provided space to allow for extensions to the proposed buildings. The new Science Schools, a single-storey brick building with an imposing classical pediment, was opened in 1904. A second storey would be added later but the building remained essentially the same.

Additional rooms and some refurbishment took place in the 1950s but it was the next decade which provided a more pressing stimulus for growth. The development of the Nuffield Scheme in the 1960s and the increase in those boys studying biology placed a strain on the existing facilities. A new extension to the schools was required and in 1971 the Parker Memorial Building was opened. It housed the Biology Department, and was designed with future expansion in mind.

With the opening of the Design Centre in 1991 and the move of classes to the new building, refurbishment took place on some of the classrooms. The Design Centre development had also provided a physical bridge between the two departments.

A major building and restoration project was launched in 1996 with an appeal to Rugbeians. Twelve years later the project was completed with the opening of the New Science Schools by HRH the Earl of Wessex, in October 2008. The opening marked more than 100 years of science buildings on the same site. **RM**

The first building specifically for Science was erected in 1858

1858.

1858 Edward Stanley 🇬🇧   **1858** Viscount Palmerston 🇬🇧

HENRY WILMOT

On March 11, 1858, **Captain Henry Wilmot** and his men were up against it in Lucknow during the Indian Mutiny. The 2nd Battalion Rifle Brigade former Rugbeian rose to the challenge and was subsequently awarded the Victoria Cross for his endeavours. Wilmot's citation said:

"That officer found himself at the end of a street with only four of his men, opposed to a considerable body. One of the four was shot through both legs, and became utterly helpless: the two men lifted him up, and although Private Hawkes was severely wounded, he carried him for a considerable distance, exposed to the fire of the enemy, Captain Wilmot firing with the men's rifles, and covering the retreat of the party."

Wilmot eventually succeeded to a baronetcy and pursued a later career as a Conservative MP, passing away from pneumonia in Bournemouth in 1901.

Awarded the VC in Lucknow during the Indian Mutiny

CHARLES DARWIN

In his book *On the Origin of Species by Means of Natural Selection*, Charles Darwin argued that organisms gradually evolve through 'natural selection'.

Darwin acquired most of the evidence for his theory during a five-year surveying expedition to South America and the southern Pacific aboard *HMS Beagle* in the 1830s.

The theory was not entirely new. It had been suggested earlier by, among others, Darwin's own grandfather Erasmus Darwin and by the French naturalist Jean-Baptiste Lamarck.

But it was Charles who was able to demonstrate a scientific, evident based explanation for evolution.

Darwin had formulated his theory of natural selection by 1844 but he was wary about broadcasting his ideas because they contradicted the biblical account of creation. In 1858, however, the British naturalist Alfred Russell Wallace produced a paper wholly independently of Darwin which also proffered a theory of evolution. Darwin could no longer remain silent. After extensive correspondence, Darwin and Wallace lectured jointly on evolution in 1858, which spurred Darwin on to prepare *On the Origin of Species*.

Published in1859, *On the Origin of Species* sold out immediately. The theory was widely embraced as a solution to so many problems in biological science but many Christians condemned the book. Controversy deepened with subsequent publications, including *The Descent of Man* in which Darwin presented evidence of man's evolution from apes. **DH**

Darwin's 'The Descent of Man' presented evidence of man's evolution from apes

1859

BEER

While access by today's Rugbeians to alcohol is strictly controlled, quality not supply was the bigger issue in the 1860s.

DB Maclaren, a pupil under Frederick Temple, wrote home:

"I like everything here except the beer which is frightful. Do you think I might have porter in bottles?"

1860.

1861 Abraham Lincoln

HMS Warrior launched in 1860 caused a sensation

BRITAIN'S FIRST IRON-CLAD WARSHIP

Launched in 1860, *HMS Warrior* was Britain's first iron-hulled, armoured warship. In 1859, the French unveiled their ironclad warship *La Gloire* which was seen to threaten Britain's supremacy at sea. Queen Victoria herself asked if the navy was adequate for the tasks that it would have to perform in wartime. Construction of *HMS Warrior* was the response.

The Royal Navy was determined to design a ship that would be regarded as a deterrent to France. She would have superior speed, armament and size, and be 60% larger than *La Gloire*. The specification required the ship should be capable of 15 knots and have a full set of sails to provide a world-wide range. Iron construction reconciled speed and protection – an iron hull was lighter than wood, giving more capacity for weaponry and power plant.

On her first voyage, *HMS Warrior* caused a sensation. Her construction offered protection from shells and her large guns changed marine warfare theory. But her life as a warship was short-lived. She was soon replaced by quicker and more heavily armed and armoured vessels and withdrawn from front-line service in 1871.

A few years later, *HMS Warrior* was mothballed. In 1924, no buyer could be found when she was put up for sale as scrap and she was converted into a floating oil pontoon at Pembroke Dock. In 1978, *HMS Warrior* was passed on to the Maritime Trust which undertook the mammoth task of restoration and, in 1987, was returned to a mooring in Portsmouth. **DH**

RACKETS COURTS

In 1860 the Head boy and head of the Games Committee, the Bigside Levée, Henry Lee Warner, wrote to the Trustees, to ask for a rackets court to be built in the School. Giving their permission, they also gave £150 towards the cost. The balance of the cost was funded by subscription by the boys. By 1861 the court, which cost some £3,000, was hosting its first matches. William Butterfield had designed a fine building, with arches and stone pillars and a fine glazed roof. A flat viewing gallery with arched openings was open to the elements. Built at a time when no national standards were in force, the playing area was reduced in size at Easter 1898 to conform to other courts. The glazed roof was completely replaced during the Easter of 1935.

The second court was proposed in late 1880, and by May 1881, Butterfield had prepared the drawings which had been approved by the Committee, and the estimate was £1,500. Due to delays in raising the required funds, building work did not start until the Easter holidays of 1883, and was completed by the summer. The first match was played in early October. A new gallery was added in the summer of 1891. **RM**

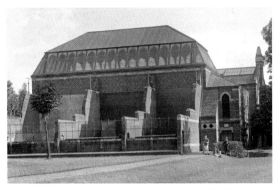

Butterfield's Rackets court cost £3,000 when opened in 1861

1861

THE DEATH OF PRINCE ALBERT

Francis Albert Augustus Charles Emmanuel of Saxe-Coburg and Gotha was aged 21 when he married his cousin, Queen Victoria, in 1840. The marriage was not a popular one but over time Albert came to win grudging respect.

After the death of Lord Melbourne, Albert encouraged his wife to take a greater interest in politics and social issues. At Albert's behest Lord Shaftesbury was invited to Buckingham Palace to discuss the contentious issue of child labour in factories.

Albert was actively involved in promoting the arts, industry, science and trade. He was the driving force behind the Great Exhibition of 1851 and encouraged Victoria to take an interest in emerging technologies.

Albert's position was constitutionally difficult but one he exercised with considerable tact. Even so, he was never universally popular in his adopted country and the title of Prince Consort was conferred only in 1857. His tactical nous was demonstrated at the very highest level in the autumn of 1861. War between Britain and the United States threatened and Albert's intervention is widely considered to have been instrumental in avoiding conflict.

When Albert died suddenly of what is now believed to have been typhoid on December 14, 1861, Victoria was devastated and adopted the black of mourning for the rest of her life. The Albert Memorial, unveiled in 1876, is among many monuments she commissioned to honour his memory. **DH**

Prince Albert, a driving force behind the arts, industry, science and trade

Lincoln…. "All men are created equal"

GETTYSBURG

On November 19, 1863, President Abraham Lincoln spoke at the dedication of the military cemetery at Gettysburg, Pennsylvania. Before Lincoln stood up, Edward Everett droned on for over two hours. In contrast, Lincoln's 272-word speech lasted only two minutes.

Lincoln articulated for a war-weary public the meaning of the Civil War. He reminded the crowd of the Founding Fathers' vision: the establishment of a nation *"dedicated to the proposition that all men are created equal"*. He addressed the country's civil war which, he said, was a test of American revolutionary ideals.

Lincoln then reiterated the purpose of the Northern war effort:

"It is rather for us the living, we here be dedicated to the great task remaining before us – that from these honored dead we take increased devotion – that we here highly resolve that these dead shall not have died in vain, that this nation, shall have a new birth of freedom, and that government of the people, by the people, for the people, shall not perish from the earth."

Afterwards, the audience was silent: some said the crowd was unsure of whether or not the President had concluded his remarks; others said that the silence betokened awe. Today, the text of the Gettysburg Address is inscribed in a wall of the Lincoln Memorial in Washington, D.C. **DH**

1863
Astronomer **George Seabroke** entered the School in this year. He arranged the purchase of the School's 8¼ inch Alvan Clark telescope and became President of the British Astronomical Society in 1900.

1863.

CRICKET & THE CRICKETER CUP

In 1867 the School's Cricket XI hosted matches against three Oxford colleges: Corpus Christi, Trinity and University. The University College side had trouble getting home when the London and North Western Railway train they were travelling back on declined to pause, as scheduled, at Bletchley. The railway company's poor performance was witheringly reviewed in *The Meteor* which commented: *"We cannot imagine what has come over the L & NW as they are always so ready to oblige anyone."*

Early days of cricket on The Close

The Cricketer Cup was originally played between the old boys of 16 Public Schools but the competition proved so popular in its first year that in 1969 it was extended to 32 teams. Forty four finals have so far produced 14 different winners, including the Rugby Meteors who won the Cup in 1973 and reached the final in 1999.

1865 Andrew Johnson
1865 John Russell

1866 Edward Stanley

1867

1867

The Meteor magazine was started by **Albert Gray** of Kilbracken in 1867, getting its name from a meteor shower the previous year.

Two Cock Houses, 1878

COCK HOUSE

Before 1850, when the School's boarding house system which had been created by Thomas Arnold was developing, School House was the largest single group of boys. The House would play their football against the 'rest of the school', a rag-tag of members of Price's, Cotton, Highton and the rest, in a contest known as the 'Schoolhouse Match'.

In 1850, School House 'condescended' to play a single house, Cotton's, and were soundly beaten for their pains. Cotton took the title of Cock House, derived from 'Cock of the House' or 'Cock of the School', a title given to the boy universally acknowledged by his peers to be the best all round. Thus humbled in 1850, School House failed for the first six years to regain their crown. The 1850 result was to be repeated for three successive years between 1878 and 1880 when Cotton, now Lee Warner's, ruled the roost.

Continuing the tradition of the mass games of earlier years, a competition called 'Cock Houses' existed into the twentieth century. The two final Cock House XVs, along with ORs from those houses (up to any number), would play anyone from the school who had obtained distinctions, and any ORs who were visiting on the day (the last day of Advent term). It was not unusual to see more than a hundred players on the Close, paying at least a nod to the official modern rules.

Other than bragging rights, there was no reward for the victor in Cock House until 1900, when the Cock House Trophy was presented. The match that year was played on November 26th and provided a comfortable win, 39-0, for School House over Collins (Kilbracken).

Today, Cock House trophies are presented across most team sports at the School, and in Athletics it is called 'The Wrigley Cup'.

WILLIAM GLADSTONE

William Ewart Gladstone was first elected to Parliament in 1832 at the age of 23. He became Prime Minister at the head of a Liberal administration in 1868.

Originally a member of the Tories, Gladstone held junior government posts before joining Robert Peel's cabinet in 1843. With Peel, Gladstone became a Liberal-Conservative following the disintegration of the Tory party in 1845-6. Twice Chancellor of the Exchequer, Gladstone joined the Liberals in 1859, becoming leader of the party in 1867.

When the Liberals won the election of 1868, Gladstone was appointed Prime Minister. He disestablished the Church of Ireland and strove to give Irish tenant farmers more rights from often absentee English landowners. He established a national system of elementary education, reformed the system of purchasing military commissions and instituted secret ballots. In 1873, Gladstone once again became Chancellor, running the two offices of Chancellor and Prime Minister in tandem. His party's heavy defeat in the 1874 General Election brought his arch-rival Benjamin Disraeli to power.

Gladstone resigned as leader only to return as Prime Minister for three further tenures in 1880-85, 1886 and 1892-94. He was subsequently responsible for the widening of the franchise and for two Home Rule Bills for Ireland. Defeat on home rule in 1893 hastened the end of his career.

1868

Charles Elsee, known by boys as 'The Bull' took over Jex-Blake's House (later Kilbracken) in Hillmorton Road in 1868. His children gave the Chapel bell in memory of Charles and his wife Mary Anne. Formally called the 'Elsee Bell', it is now known as the 'Boomer'.

1868

1867

1868 William Gladstone 🇬🇧

1868 Benjamin Disraeli 🇬🇧

HENRY HAYMAN

Dr Henry Hayman's four-year shift as Head Master from 1870 is described by School historian JB Hope Simpson as a 'calamity'. He was opposed from the start and his tennure ended in a bitter court case.

Like Tait following Arnold, Hayman was always going to be on the back foot as the Trustees' chosen successor to Temple.

But when everyone, including your predecessor, is vehemently opposed to you, the omens are not good.

Obstacles facing Hayman from the off included his perceived lack of intellectual ability, high quality rivals, an undistinguished record, and insufficient connections with the School.

The quality of Hayman's academic abilities hinged on him missing out on a First at Oxford, despite being a scholar of St John's College and later a Fellow.

This scholastic stain was described by Temple, in a withering example of damning faint praise, as a 'good double second'.

At other times at other schools, being an Oxford Fellow might have been enough to counter critics.

But Hayman's cause was not helped by the fact that other candidates included the then Secretary to the Civil Service Commission, Theodore Walrond (an OR and Temple's favoured candidate) and John Percival, former Rugby master, successful head at Clifton College and possessor of a Double First in mathematics and classics.

Doubts about Hayman's qualification to lead the School stemmed from his three previous positions as Head at St Olave's grammar school in Southwark, Cheltenham Grammar School and Bradfield College – and his

1869
In this year, a writer in *The Meteor* appealed for lockable cupboards to be installed at the School's rackets courts, after a spate of thefts of players' footwear.

application being accompanied by apparently out-of-date testimonials.

The protests against Hayman were led by the School's assistant masters who delivered their verdict on his forthcoming appointment in writing while he was still at Bradfield.

Their sea of charges against him included the passage:

> *"The differences between Rugby on the one hand and…St Olave's and Cheltenham Grammar School on the other, are not so few or so slight that fitness for the duties of one implies fitness for those of the other…We submit that there was the strongest presumption beforehand that if you had applied to some of the writers for Rugby testimonials, you would not have obtained them."*

The furore surrounding Hayman went on, but he was appointed anyway, with as much opportunity as any previous Head to make a success of it. But it was not to be and the

Henry Hayman: Head Master from 1870 to 1874

doubters were proved right.

At the business level of the school, numbers declined, as they had with Tait, and there were discipline issues and complaints from parents.

These practical difficulties were not helped by Hayman believing he could not trust two School House tutors EA Scott and James Robertson, which then led to difficult and protracted wrangling and dispute in public.

This complex quarrel culminated in a statement from the Governing Body (which had replaced the Trustees) in November 1872: *"If Dr Hayman is not prepared to act in future in a spirit of cordial good will towards Mr Scott, the Governing Body think it is due to the interests of the School*

that he should lose no time retiring from the office of Head Master."

Although time was lost following this statement, the die was cast against Hayman and in December 1873 the Governors wrote: "*…upon a review of the administration of the School…they are of the opinion that Dr Hayman is not a fit and proper person to hold the position of Head Master of Rugby School, and that it is for the interests of the School that he should cease to hold that office… from 7th day of April next."*

Hayman's undistinguished reign as Head Master formally ended in 1874 but not before he unsuccessfully challenged the decision.

Writing in *The Times* in March 1874 Hayman declared with resignation but defiance:

"After an argument of six days duration, the Court of Chancery decided it could not interfere with a sentence of dismissal…I shall not attempt to appeal against that decision. Enough has transpired to vindicate my character and conduct, both as a Head Master and a gentleman."

Hayman did not become Head of another school, accepting instead an offer from Disraeli of a lucrative church living in Aldingham, Lancashire, where he died in 1904 – a long way from Rugby.

1870

THE DEATH OF DICKENS

Born in 1812, the great Victorian novelist Charles Dickens was sent to school at the age of nine. But his good fortune did not last as his father John, a naval clerk who dreamed of striking it rich, was imprisoned in the Marshalsea for debt.

The whole family, apart from Charles, was incarcerated. He was set to work in Warren's boot-blacking factory at 6/- a week. This was an experience he never forgot and later featured it in *David Copperfield* and *Great Expectations*.

Dickens began his literary career as a journalist, becoming parliamentary correspondent for the *Morning Chronicle* in 1833. Under the pseudonym 'Boz', he published sketches and in 1836 married Catherine Hogarth, his publisher's daughter. His bestseller *Pickwick Papers* was published that year.

In addition to his many novels, Dickens published an autobiography, edited, produced travel guides and worked with several charities. He enjoyed the limelight, literally, writing and performing in plays. Travelling, extensively, he visited the United States twice where his 76 readings earned him $95,000, the equivalent of well over £1 million today.

In 1858, he was estranged from his wife by whom he fathered ten children, living instead with his mistress, the actress Ellen Ternan. In 1865, Dickens was in a train accident from which he never fully recovered. Though fragile, he continued to tour until 1870, when he had a stroke and died at Gad's Hill, his country home in Kent. He is buried in Poet's Corner at Westminster Abbey. **DH**

1874-1899

GOLDEN YEARS

1874 THOMAS JEX-BLAKE BECOMES HEAD	**1874** BENJAMIN DISRAELI
	1875 THE SUEZ CANAL
1876 THE RUGBEIAN SOCIETY	**1876** ADVENT OF THE TELEPHONE
1877 LAWN TENNIS THE TEMPLE READING ROOM (TRR)	**1877** PHONOGRAPH
1878 AUSTEN CHAMBERLAIN LAWRENCE SHERIFF SCHOOL	
1879 WILLIAM WADDINGTON	**1879** ZULU WAR EDISON
1885 NEW BIG SCHOOL (NBS) & THE MACREADY THEATREE	
	1886 FIRST PETROL-DRIVEN MOTOR CAR
1887 JOHN PERCIVAL BECOMES HEAD	**1887** SHERLOCK HOLMES
1888 TOWN HOUSE MATTHEW ARNOLD	
1893 TUDOR	**1893** THE LABOUR PARTY
1894 KNOX PUNCH	
1895 WYNDHAM LEWIS HERBERT JAMES BECOMES HEAD STAFF UNDER JAMES	**1895** THE ARREST OF OSCAR WILDE
1896 KANWAR SHUMSHERE	
1897 ARTHUR RANSOME	
	1899 THE BOER WAR

THOMAS JEX-BLAKE

Thomas Jex-Blake: Head Master from 1874 to 1887

Thomas Jex-Blake, Head Master for thirteen years after Hayman, can be credited for steadying the School ship after turbulence and decline.

The Jex-Blake reign from 1874 to 87 is remembered benignly, although he was arguably too soft on discipline, and numbers fell during his final years.

Raised on the south coast, Jex-Blake entered the School in the 1840s. Despite early laziness and some eminent peers like GJ Goschen, he proved a good enough cricketer to play for the XI, a good enough runner to win the Crick and a good enough student to win an Oxford scholarship.

After gaining a Double First in classics and being elected a Fellow at Queen's, he returned to Rugby (following a short stint at Marlborough), taking on Bradley's boarding house in 1857.

In 1868 he became Principal of Cheltenham College, before making the journey to Rugby for the third time in 30 years, this time as Head Master.

Jex-Blake was a strong supporter of art education and in 1879 oversaw the opening of the first art museum within any English school, at the Temple Reading Room.

The museum curator was TM Lindsay, one of several distinguished men who joined the School under Jex-Blake, including future Bishop of Madras Henry Whitehead and Rupert Brooke's father, WP Brooke.

The foundation of Lawrence Sheriff School was a major project for Jex-Blake during his time as Head Master with plans progressing to buy a suitable site just a year after his arrival.

The aim of the new venture was to create a local grammar school more closely following the original intentions of Rugby's founder.

Appointing HT Rhodes, who had been at Rugby under Tait, as the first Head Master, establishing and growing the new school was a key responsibility for Jex-Blake and his successors, until a separate Board of Governors was set up in 1906.

While not engaged with effectively running two Schools, Jex-Blake did manage to introduce, or at least formalise, one other innovation at Rugby – evening 'House Prep'.

Although this step may have contributed to the School maintaining good academic standards, including 80 Oxbridge places, Jex-Blake's reluctance to give orders or discipline those boys who needed it, gradually reduced Rugby's reputation among leading public schools.

Leaving to become Rector of Alvechurch, Jex-Blake was recommended by Lord Salisbury to the Deanery of Wells in 1891, where he remained until 1910 and died in 1915.

School historian JB Hope Simpson felt that despite a decline in numbers *"Jex-Blake cannot be written off as a failure"*.

The Dictionary of National Biography also recorded that

"By tact and wisdom, and with the help of old friends, Jex-Blake restored the school to prosperity, his courteous manners and knowledge of the world being helpful to Rugby in its relations with parents and with the county."

It added, however: *"As a Head Master he was mild and benevolent, with a kind manner, which gained him popularity with the boys. He avoided rows with the masters. But some felt he lacked firmness. He was reluctant to resort to expulsion or to enforce rules about superannuation; nor did he use corporal punishment."*

1874.

1874 Benjamin Disraeli 🇬🇧

BENJAMIN DISRAELI

Benjamin Disraeli, writer, politician and bon viveur, became Prime Minister for the second time in 1874 having briefly held office in 1868. Initially suspicious of Disraeli's raffishness, Queen Victoria wrote: *"Mr Disraeli is Prime Minister. A proud thing for a man risen from the people."*

'Dizzy' was the son of a Jewish Italian writer, brought up an Anglican. This allowed Benjamin to pursue a political career which otherwise would have been unthinkable as Jews were excluded from Parliament until 1858.

In 1874 the Conservatives returned to power and 'that Jew' – as Gladstone's wife called him – became premier for the second time at the age of 70. Disraeli and a talented ministerial team undertook a wide range of legislation, much of it addressing fundamental social issues such as the Factory Acts (1874, 1878) and the Poor Law Amendment Act (1878). The Climbing Boys Act (1875) strengthened the ban on employing children as chimney sweeps. The Artisans Dwelling Act (1875) allowed local authorities to destroy slums, replacing them with decent housing for the poor. The Public Health Act (1875) provided sanitation such as running water and refuse disposal.

Disraeli retired following the Liberals' election victory in 1880 and died a year later. **DH**

1875

Suez, a shipping canal constructed through 100 miles of desert

THE SUEZ CANAL

The driving force behind the construction of the Suez Canal was Ferdinand de Lesseps, a former diplomat, who faced considerable political and financial odds before work could begin.

In 1854, de Lesseps secured the consent of Said Pasha, the Viceroy of Egypt, for a shipping canal to be constructed through the 100 miles of desert between Africa and Asia. A prospectus was circulated but shares in the company were slow to sell, other than in France.

The project was thought to be intrinsically risky. In addition, Britain regarded France's increasing influence in this region with suspicion. Besides declining the share offer, Britain organised a boycott which caused a shortage of investors. The project was saved only when Said himself agreed to buy the remaining unsold shares.

After almost eleven years' construction, the canal was opened in November 1869. Said had died in 1867 to be succeeded by his nephew Ismail. In the first year of operation, three-quarters of the vessels using the canal were British.

By 1875, Ismail had incurred massive debts in trying to modernise Egypt. He offered his country's 44% stake in the canal for sale. Against the advice of his ministers but with the support of Queen Victoria, Prime Minister Benjamin Disraeli bought the shareholding for £4 million, an interest retained until 1956.

As a consequence, the purchase established British influence over the waterway, providing a shorter route to its empire and the oilfields of the Persian Gulf. **DH**

THE RUGBEIAN SOCIETY

The Rugbeian Society was officially formed in 1876, when fifteen Old Rugbeians met formally at the Charing Cross Hotel, in London.

They resolved that the Society should *"assist and promote the School Games, and so form a bond of Union between past and present Rugbeians"*.

In the early days, the Society maintained the 'bond of union' by focusing on School games. Annual grants were made for the upkeep of grounds and grounds machinery, although not always successfully.

In 1893, the Cricket sub-committee recommended *"the purchase of a horse for the roller, costing £25"*. Next year's minute reads: *"The School horse presented to the School, having turned out unsatisfactorily from an equine as well as financial point of view, was sold for £5."*

In 1900, the Society marked the new century by placing the Webb Ellis Memorial Tablet on the Doctor's Wall at a cost of £18. With delicious hindsight, the rules were amended in 1902, permitting the Society to spend money on memorials.

In 1901 the Society's Cricket sub-committee had eighteen members and concerned itself almost entirely with the award of bats for the Rugby vs Marlborough match at Lord's.

The first 'OR Letter' was published in 1910 and a Reunion was held at the School in 1919. But there is then no further mention of Reunions, other than dinners, until 1946.

GAFM Chatwin (SH 1893-1900 and Staff 1904-1941), became Editor of the OR Letter from 1913 and Society Secretary from 1919 to1937. MET Wratislaw (T 1888-92) became acting Secretary and Editor from 1940 to 1946.

AR Tatham (SH 1906-11 and Staff 1917-52) was Secretary and Editor from 1946 to 1966, and Ian Miller (Sh 1931-35 and Staff 1950-80), edited the OR Letter, now the *Floreat*, from 1966 to 1994. During this time, Sir Patrick Dean was President of the Society.

One of the Society's more colourful Secretaries was Hubert Snowden (SF 1928-32). He became Secretary of the Society for over 20 years from 1972 to 1993. With his distinctive bowling action and golf swing, neither of which harmed his performance in either game, he ran the Society with panache from his position as Headmaster of Hildersham House in Broadstairs, Kent. John Marshall (M 1942-47 and Staff 1959-94) took over from Hubert as Secretary from 1993 to 2003.

The Society has continued to run appeals for School causes such as memorials in the Chapel, the James Pavilion, the building of the three Standard Squash courts, and in 2009 the building of two new Fives courts after a 20-year absence.

The OR Trust, gives about £16,000 each year to support a boarding bursary through the Arnold Foundation. The rules dictate that these must be of direct benefit to pupils, and in the past took the form of small grants.

The Society continued with its focus on sports by forming the OR Golfing Society in 1924, followed by the Rifle, Lawn Tennis and Cricket Clubs (which later became known as The Meteors), and after the Second World War, the Sailing and Hockey Clubs. Today there are thirteen Sports Secretaries and Managers.

In 2001, Head Master Patrick Derham was concerned that the relationship between the School and its former pupils was not as strong as it should have been, so he and Michael Fowle, then Chairman of the Board of Governors, agreed some fundamental changes to the Society when Peter Berners-Price (St 56-61) became President in 2013.

This step made the Presidency a four-year appointment, introduced a membership fee, reduced the Society committee from 65 to twelve members, and dropped the word 'Old' from its name so it could represent all those who support the School, including teaching staff.

A number of focused social events were created to encourage Rugbeians to come together on an annual basis. These include a 50th Anniversary Dinner, hosted by the School at the School, as well as 25th, 10th, 5th and 1st Anniversary Year events held in London.

An OR Day was first held at the School in May 1972, but these have now been replaced by House Reunions. Two House Reunions take place each year and these have become very popular events that bring together current and past pupils of the House, as well as their Housemasters, Tutors and Matrons. With a total of fifteen boys' and girls' Houses at the School today, this means that House Reunions come round every seven years.

The Society continues to foster 'the bond of union' through its sports societies as well as its social events but an important new dimension, the Business & Professional Network, was introduced by the 'new look' Committee in 2003. This encourages Rugbeians *'to share and develop areas of mutual business interest, and to make themselves available as mentors to boys and girls at the School through the Careers Department, and to other ORs who might be seeking help from time to time.'*

Today, some 50 work placements are offered by Rugbeians each year. This figure is set to rise in the future, offering young Rugbeians the chance of work experience they might not otherwise be able to access.

In 2003, Nick Hills, (C 1961-66), became the Society's first salaried administrator. He was succeeded in 2005 by Julie Bott who held the role until 2010, since when Tracey Ahmet has held the position as Executive Secretary. In their new Society roles, they have supported the Presidencies first of Peter Berners-Price and then Ben Habib (M 79-84), Fiona Hughes d'Aeth, the Society's first female President (D 80-82), who ran the Society very successfully from Dubai, and Simon Penniston (C 65-70).

The Rugbeian Society

1876.

ADVENT OF THE TELEPHONE

In 1876, Alexander Graham Bell filed a patent application in the United States for his invention, of the telephone, only a matter of hours before another inventor advised the U.S. Patent Office of his intention to seek a patent for a similar device. Bell, having filed first was, awarded patent number 174,465, granting him proprietorship over the equipment and principle of a telephone system.

Days later, Bell successfully tested his device, summoning his assistant from another room by saying: *"Mr Watson, come here; I want you."* Within the year, Bell was able to test the telephone over a two-mile stretch between his home in Boston and Cambridgeport.

Born in Scotland in 1847, Bell was trained to succeed his father who was a leading speech therapist. The family moved to Canada in 1870 and Alexander

became a roving ambassador, demonstrating his father's techniques for teaching speech to the deaf. In 1872, Bell opened his own school in Boston where, the following year, he became a professor at the university.

In his leisure time Bell experimented with sound, becoming convinced that speech could be transmitted via an electrical system. Working with a mechanic, Thomas Watson, Bell produced a prototype, but the sounds were indistinct.

In 1877, the Bell Telephone Company was formed and, within months, hundreds

of legal challenges to its monopoly began. Bell's claims were upheld by the Supreme Court and the company enjoyed success until the expiry of the patent in 1894 when competitor companies were able to enenter the field. **DH**

LAWN TENNIS

A Lawn Tennis Club was founded at the School in spring 1877 by the
Bigside Levée, but only after considerable debate on the subject and letters
to *The Meteor*. In 1878 club members competed in a tournament, with prizes
of 15 and 30 shillings up for grabs.

1877.

1877 Rutherford Hayes

THE TEMPLE READING ROOM (TRR)

Head Master Jex-Blake held a strong belief of the value of art in education.
He pressed the Governors on the necessity of building an art museum, reading
room, and a Curator's house, and his plans were accepted in 1877. In 1878,
the Art Museum and Temple Reading Room were opened. The building by
Butterfield had cost some £9,000. This was the first art museum to be built in
a school in Britain. The stained glass windows contained the names of Rugby
boys and masters who had become Bishops. The building held numerous
loan exhibitions over the years, including many from the British Museum and
the Victoria & Albert. Casts of the Elgin Marbles were moved from New Big
School and hung on the stairs in 1888.

   A new Drawing School was created next to the TRR. Known as the Tin
Tabernacle, it was lined with wood, and heated by hot water from the Reading
Room. Started in late December 1887 and completed in January 1888, the
building was demolished in 1936 after the Art Museum was moved over to
the Old Sanatorium and the space became free to house the Art School. Over
the decades, boys would be taught by talented artists including RB Talbot
Kelly, and BB (Denys Watkins-Pitchford), and by the 1960s the Art Museum
had moved back to the Upper TRR. In 1993, the building was completely
refurbished to create the main library for the School, and it was re-opened
in 1996 by former Foreign Secretary Douglas Hurd. **RM**

PHONOGRAPH

The first phonograph was invented by Thomas Edison in 1877 at his Menlo Park laboratory in New Jersey. He was awarded US Patent Number 200,521 the following year.

Edison's invention was a by-product of his work in telephony and telegraphy in which he was a rival of Alexander Graham Bell. Edison had developed a means of capturing Morse code messages sent by telegraph using indentations on a roll of paper. He thought something similar might be achievable with the telephone, utilising the vibrations of the diaphragm.

Edison devised a system that transferred the vibrations to a needle which then inscribed a groove in tin foil wrapped round a rotating cylinder. A needle on the other side of the cylinder could then play back what had just been recorded but, after just a few replays, the tin foil would disintegrate.

The machine was ready for demonstration in late 1877. *Scientific American* recorded in its issue of December 22 that:

"Mr Thomas A. Edison recently came into this office, placed a little machine on our desk, turned a crank, and the machine inquired as to our health, asked how we liked the phonograph, informed us that it was very well, and bid us a cordial good night."

1878

A Knight of the Garter and winner of the Nobel Peace Prize

AUSTEN CHAMBERLAIN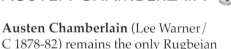

Austen Chamberlain (Lee Warner / C 1878-82) remains the only Rugbeian to have won the Nobel Peace Prize.

His ministerial appointments included civil lord in the Admiralty, Postmaster General and two stints as Chancellor of the Exchequer, the second of which, from 1918 to 1921, dealt with managing Britain's enormous debts following the First World War.

Chamberlain also led the Conservative Party briefly in the early 1920s while it remained in coalition with Lloyd George, before being replaced by Andrew Bonar Law who became Prime Minister.

His greatest achievements, however, came when he served as Foreign Secretary from 1924 to 1929 under Stanley Baldwin, helping to steer through the Locarno Agreements, by which Britain, alongside six other European powers, signed a range of pacts and treaties to prevent further war in Europe.

For this Chamberlain was made a Knight of the Garter and received the Nobel Peace Prize.

Austen having entered Rugby in 1878, his famous father Joseph at one point intervened to stop him being beaten. After Rugby, Austen went to Trinity College, Cambridge before entering the House of Commons in 1893, where his maiden speech was praised by Gladstone.

Chamberlain maintained links with his old school and served as Chairman of the Governing Body from 1907 to 1937.

He supported Churchill's calls for Britain to rearm but died in 1937, two years before his half-brother declared war on Germany.

1878

LAWRENCE SHERIFF SCHOOL

Lawrence Sheriff's intention in 1567 was that

"for ever there should bee a free Grammar Schoole .... to serve Chiefly For the Children of Rugby and Brownsover aforesaid and next for such as bee of other places thereunto adjoyneing."

By the 1820s, however, more and more pupils at Rugby were joining the School from some distance, their parents moving into the town to improve their chances. They became known in the town as 'sojourners' and came mainly from gentry or professional families, particularly clergy and army or navy officers.

In 1860 sojourners provided about three-quarters of the town's entry to Rugby School. This led the *Rugby Advertiser* to complain that:

"the present school does not supply the education required by the children of Rugby"

The Clarendon Commission, set up by Parliament in 1861 to enquire into the state of the major public schools, found Rugby had a national reputation for drawing boys from all over the country, with sojourners enjoying most of the benefits of the Free Foundation.

In 1864 Head Master Frederick Temple put forward his own proposal for meeting growing objections from the town. He suggested a separate Lower School specifically for the boys of Rugby and Brownsover. It would have 50 free places but also be open to fee payers.

More meetings followed with impassioned debates about admissions, age of entry and the place, if any, for charging school fees. Proposals were approved by the Public Schools Commission in 1875 with organisation of the new school left entirely to Rugby School, effectively the Head Master Dr Temple. Land was acquired and buildings planned which are in use today.

Finally, in 1878 the Lower or Subordinate School of Lawrence Sheriff opened its doors to 58 boys of varying ages over eight.

The original thatched cottages of Whitehall still stood roughly where the roundabout in Hillmorton Road stands today.

The names of nearby roads gave clear clues as to the rural nature of the School's surroundings. Whitehall Road was Bridle Lane, and Bath Street, Pigstye Lane.

Battles waged between Lawrence Sheriff boys and boys from local elementary schools – snowball fights in winter, and all round the year skirmishes involving catapults and brickends. One was so vicious that two masters and many boys required hospital treatment.

The Rugby School influence on the development of the new school was evident from the start. All staff appointments were made or approved by the Head Master of Rugby. Lawrence Sheriff School's first Headmaster, HT (Henry Tull) Rhoades (1878-1889) had formerly been Head Boy at Rugby. Drawing was taught by Rugby School's Drawing Master JL Tupper, Elementary Chemistry by Rugby's Laboratory Assistant AP Smith, Drill by Sergeant Hare of Rugby School's Rifle Volunteers and Music by FK Stroh, Organist of nearby (but now gone apart from its churchyard) Holy Trinity Church. He also taught at Rugby.

Rhoades resigned in 1889 and moved to be assistant at Rugby School. The staff of the Lower School presented him with an illuminated address congratulating him on his 'advancement'. This was no ironic farewell as most of Rugby's Classics Masters were then paid ten times as much as the Lower School assistants.

The appointment of a new Head Master signalled a determination to ensure that the organisation of Lawrence Sheriff School remained close to Rugby.

The new Head Master was Henry Victor Weisse who had reportedly made a 'brilliant' career as a boy at Rugby, winning an Open Scholarship at Christ Church, Oxford. He had also taught briefly at Rugby in 1889.

The *Rugby Advertiser* reported a mixed reaction from the town to the appointment of Mr Weisse. He owned a reflecting telescope and was familiar with Modern Languages which suggested a 'modern scientific type'. But his rigid, autocratic methods of discipline and decision-making attracted hostility. Weisse also commented darkly on persistent opposition and the absence of support from a powerful figure whom he declined to name but was widely believed to be Jex-Blake (Rugby's Head Master). Matters improved when Dr James replaced Blake, the former finding a Lower School with no Governing Body, no Clerk, no Accountant and no funds. Weisse did all he could with scant authority to take big decisions, on a salary of £120 per annum.

Thus began what would one day be nationally known as Lawrence Sheriff School. It moved through its first two decades as 'The Lower or Subordinate School of Lawrence Sheriff'. Today it thrives as an 'outstanding' school (OFSTED's word), regularly appearing in the top half dozen of national league tables.
DH

WILLIAM WADDINGTON

William Waddington is, unsurprisingly, the only Rugbeian to have won the Boat Race and become Prime Minister of France.

Waddington was born in 1826 to Thomas Waddington, a cotton industrialist with a large business in France. After attending Rugby under the supervision of his uncle Walter Shirley, he went up to Cambridge. There he won the Chancellor's Gold Medal and was a member of the winning Boat Race crew in 1849.

On returning to France, Waddington turned to archaeological research and writing about religion, before being elected as a Deputy in the French parliament in 1871.

Briefly serving as Minister for Public Instruction in 1873, he became a Senator in 1876 and in 1879 served as Prime Minister for less than a year. For ten years from 1893 Waddington was the French ambassador in London before losing his seat in the Senate and dying the following year.

1880 William Gladstone

1881 Chester Arthur

1881 James Garfield

1879

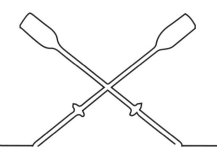

The death of Lieutenants Melvill and Coghill at the Battle of Isandlwana

ZULU WAR

January saw imperial forces operating in two theatres of war. In Afghanistan, the British army occupied Kandahar. In southern Africa, Zulu troops marshalled by King Cetshwayo massacred 1,700 British troops at Isandlwana. The rearguard of Cetshwayo's army went on to attack the 120 men left at the British outstation at Rorke's Drift but, though heavily outnumbered, the imperial forces managed to drive off their attackers. In the Anglo-Zulu war, fortunes ebbed and flowed. In March alone, the Zulus defeated the British at Intombe and Hlobane, whilst at Kambula the British overcame a Zulu force of some 20,000. By July, however, the war was effectively over with the British victory at Ulundi. **DH**

THOMAS EDISON

1879 saw the first successful test of an incandescent light bulb. Thomas Edison had filed his first US patent for 'Improvement in Electric Lights' the previous year. Whilst 22 others may have a claim to be the inventor of the incandescent lamp before Edison, his was the first practical device. Under test in October, his lamp shone for thirteen and a half hours.

In Britain, Edison's success had been pre-figured a month earlier when, for the first time, the Blackpool Illuminations shone. **DH**

Thomas Edison, inventor of the incandescent lamp

NEW BIG SCHOOL (NBS) & THE MACREADY THEATRE

As school numbers grew through the 19th-century, the original buildings struggled to accommodate the boys. Old Big School was becoming too small to be comfortable for Founder's Day and Speech Day celebrations. As the buildings of New Quad were being completed in 1885, the Head Master, Jex-Blake, had William Butterfield submit plans for a New Big School to provide the much-needed space. The building consisted of a large school or classroom, on the upper floor, with a further three schools below. The completed building first echoed to the sound of Speech Day and the School's concerts in 1886 and, for the first time in many years, the whole School was able to gather together in one place. Despite its size, by the first decade of the new century it was proving to be too small and would be superseded by the Temple Speech Room in 1909.

Much of the interior fittings were moved across the road, including the Bryceson organ. 'New Big' still provided space for lessons, concerts and dramatic performances and was in use as such until the 1970s. Plans for a completely new School Centre with octagonal theatre, cafeteria and pottery workshops proved too expensive, with spiralling costs

brought on by the oil crisis of 1974. A less expensive solution was to convert New Big School and by 1975 the Macready Theatre was born. It was named after William Charles Macready who entered Rugby, at the age of ten, in 1803. Macready became one of the greatest actors of his generation. **RM**

1885

1880s
Baron Charles-Pierre Frédy de Coubertin visited Rugby and was later inspired to rekindle the Olympic Games.

"How often, at dusk, alone in the vast Gothic Chapel at Rugby, with my eyes fixed on the funeral slab inscribed simply with the name of Thomas Arnold, have I thought to myself that here was the corner stone of British Empire."

Pierre de Coubertin

1885 Grover Cleveland   **1885** Marquess of Salisbury 🇬🇧   **1886** William Gladstone 🇬🇧

FIRST PETROL-DRIVEN MOTOR CAR

In 1885, German mechanical engineer, Karl Benz designed and built the Benz Patent-Motorwagen, the world's first practical motor car to be powered by an internal-combustion engine.

Benz's wife Bertha had financed the project but because under German law a married woman could not hold a patent. It was Karl who, on January 29, 1886, applied for a patent for the first three-wheeled, petrol-powered car. He officially unveiled his invention to the public six months later on July 3, on the Ringstrasse in Mannheim.

Sporting a single-cylinder, 954cc, 4-stroke engine, the vehicle included features still in place today, including a weight-balanced crankshaft, electrical ignition and water cooling. It achieved a top speed of 16 kmh (about 10 mph), generating 0.55 kW (about three-quarters of one horsepower). In November 1886, the Imperial Patent Office granted Benz patent number 37435 and production of the vehicle for sale began.

Benz built his first four-wheeled car in 1891, which accelerated development. In 1894, the Benz Velo was unveiled and 1,200 were manufactured, making it the first inexpensive, durable, mass-produced car. By 1900, Benz's company had developed to become the world's largest manufacturer of motor vehicles. **DH**

The Benz Patent-motorwagen: A weight-balanced crankshaft, electrical ignition and water cooling are features still in place today!

1886.

1886 Marquess of Salisbury 🇬🇧

1887

SHERLOCK HOLMES

A Study in Scarlet, the 1887 detective novel, introduced readers for the first time to Sir Arthur Conan Doyle's greatest fictional character, the amateur detective Sherlock Holmes, and his biographer and friend Dr John Watson.

The story first appeared in *Beeton's Christmas Annual* for 1887 and took its title from Holmes's description of the murder investigation on which he was engaged as a 'study in scarlet'. *The Study* was the first detective novel to feature the use of the magnifying glass in an inquiry, but the story attracted very little public interest on its appearance.

A further novel appeared in *Lippincott's Monthly Magazine* in 1890 before a series of short stories in *The Strand Magazine* in 1891 cemented the character's immense popularity. The character of Sherlock Holmes is thought to have been based on Dr Joseph Bell, a renowned forensic scientist for whom Conan Doyle had worked in Edinburgh. By 1927 when the canon was complete, four full-length novels and 56 short stories featuring Holmes and set around the turn of the 19th and 20th centuries had been published. Since then, the stories have been rendered innumerable times in cinema and on television.

Conan Doyle's creation has passed wholesale into the public imagination. Professor John Moriarty is the embodiment of evil genius. Irene Adler has caused many to wonder about Holmes's – and Conan Doyle's – attitudes to women. Tourists continue to search in vain for 221B Baker Street while Holmes' engagement with the 'irregulars', informers drawn from the underclass, continues to exercise social historians. **DH**

JOHN PERCIVAL

John Percival's contribution to reviving Rugby at a time of need was arguably no less significant or important than Arnold's.

Although twice passed over for the top job in 1869 and 1874, he was the only candidate considered and interviewed by the Governors when Jex-Blake left in 1887.

While for some Head Masters running Rugby was the high point of their careers, Percival arrived with serious educational accomplishments firmly under his belt.

After a village and grammar school education in Westmorland, Percival became an Oxford scholar where he shone in classics, maths and history (although he nearly burnt out through over work in the process).

After Percival was ordained in 1860, Temple appointed him to the Rugby staff, where he got into trouble with the School Marshall for 'giving boys beer when he entertained them to breakfast'.

Despite this hiccup, Temple recommended him after just two years to become the first head of Clifton College, where he made his name before moving to become President of Trinity College, Oxford, in 1878.

Inheriting a school in need of firm government, Percival wasted no time at Rugby, according to historian JB Hope Simpson:

"Very rapidly he took the measure of the School, hardly less rapidly of individual boys. He found a School which he considered idle and one in which there was a good deal of evil – and he regarded idleness as immoral and hated evil with single-minded intensity that made him frightening."

Examples of Percival's 'intensity' were clear and unambiguous: within a year he expelled five boys and he flogged another for 'persistent idleness'.

In the classroom he insisted on more tests and outside it he curbed the number of distinctions awarded for minor games.

Percival expected the VIth to exercise discipline and told new boys *"Eh – I shall be watching you every day of your lives."*

The new Head Master's approach was not just sound and fury. He improved quality by getting ORs to fund scholarships. He modernised learning and teaching through 'bifurcation', splitting the Upper School into classical and modern sides.

To help academic improvement Percival made good staff appointments, with many going to headships beyond Rugby, including George Smith (Dulwich), J Lewis Paton (Manchester Grammar), Frank Fletcher (Marlborough and Charterhouse) and R Waterfield (Cheltenham).

More imaginatively he appointed in 1888 Marie Bethell Beauclerc to teach shorthand, the first appointment of either a female or shorthand teacher in any English boys' public school.

Under Percival, numbers as well as standards rose and he maintained a constant and severe watch over every aspect of the School. Yet at a price, according to Hope Simpson:

"And so Percival restored Rugby's greatness. But he did not create a happy School, and there is a reverse side to the coin even of his efficiency. So intense was his moral earnestness and passion for righteousness that he was unwilling to allow any liberty. He feared it…He was a task-master who exacted the last ounce of work from his pupils…"

While life under Percival was clearly no picnic (the death of a pupil during a run even led to press criticism) he continued to improve the School.

He helped day boys form their own 'Town' house and started the Rugby School Mission in 1889, adopting the Arthur Walrond's Boys Club in Notting Dale.

This good work was offset slightly by some odd likes and dislikes (including disapproving of exposed knees on the games' field!) and strong public views on topics including supporting the disestablishment of the church in Wales.

In January 1895 Percival accepted Lord Rosebery's offer to become Bishop of Hereford (which was opposed by Queen Victoria, who didn't like his stance on the Welsh Church). Before departing to London for his consecration on March 24, he watched a huge gale fell seventeen great elms on The Close.

The metaphor was fitting, according to Hope Simpson: *"He had himself blown like a whirlwind through the life of Rugby, and his work was done. He had brought discomfort and discontent for the idle and the self-satisfied, he had jerked a placid community into intense activity, he had subjected the School to a strain almost beyond bearing. But he had done what he had been put there to do…"*

In character with his time at Rugby, Percival was equally active in his new career beyond the School. He opposed British concentration camps during the Boer War, supported university degrees for women, controversially invited non-conformists to take Holy Communion to mark the coronation of George V, chaired

the first meeting of the Workers' Educational Association and supported Lloyd George's 'People's Budget' in 1909.

Disappointed to be too old to succeed to York, Percival retired to Oxford in 1917 and died the following year.

John Percival: Head Master from 1887 to 1889

TOWN HOUSE

The Day Boys' House can trace its origins to the foundation of the School in 1567. Officially recognised as a 'House' in 1888, and given its own tutors in 1891 (previously they shared the School House Tutors), Town boys gained their first house building in 1902, when the first 'Town Room' was built. *The Meteor* described it as 'certainly not pleasant to look at'. Before this date, the boys looked to the shop Pepperdays, at the top of the High Street, as their home. The boys would change for games on the front steps of the shop, place their 'off games' notes in a cash box on the counter and read house notes from a notice board within the shop itself. After the Second World War, when Kilbracken moved to its current site, Town moved to Hillmorton Road. The old Town Room became the Bursary until 2004, when the School Bookshop, now the School Shop, took over the premises. The current Town building was opened in September 1971 and the old Hillmorton Road building was demolished in 1972. A first phase of refurbishment was completed in 2004, with the final phase completed in 2005. Town House and School House have kept their original names unchanged.

Town House alumni include **William Webb Ellis**, creator of rugby football… **Edward Cave**, founder of *The Gentleman's Magazine*… **Roger Allan Wallis**, composer of Sweden's 1969 Eurovision Song Contest entry… and **Andrew McCarthy**, geneticist involved in the discovery of a 'Master Switch' gene, linked to diabetes and obesity. **RM**

1888

MATTHEW ARNOLD

Being the son of Thomas Arnold was not the easiest of tasks but **Matthew Arnold** (24 December 1822 – 15 April 1888) succeeded in making his own mark on Victorian England. His regular profession was as a schools' inspector, a role which involved drudgery but considerable rail travel and therefore time to write. His output encompassed contemporary social issues and poetry including *Dover Beach*, which begins

The sea is calm to-night
The tide is full, the moon lies fair
Upon the straits; on the French coast the light
Gleams and is gone; the cliffs of England stand,
Glimmering and vast, out in the tranquil bay.

Like his father Arnold had a weak heart, and died of heart failure while running to meet his daughter at a railway station. It is perhaps fitting that he wrote *'Truth sits upon the lips of dying men.'*

Matthew, the son of Thomas Arnold

1889

The annual Rugby v Marlborough cricket match at Lord's cricket ground in London featured one of the School's rising stars, **PF 'Plum' Warner**, in 1889. Warner played in the Marlborough match four times but never won. He did, however, go on to captain Middlesex and England, regaining the Ashes in 1903-4.

1889 Benjamin Harrison

1893

THE LABOUR PARTY

The Reform Acts of 1867 and 1884 gave British male householders the vote. In elections, the choice lay between Conservative or Liberal but a number of working-class candidates, with trade union backing, stood as Liberal-Labour candidates. At the election of 1885, eleven of these became MPs.

A growing number of socialists like Keir Hardie, the Liberal-Labour MP for West Ham, became convinced the working class needed its own parliamentary representation. This feeling was especially strong in the north where the Scottish Labour party was founded in 1888 and the Manchester Independent Labour Party in 1892. Many other Labour organisations sprang up all over the country and following a conference in Bradford in 1893 this led to the formation of the Independent Labour Party. Led by Keir Hardie, the ILP's principal objective was *"to secure the collective ownership of the means of production, distribution and exchange"*.

By 1895, the Independent Labour Party (ILP) had 35,000 members. In that year's General Election it put up 28 candidates but polled only 44,000 votes nationally. All its parliamentary candidates were defeated but the ILP met with increasing success in local elections and West Ham became the first Labour-controlled council in 1898. In 1900 Keir Hardie became the ILP's first MP when he was elected to represent Merthyr Tydfil. **DH**

TUDOR

Tudor House was the only major construction work during John Percival's time as Head Master. It was the second of only two purpose-built boarding houses, and also the last major building work to be carried out in the 19th-century. It was opened by George Stallard in 1893 and has remained on its current site to this day. Bought by the school in 1913, for £11,000, it was permanently named Tudor in 1931. In 1962, one week before term started, a major fire destroyed the dormitories. In September 2000, by which time the decision had been made to convert the building to a girls' house, the few remaining boys, along with their Housemaster, moved to Whitelaw.

Tudor alumni include **Wyndham Lewis**, writer and artist, and actor **Anthony Quayle**. **DH**

1892 William Gladstone 🇬🇧

1893.

1893 Grover Cleveland 🇺🇸

1894

1894 Earl of Rosebery 🇬🇧

Edmund Knox, editor of Punch from 1932-1949

KNOX PUNCH

Rugbeian poet and satirist **Edmund Knox** (1881–1971), wrote under the pseudonym Evoe and was editor of *Punch* 1932-1949.

His classically written satirical verse included a poem called *Desperate Measures (A song of the Heat)* which began:

'Tis not enough that I be laid
Under the lime-trees' scented shade;
'Tis not enough, O Muse
That from these hands the heavenly lyre
Must fall, because its strings are fire,
'Tis not enough; I still perspire,
I positively ooze.

WYNDHAM LEWIS

Described by Dr Alan Munton of Exeter University as *"one of the most important British artists of the twentieth century"*, Rugbeian Wyndham Lewis was also an art critic, novelist and short-story writer, cultural commentator, political theorist and philosopher.

Wyndham Lewis (1882-1957) co-founder of the Vorticist movement in art, and edited the literary magazine the Vorticists, *BLAST*. His novels include *Tarr* (set in Paris), *The Human Age*, and the trilogy *The Childermass* (1928), *Monstre Gai* and *Malign Fiesta*.

"One of the most important British Artists of the twentieth century"

1895 Marquess of Salisbury 🇬🇧

1895

HERBERT JAMES

With a long flowing white beard and stout, short build, **Herbert 'H.A' James** looked like the long-lost brother of Santa Claus and Edward VII.

James was the first Rugby Head to be nicknamed the 'Bodger' (a word for successors that continued until the 1980s) and also perhaps the only one knowingly dreamt about by Rupert Brooke.

As a member of the Bloomsbury Set, Brooke told Geoffrey Keynes (brother of the JM):

"I was in the Gardens of Heaven walking between great odrous beds of helchrys and asphodel. Turning a corner I met the present Head Master of Rugby School in his shirt-sleeves. He was digging up all the beautiful flowers. I hit him severely on the nose."

James came to Rugby via grammar school in Wales, a scholarship to Oxford, presidency of the Oxford Union and a Double First in Classics.

His pre-School career included an assistant mastership at Marlborough, a fellowship at St John's Oxford, eleven years as Headmaster of Rossall (where he was unpopular among students), three years as Dean of St Asaph and Principal at Cheltenham. James' approach to leading Rugby was in sharp contrast to Percival's. Coldness became warmth, constant supervision of masters became trust in their ability.

Rival fans of the two men promote the merits of each but in their own way both men were successful.

Although remote from his pupils, only speaking to them individually during confirmation interviews, James was revered and respected.

He also (unusually compared to other Rugby Heads) had a range of outside interests beyond education and religion, although he was an ordained priest.

These included being a useful bowler for Monmouthshire during the holidays and having a passion for golf, stamp collecting and foreign travel on mule or horseback in Greece and Algeria.

On top of this he wrote hymns and, perhaps a little incongruously, hundreds of limericks.

James' brilliant and colourful masters included WP 'Tooler' Brooke, and Linnaeus 'Puff' Cumming who presided over riotous laboratory lessons.

During James' headship, numbers at the School rose to over 580, although they slipped back in his final years.

Perhaps his most visible legacy, however, apart from introducing central heating in boarding houses and appointing a full-time School doctor, was the building of the Temple Speech Room, following a subscription appeal among Rugbeians.

The TSR was opened by King Edward VII on July 3, 1909, the first reigning monarch to visit the school in its then 343-year history.

Whether or not James was the equal of his predecessor in academic or moral rigour is irrelevant given how the School expanded physically and in numbers during his time. And there was no drop-off in the quality of the boys it produced either, with James' pupils including not just Brooke but socialist historian RH Tawney (after whom the Tawney Society is named) and future Archbishop of Canterbury, William Temple, son of Frederick.

When James left Rugby in December 1909 to become President of St John's College, Oxford for 22 years before his death, the School was arguably in better shape than ever –

just five years before the First World War took the lives of Brooke and over nearly 700 other boys.

Before he died in 1931, James was made a Companion of Honour by King George V in 1926. A dinner for over 200 to mark the award was attended by the great and good, including former Foreign Secretary, former pupil and School governor Austen Chamberlain, who described him as *"one of the greatest and most forceful characters who had ever devoted himself to education"*.

James' obituary in *The Times* added that he was

"…equally effective and esteemed in the class-room and the pulpit, in the School House of Dr Arnold, and on the playing fields."

Herbert James: Head Master from 1895 to 1909 and the first Head to be nicknamed 'The Bodger'

1895.

STAFF UNDER JAMES

Staff at Rugby during the time of 'Bodger' Herbert James (1895-1909) were known for their eccentricities.

A dog belonging to WP 'Tooler' Brooke used to sit in a wastepaper basket during lessons, while his master had the unusual habit of awarding marks from nought downwards.

Housemaster and Classics teacher Robert Whitelaw used to invite boys to ride with him on a double-saddled tricycle.

Meanwhile the celebrated laboratory lessons of Linnaeus 'Puff' Cumming, who was of sizeable stature, were remembered in verse:
"Beloved at Rugby, this old chap
So good and kind,
When he has gone away a gap (!)
Will leave behind."

Oscar Wilde and the Ballad of Reading Gaol

ARREST OF OSCAR WILDE

In 1895, Oscar Wilde was taken to Reading Gaol after being convicted of sodomy. Wilde's private life was drawn to public attention because of a feud with Sir John Sholto Douglas, Marquess of Queensbury, whose son Lord Alfred Douglas was intimately involved with Wilde.

Homosexuality was a criminal offence at this time in Britain and Wilde had veered between hiding his personal orientation and attempting to gain some measure of public acceptance. A violent homophobe, Sir John Douglas had sounded off in public about Wilde who felt compelled to sue for libel.

Giving evidence, he said that Wilde had solicited a dozen rent-boys to commit homosexual acts between 1892 and 1894. After three days, Wilde's barrister withdrew the suit as Wilde's guilt was self-evident and shortly after, a warrant was issued for Wilde's arrest on indecency charges.

Spurning several opportunities to flee to France, Wilde decided to stand trial. At a preliminary hearing, chambermaids testified that they had seen Wilde in bed with young men and bail was denied.

A mistrial having been declared when a lone juror refused to convict, a second trial began on May 21. Whilst many potential witnesses refused to give evidence, Wilde was found guilty and sentenced to two years of hard labour.

Wilde served his sentence before leaving the country for good. Released from prison in 1897, he left for Paris where he started writing again, producing *The Ballad of Reading Gaol*, based on his prison experiences. He died of meningitis in 1900.

Pembroke College, Cambridge

KANWAR SHUMSHERE

Kanwar Shumshere was the oldest surviving Kent cricketer when he died in 1975. Remarkably Shumshere played for the XI at Rugby in 1896, a year before Queen Victoria's Diamond Jubilee.

At Pembroke College, Cambridge he played one match for the University and then four for Kent over two years.

His solitary varsity appearance was a three-day match from June 6-8, 1901 against Surrey in which he scored 16 and 18.

In a match for Kent against Worcestershire at the Oval he top scored with 45 and helped Murrell to add 115 in 55 minutes for the seventh wicket.

Noted as a batsman with a strong defence, and a good fielder, Shumshere later trained as a doctor at Barts in London, qualifying in 1905.

He then entered the Indian Medical Service in 1906, became a Lieutenant Colonel in 1926 and retired eight years later.

"At the time of his death in New Delhi,
he was the oldest surviving Kent cricketer."

1896.

ARTHUR RANSOME

As a young journalist Rugbeian Arthur Ransome reported on the 1917 Russian Revolution for the *Daily News* newspaper.

Ransome's time in Russia won him a place in the files of MI5 who wondered if he was a spy, and in the heart of Evgenia Shelepin, secretary to Soviet Union co-founder Leon Trotsky.

An MI5 document from 1918-1919 describes Ransome as *"a keen supporter of Trotsky and… an ardent Bolshevik"* but the authorities' suspicion was not formally pursued.

From the thrill of covering a country in tumult, Ransome came back to England, married Evgenia and settled down to write *Swallows and Amazons* and a raft of children's books that endure in popularity today in print and on screen.

Ransome was born on January 18, 1884 in Leeds and educated in Windermere and at Rugby. He was happy at Rugby but during his time there, sadly lost his father, Cyril, who was only 46 when he died from a bone infection.

While at Rugby, Ransome's family spent their summers at Nibthwaite, to the south of Coniston Water where he fell in love with the Lake District and fishing.

After leaving Rugby in 1901, Ransome studied for a chemistry degree but gave it up for a junior job in a publisher's office.

He published *Bohemia* on London's artistic scene in 1907 and several other titles. Following a failed marriage (which produced a daughter, Tabitha, from whom Ransome was later estranged), he headed for Russia where he met leading revolutionaries including Lenin and Trotsky.

Settling back in England in 1924, Ransome earned his living as a correspondent covering foreign news and angling for the *Manchester Guardian*. He married Evgenia the same year, following a difficult divorce from his first wife.

Swallows and Amazons, published in 1930, was the first of a series of children's adventure stories published over the following sixteen years. One title, *Pigeon Post* in 1936, won the Carnegie Medal for best children's book in 1937.

Ransome's books, set mainly in the Lake District and the Norfolk Broads, presented children with endless summer days on boats and lakes, far from the watchful eyes of adults, and a series of strong juvenile characters like Titty, Susan and Nancy.

In October 1965 Arthur Ransome became seriously ill and he died on June 3, 1967, aged 83. Evgenia following eight years later. The *Guardian's* obituary on Ransome called him *"a man built for happiness"*.

Arthur Ransome: From Lenin and Trotsky to Swallows and Amazons

1897

1899

Fought between Britain and the 'Boer' colonies of the South African Republic to maintain control of the Transvaal's gold mines

THE BOER WAR

The Boer War was fought between Britain and the self-governing Afrikaaner (Boer) colonies of the South African Republic (the Transvaal) and the Orange Free State. At the outbreak, Britain ruled the two colonies of the Cape and Natal. Hostility between the two sides was longstanding and had been greatly exacerbated by the Jameson Raid of 1895, a botched attempt to overthrow the SAR government and to install a pro-British regime in the Transvaal.

The war began on October 11, 1899, following a Boer ultimatum demanding the British stop building up their forces in the region. The Boers had refused to grant political rights to non-Boer settlers known as Uitlanders, most of whom were British. They had denied any civil rights to Africans. There was also an economic imperative: at a time when the international financial system was based on the gold standard, control of the Transvaal's gold mines was an issue.

The conflict proved to be more than a 'white man's war'. Large numbers of Africans and other non-Europeans were involved. These included Mohandas Karamchand Gandhi, then living in South Africa, who served as a volunteer stretcher-bearer in 1900. On the British side, troops came from Britain and from other parts of the empire, including Australia and Canada.

Winston Churchill covered the conflict as a war correspondent and was famously captured and escaped.

1900-1910
HOPE AND GLORY

1901   THE DEATH OF QUEEN VICTORIA

1903   FIRST FLIGHT

1904   SIR ARTHUR BLISS & OTHER MUSICIANS

1906   THE SAN FRANCISCO EARTHQUAKE

1908   MODEL T FORD
"SCOUTING FOR BOYS"

1909   THE TEMPLE SPEECH ROOM (TSR)

1910   AA DAVID BECOMES HEAD

1912   CAPTAIN SCOTT
TITANIC

1913   SUFFRAGETTES

THE DEATH OF QUEEN VICTORIA

Queen Victoria died at Osborne House on the Isle of Wight on January 22, 1901, aged 81. After suffering a series of strokes a few days earlier, the Queen was confined to bed. Although rallying slightly, she faded towards evening on the day of the death and passed away at 6.30pm.

At her bedside were her children and grandchildren including her son who would succeed her as King Edward VII and her grandson German Kaiser Wilhelm II.

The late queen left detailed instructions about what she wanted in her coffin. These included her late husband's dressing-gown, a plaster cast of his hand, her wedding veil and a picture of her faithful Scottish servant, John Brown.

Responding to the event, the *Economist* wrote:

"There is a perceptible note of apprehension in the public mind, caused by the death of the Queen, which is a little exaggerated. Of the magnitude of that loss and its irreparable character there can, indeed, be no doubt whatever. The steady good sense of Queen Victoria, which latterly rose to sagacity; the unprecedented length of her reign, its marvellous good fortune scarcely broken by the catastrophe in Afghanistan or that unique disaster the great Mutiny in India, or the unexpected strain of the present war; and the remarkable relation as of a mother with sons which, after the Prince Consort's death, grew up between the Queen and her peoples, had evoked a warmth of loyalty, which acted throughout the Empire as a binding force, and immensely increased its prestige among the nations."

The funeral of Queen Victoria in London who was succeeded by King Edward VII

1901 Edward VII

1901

1901 Theodore Roosevelt

1903

The first flight lasted 12 seconds and changed history forever

FIRST FLIGHT

It took place 20 feet off the ground a week before Christmas 1903, lasted twelve seconds and changed history for ever.

That was the feat of Orville and Wilbur Wright when they made the first successful powered flight by an aircraft.

The brothers had been testing aircraft since the late 1890s at Kitty Hawk Beach in North Carolina, starting with gliders and then adding power.

With no existing engine available that was light or powerful enough for the job, they decided to build their own 12hp engine with the help of machinist Charles Taylor.

With a new aircraft for their engine, the brothers headed for Kitty Hawk and made the first attempt on December 14. The engine stalled and the aircraft was damaged.

After three days of repairs they tried again, this time making history at 10.35am when they remained airborne for 120 feet.

Today, the plane the Wright brothers used can be seen at the National Air and Space Museum in Washington, D.C, ironically just a short distance away from the Pentagon, where US military commanders today control thousands of jet fighter aircraft across the globe.

SIR ARTHUR BLISS & OTHER MUSICIANS

Rugbeian composer and conductor Sir Arthur Bliss is best known for his 1921-22 work *A Colour Symphony*.

Born in 1891, Bliss entered Rugby in 1904. His early compositional work was unconventional and modernist but his later output was seen as more traditional and conversative.

During the Second World War, Bliss became director of music for the BBC and after the war was appointed Master of the Queen's Music in 1953.

Sir Arthur Bliss,
Master of the Queen's Music

Other classical music Rugbeians have included choir director, organist and composer **Sir Sydney Hugo Nicholson**, founder of the Royal School of Church Music… composer **Robin Milford** (1903-1959)… operatic tenor **John William Kentish** (1910-2006)… and organist and composer **Richard Hey Lloyd** (born June 25, 1933).

Contemporary music Rugbeians include **Pete Kember** of *Sonic Boom*… **Faris Badwan** and **Tom Cowan** of *The Horrors*… **Freddie Cowan** of *The Vaccines*… and **Dan Haigh** and **Alex Westaway** of *Fightstar*.

1904.

1905 Henry Campell-Bannerman

*Buildings were crumbling as one might crush
a biscuit in one's hands*

THE SAN FRANCISCO EARTHQUAKE

It killed between 700 and 3,000 people, destroyed 80% of the city and is still the greatest loss of life from a natural disaster in California's history.

At around 5.12am on April 18, 1906, San Francisco was hit by a foreshock, followed around 20-25 seconds later by an earthquake estimated at over 8 on the Richter scale when the northernmost 296 miles of San Andreas fault ruptured.

The quake ignited fires which burned for three days and destroyed 490 city blocks totalling 25,000 buildings. 250,000 people were left homeless.

One eyewitness said the quake 'was as if the earth was slipping gently from under our feet'.

"Then came the sickening swaying of the earth that threw of us flat upon our faces. We struggled in the street. We could not get to our feet. Then it seemed as though my head was split with the roar that crashed into my ears. Big buildings were crumbling as one might crush a biscuit in one's hands. Ahead of me a great cornice crushed a man as if he were a maggot – a labourer in overalls on his way to the Union Iron Works with a dinner pail on his arm."

1906.
1908.

The "Tin Lizzy" launched by Henry Ford in 1908

MODEL T FORD

The Irish band *Thin Lizzy* took their name from a cartoon character in turn named after Tin Lizzie, the nickname for one of the world's most successful cars, the Model T Ford.

Launched by Henry Ford on October 1, 1908 at his factory in Detroit, the car gave ordinary American people affordable wheels and the opportunity to travel. Over the next nineteen years 16.5 million Model Ts were sold, putting it in the top 20 of best-selling cars of all time.

Assembly-line production allowed the price of the touring car version to be lowered from $850 in 1908 to less than $300 in 1925.

The Model T had a 22-horsepower, four-cylinder engine and was built using a new kind of heat-treated steel. This made it light at just 1,200 pounds, fast at 40 miles per hour and flexible enough to run on gasoline or hemp-based fuel.

"SCOUTING FOR BOYS"

Robert Baden-Powell wrote *Scouting for Boys* in 1908 after first-hand experience of the potential and skills of young people during the Boer War.

Training boys aged between twelve and fifteen to be postmen, messengers and stretcher bearers at the siege of Mafeking, he returned to England and wrote *Aids to Scouting*, a guide to field observation and deduction. *Scouting for Boys* updated this work.

Since its appearance, the book has sold over 100 million copies in more than 80 languages, putting it on a par with sales of books by Lewis Carroll.

Scouting for Boys offered instruction on a wide range of practical subjects including lighting fires, building boats, stalking animals, chivalry, manners, self-discipline and improvement. It can still be bought for under £10, nearly 110 years after first appearing.

1908.

The Temple Speech Room on the corner of Barby and Hillmorton roads

1908 Herbert H. Asquith 🇬🇧   **1909** William Taft 🇺🇸

The new Temple Speech Room was opened in July 1909 by King Edward VII

THE TEMPLE SPEECH ROOM (TSR)

The death of former Head Master and Archbishop of Canterbury Frederick Temple in 1902 was a great loss to Rugby.

By 1903 a Memorial Committee had been set up and by 1905 was proposing 'a still newer Big School' to replace Butterfield's New Big School. Although only opened in 1885, New Big School had become too small for a growing school.

Rugby wanted a building which was big enough to hold the whole school and visitors on Speech Day. The need for an enlarged Big School, and a memorial to Temple produced the Temple Speech Room, the main concert and assembly hall.

In 1905 Thomas Jackson was engaged as architect and the proposed building given its name - The Temple Speech Room. Whilst the work of building gathered pace, New Big School was plundered, with the portraits and even the 1890 Bryceson organ being moved across the road. The strikingly modern casing was replaced in 1911 by a more traditional design. The fine marble bust of Arnold by Arthur Gilbert joined the caravan. By July 1909, much of the interior of NBS had crossed the road.

By 1908 a proposal to place stained glass in the windows was put forward, each one to be a gift from an OR. Portraits of Arnold and Lawrence Sheriff would be added to the transepts. Further proposals

for a commemorative tablet, a bust and Temple's coat of arms were accompanied by the proposal that, in line with other schools, subscriptions should be sought for chairs to fill the hall.

The suggestion met with approval and by 1909 H.A. James, the Head Master, was asking for one guinea, which would provide *for a solid oak chair, and for the donor's name and year of entry to Rugby, to be carved on the back.* Cushioned seats were provided in the 1930s through the generosity of an OR who had presumably suffered long sessions on the unadorned oak seats. The windows were all funded by W B Gair. The bust of Frederick Temple, a copy of that by Sir George Frampton, was given by Mrs Temple and her sons.

The Speech Room was finally opened on July 3, 1909, when the Speech Day ceremony was 'mercifully curtailed'. Edward VII, the first ruling monarch to visit the School, arrived to enthusiastic cheers from the waiting crowds. The Head of School, H J B Clough, in a seemingly unscripted moment, set the King a challenge.

"Finally, may I venture to remind your Majesty, that it is a kingly prerogative to command an addition to our hard-earned holidays. Should your Majesty be pleased to exercise it on our behalf, it

will be a kindness long to be gratefully remembered by the School."

After a hurried conversation between the King and the Head Master, and with a barely concealed grin, His Majesty in his reply said,:

"I am glad to tell you that my visit will be commemorated later on by the addition of a week's holiday to one of your vacations."

This produced cheers and laughter from the entire audience.

A fire in 2000 destroyed part of the stage and one of the grand pianos. During the cleaning and restoration work which closed the building for a year, the balcony was enlarged and given a second staircase. The stage now included a lift for removing pianos and props. The old oak chairs were largely replaced by new and more comfortable seating.

In January 2006, just before term began, a small section of the ceiling above the stage collapsed, and asbestos was discovered. The building was yet again closed, for asbestos removal and further restoration work. The TSR reopened again in September 2007. **RM**

1910

AA DAVID

At a joint memorial service held in May 1915 to mark the loss of scholar-poet Rupert Brooke and England Rugby star Ronnie Poulton-Palmer, Rugby Head Master, the Reverend AA David, delivered the sermon.

"…If we were asked to describe what highest kind of manhood Rugby helps to make, I think we should have Ronnie in mind… God had endowed him with a rare combination of graces and given him an influence upon men such as very few in one generation…"

As Head Master, AA David steered Rugby through a much more significant and difficult period than many before him.

An Oxford Queen's Scholar with a double first in Classics, David had already taught at Rugby in the 1890s before becoming Head Master of Clifton in 1905.

Arriving at Rugby in 1910, David inherited a School that was on one level stable and successful but below the surface needing change.

Much of David's pre-war focus was on replacing Housemasters (in particular ensuring the School bought the boarding houses boys lived in) and improving staff pensions.

He also tackled learning and teaching, introducing sets at all levels, improving science, and putting Lower Middle form teaching under one master.

Within these changes, he tackled the tricky issue of the retirement of Robert Whitelaw, who had run the XX for 43 of his 47 years at the School, with admirable energy and success.

A prickly character, Whitelaw asked David not to mention him on Speech Day when he retired in 1913, and complained forcefully when the Head Master overruled the request.

The First World War in one way did not have an impact on the School. Numbers fell at first but were at record levels by 1918. But the human cost was inevitably immense with nearly 700 boys lost during the the conflict.

At the School itself, there was a surge of patriotism when the War started and boys flocked to join the School Corps.

During the long War years, there were changes in the School's domestic regime, including economies on bread and sugar to divert money for comforts for troops on the front line, with squads helping local farmers to pick potatoes.

House suppers were abandoned, town food shops placed out of bounds and food parcels from home forbidden.

Armistice Day in 1918 was greeted in enthusiastic fashion, with impromptu School celebrations including a concert from a makeshift eleven-strong orchestra assembled on the Bradley rooftop.

The work of David and his team to keep the School running was recorded by the Governing Body on the first anniversary of the Armistice:

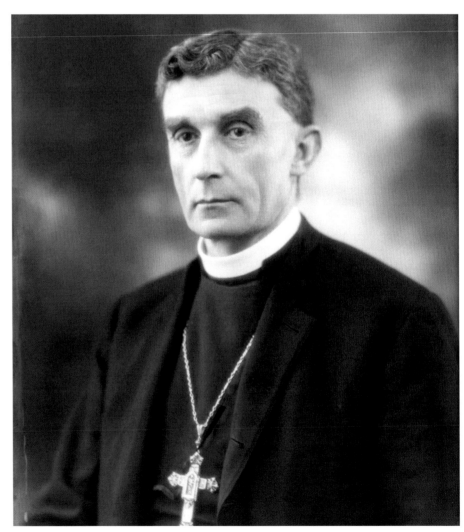

AA David: Head Master from 1910 to 1921

1910 George V

"To Dr David…they wish to express their gratitude for the wisdom, tact and unfailing energy which he has uniformly displayed and which make his name a conspicuous one in the illustrious list of Rugby Head Masters."

David's wartime contribution, however, was perhaps as of nothing compared to his selfless decision to buy, with the School's housemasters, land on both sides of Barby Road when it came up for sale. At the time the Governing Body did not have the necessary funds although in 1919 it was persuaded to take it over.

This decision enabled the School to maintain a large swathe of green land from The Close southwards for nearly two miles.

In 1921, David was offered the post of Bishop of St Edmundsbury and Ipswich, and Liverpool two years later.

He retired to Cornwall in 1944 and died aged 83 in 1950.

1911

J Nettleton (Tudor 1911-14) recalled being beaten for sharing a fruit cake sent to a fellow boarder by his mother. The boys had broken the School's 'Stodge Rules' which decreed that they should be in training for sport rather than scoffing cake.

1912

CAPTAIN SCOTT

British Antarctic hero Captain Scott faced two setbacks on his last trip across the snow and ice, one of them fatal.

After making a name for himself on the National Antarctic Expedition of 1901-4, during which he went further south than anyone had before, Scott assembled funds and crew for an attempt on the South Pole.

Leaving Cardiff Bay on board *Terra Nova* in June 1910, Scott and his team reached the Pole on January 17, 1912 only to discover they had been beaten there by Norwegian explorer Roald Amundsen.

Amundsen had successfully used dogs while Scott's horses had died during his attempt, forcing his team to pull their own sledges.

On their gruelling return journey, Scott and his four colleagues, Wilson, Evans, Oates and Bowers, were hit by unseasonably cold temperatures.

While Oates and Evans died en route, the remaining three perished from starvation and exposure on March 29, just short of their supply depot.

The bodies of Scott and his colleagues were discovered eight months later, still in the tent where they died.

Since then 'Scott of the Antarctic' has widely been regarded as a national hero, despite failing to reach the Pole first and dying on the way home.

Scott left behind a note for his wife asking her to encourage their young son to take an interest in nature, if he failed to return. Peter Scott, later Sir Peter, went on to be a celebrated conservationist, artist and founder of the Wildfowl and Wetlands Trust.

Captain Scott, father of Sir Peter Scott

THE TITANIC

The wreck of *RMS Titanic* rests today 12,415 feet below the sea, 300 or so miles off Newfoundland on the route from Ireland to New York.

The most famous, largest and advanced ship of its kind in the world at the time, *Titanic* set out from Southampton on April 10, 1912 carrying more than 2,200 passengers of all classes, including some of the world's richest.

At 11.40pm on April 14 she struck an iceberg, ripping her side open and flooding supposedly watertight compartments.

Titanic's inadequate lifeboat supply, which was poorly distributed at the scene of the disaster, offloaded 705 survivors.

The remainder, including Captain Edward Smith and the boat's architect Thomas Andrews, went down with the ship.

Inquiries into the loss of *Titanic* took place on both sides of the Atlantic, leading to a host of improvements in maritime safety, many of which remain in place today.

The ship's final resting place was located in 1985 and thousands of artefacts have been salvaged.

Titanic was also the subject of a 1997 Oscar-winning film starring Leonardo di Caprio and Kate Winslet.

1913

SUFFRAGETTES

The suffragette campaign to win the right for women to vote in elections is remembered for its charismatic leader Emmeline Pankhurst and its militant campaign of direct action.

Although not as famous as Pankhurst, Emily Wilding Davison is connected with the movement's most infamous, and perhaps tragic, direct act when she stepped in front of a racehorse owned by King George V at the Epsom Derby on June 4, 1913.

Davison, who had already been jailed nine times and force-fed while locked up nearly 50 times, died from her injuries four days later at Epsom Cottage Hospital.

At her funeral in London ten days after the Derby, thousands of suffragettes turned out to honour the woman who had given her life to their cause.

Speculation has surrounded Davison's decision to step in front of Anmer, the King's horse. It was widely believed she clearly knew the mortal danger she faced and had attempted to bring Anmer down.

But analysis of newsreel footage of the event now suggests Davison was actually trying to attach a suffragette banner to the bridle of the horse, a theory reinforced by the fact that she was carrying a return train ticket.

Although interrupted by the First World War, the suffragette campaign succeeded in winning votes for women over the age of 30 in 1918 and all women over 21 in 1928.

The suffragettes, led by Emmeline Pankhurst fight for the women's right to vote

1913 Woodrow Wilson

1914-1924
IF I SHOULD DIE

1914 GEORGE DYSON MAURICE HANKEY	**1914** THE FIRST WORLD WAR
1915 RUPERT BROOKE HARRY RICARDO	
	1916 THE EASTER RISING
	1917 THE RUSSIAN REVOLUTION
1918 STARTING GUN	
	1919 TREATY OF VERSAILLES
1920 DICK FRANKS JIM CASSELLS PERCIVAL GUILDHOUSE	
1921 WILLIAM VAUGHAN BECOMES HEAD HOCKEY	
1922 THE STODGE THE MEMORIAL CHAPEL	**1922** THE BBC
1923 THE MUSIC SCHOOLS	

THE
WORLD
AT WAR

The First World War began on August 4, 1914, and the public schools' sacrifice was probably only matched by the colleges at Oxford and Cambridge.

About 3,500 serving Rugbeians received a postcard from their alma mater saying: *"Each day at noon work stops while the chapel bell rings and one thinks of you and wishes you well."* The Head Master read out the casualty list once a week. The numbers grew ever longer and their depressing impact caused him to abandon the practice.

By the end of 1914 Rugby had lost 63 former pupils, rising to nearly 700 by the end of 1918. Ninety of these are recorded on the walls of the Menin Gate in Ypres and on the Thiepval Memorial on the Somme who lost their lives in these areas of the war.

1914.

The First World War was primarily a soldier's war and the cards were heavily stacked against you if you were a junior officer. Seventy-eight per cent of Rugby's casualties were Captains, Lieutenants and Second Lieutenants.

Rugbeians Lieutenant-General **Samuel Lomax** (B 1869-72) aged 59 and Lieutenant-Colonel **Arthur Percival** (SH 1887-89) aged 44 were killed by enemy shell fire, and Brigadier-General **Ernest Pratt** (W 1877-79) aged 55 died of gas poisoning. It may well be that Lieutenant-Colonel **Jasper Richardson** (SF 1864-65) was the oldest member of the British Army to die in the Great War three days short of his 69th birthday. One hears of youngsters lying about their age to enlist. Richardson concealed his real age to serve at the front. He survived until March 1918 when, a few miles east of Bapaume, he was struck by multiple shell splinters. He had left Rugby in 1865.

Forty-five Rugbeian airmen died, as well as members of the Royal Navy and Royal Marines, including **Rupert Brooke** (Brooke 1901-06) and **William Denis-Browne** (K 1903-07) from the Royal Naval Division.

Major **William Abell** (SH 1887-90) fell in action at Oburg, near Mons, on August 23, 1914. He was Rugby's first casualty and comes first alphabetically in the list of Rugbeians on the *Registers* in the Memorial Chapel. By the last day of December in that opening year three nineteen year olds had been lost but ten were over 40 and eighteen were in their thirties.

Lieutenant-General **Sir William Franklin** (SH 1870-73) was 58 and left a widow and three children. In those first five months the conflict had created 24 Rugby widows and 39 orphans. Rugby also lost her first Victoria Cross holder of the war. Lieutenant **Frank de Pass** (SF 1901-04) 34th Poona Horse, who fell

at Festubert, France. Captain **John Norwood** (B 1891-94) had won his VC outside Ladysmith in 1899 in the South African War. He was killed on his 38th birthday near Sablonnières. One of the saddest references concerns the Smeathman brothers, Lieutenants **Julian** (St 1902-05) and **Cecil** (St 1903-08) separated by a year but both in Stanley House. On October 24, 1914 Julian was killed in the first battle of Ypres. A few hours later that day Cecil died of wounds in the base hospital at Bailleul. Brothers **Henry** (St 1907-12) and **Everard** (St 1909-13) Handford fell side by side at Vermelles on October 14, 1915. Both were in Stanley House, the same Cambridge college and the same battalion of the same Regiment. The Chaworth-Musters and Buckley Roderick families were linked by three years. Both families lost Rugbeian brothers in 1915, 1917 and 1918. In 1915 brothers **Meaburn** (M 1892-95) and **Geoffrey Staniland** (M 1895-97) died and now lie together in Dranoutre churchyard, Belgium. **Alick Hunter** (B 1888-91), despite being 44, was only a Cadet; his brother **Douglas** (B 1888-90) a Lieutenant-Colonel aged 48. Both succumbed to the hardships of war, dying in 1918 and 1921 respectively. One cannot imagine the feelings of Mrs Lupton as she received the news of her three sons killed in 1915, 1916 and 1917. **Maurice** (K 1902-06), **Lionel** (K 1906-10) and **Francis** (K 1900-04) were followed by nephew **Charles** (K 1912-16) in 1918. Another relative, **Arthur** (K 1899-03), won the Military Cross and Croix de Guerre and survived. All were Kilbracken lads. The two worst days for British casualties were July 1, 1916 (the Somme) and September 25, 1915 (Loos), with Rugby losing 25 over both battles.

Rugbeians came from as far afield as Ceylon, Fiji, Australia and Canada and their final resting places can be found in East Africa, Mesopotamia,

Rugby's Clifton Road cemetery and the bottom of the North Sea. Four Heads of School, eight winners of the Crick, 54 members of the XV, three Rugby Football Internationals and six members of the winning Ashburton Shield VIII of 1912 died. Captain **Frederick Selous** (C 1865-68) aged 65, the famous big game hunter, is buried in today's Tanzania. A year later to the day, on January 4, 1918, his son, also **Frederick** (SH 1912-15), aged nineteen, R.F.C. was shot down near Arras. Second Lieutenant **Havilland le Mesurier** (C 1908-13), at six foot six inches, must have made an inviting target as he went over the top at Delville Wood.

Future school staff also served. **Richard Talbot Kelly** (K 1911-14) was a Kilbracken boy. He observed and sketched the horrors on several fronts for nearly three years. Severely wounded he was invalided home and later became a distinguished Art Master at Rugby.

Second Lieutenant **Harold Woolley** was also on the staff after the war. In April 1915, at Hill 60 near Ypres, he became the first Territorial officer to win a Victoria Cross in the war. Second Lieutenant **Leonard Colbeck** taught at Rugby from 1907 until 1911. Commissioned in the Royal Field Artillery, he won the Military Cross in 1917 and died the following year. Captain P.F 'Plum' Warner thought him one of the finest batsmen of his generation. Schoolmasters Second Lieutenant **H.S Wilson** and Lieutenant-Colonel **H. Podmore** (K 1901-06) never returned to Britain.

Gaston Emile Bernheim (B 1907-09) 2nd Artillery Regiment, French Army fell to shell fire in the Champagne region. He died with a degree from Exeter College, Oxford and a Croix de Guerre. His image in Volume II of the *Memorials* comes complete with kepi and cigarette. Conducteur **Cyril Danger** (St 1912-17) joined the French Red Cross after rejection by the British Army. He died in 1920 as a result of septic infection contracted on active service. **Patrick Lysaght** (SF 1906-09) left Rugby in 1909. Part of a Quaker family, he volunteered on the outbreak of war as a non-combatant with the Friends' Ambulance Service. He was killed in December 1914, aged 22, and is buried in an Amiens cemetery.

Eleven Rugbeians died in November 1918 before 11am on the eleventh day of that eleventh month. We have travelled from Major Abell to Captain **A E Stehn** (W 1909-13). Arthur Stehn had been a popular volunteer at the Rugby Clubs Mission in Notting Dale before the war. He crossed to France in November 1914 and survived until November 8, 1918, the last Rugbeian to fall at the front.

GEORGE DYSON

Organist **George Dyson** only stayed at Rugby a year but was a popular member of staff.

It is said his decision to arrive at his interview in 1914 on a motorcycle impressed the selection committee who felt it would 'appeal to the boys'.

Arrived for his interview on a motorcycle!

1914

MAURICE HANKEY

Maurice Pascal Alers Hankey (Collins 1890-95), 1st Baron Hankey, GCB,GCMG,GCVO,PC,FRS was a British civil servant who gained prominence as the first Cabinet Secretary and who later made the rare transition from the civil service to ministerial office. He is best known as the highly efficient top aide to Prime Minister David Lloyd George and the War Cabinet, that directed British strategy making in the First World War, and the founder of cabinet government in Britain. He is the author of *Supreme Command 1914-1918*.

RUPERT BROOKE

Poet **Rupert Brooke** died on April 23, 1915, 299 years to the day after another master of the English sonnet, William Shakespeare.

In September 1914, Brooke had joined his regiment and took part in the unsuccessful defence of Antwerp. The following February, as a friend of the Asquiths, he convalesced from flu at 10, Downing Street. In the following spring he joined the expedition setting out for the ill-fated Dardanelles campaign. Although he suffered during the voyage from sunstroke and dysentery he refused the comfort of a staff job away from his men.

On Saturday, April 17, 1915 Brooke received a letter saying that his sonnet, *The Soldier*, had been recited by the Dean of Westminster during a service at the Abbey two weeks earlier.

The Dean at the time was Henry Ryle, who later developed the idea of a tomb in memory of the Unknown Soldier and wrote the inscription that appears on it.

On Tuesday, April 20, Brooke fell ill after a mosquito bite on his upper lip became inflamed. The bite turned to blood poisoning and two days later Brooke was transferred to a French hospital ship. He was the only patient for the twelve doctors and surgeons on board.

The following day his temperature rose and Brooke died in the late afternoon. He was buried in an olive grove on the Greek island of Skryos before midnight on the same day.

Born on August 3, 1887, Brooke was the son of William 'Willie' Brooke and Mary Cordell. His parents met at Fettes College in Edinburgh but had to leave after their marriage in 1879 as the school had no married quarters.

Willie Brooke joined Rugby where he became Housemaster of School Field in Hillmorton Road.

Rupert excelled academically and was a member of the XV and cricket XI. He also grew his hair long and dressed more flamboyantly than his peers.

Brooke was a member of an Upper Bench literary group called Eranos and in June 1904 was a prime mover and contributor to a literary magazine at the School called *The Phoenix*.

In 1906 Brooke won a scholarship to King's College, Cambridge, where his circle of friends included Virginia Woolf, EM Forster and the poet Frances Cornford, granddaughter of Charles Darwin.

At Cambridge Brooke wrote that he

"had been happier at Rugby than I can find words to say. As I looked back at five years I seemed to see almost every hour golden and radiant, and always increasing in beauty..."

1915

In 1910 Brooke briefly returned to Rugby following the death of his father and served as Housemaster of School Field for a term, although he was not on the staff.

Brooke was a passionate man, pursuing love affairs with both sexes, and was an active supporter of socialism, joining the Fabian Society and campaigning for Poor Law reform. After graduating he was elected a fellow of his college and continued to write and publish poetry.

Aside from *The Soldier*, with its haunting opening line: *"If I should die think only this of me"*, Brooke, is also remembered for another war sonnet, *The Dead*. This includes the opening lines: *"These hearts were woven of human joys and cares, Washed marvellously with sorrow, swift to mirth."*

Today Brooke's memory is marked through a statue, a road and pub in Rugby, a memorial wall at Rainsbrook Cemetery, a statue in Brooke Square, Skyros and at his grave in west Skryos.

Rupert Brooke House for sixth-form girls at Rugby was opened in 1988 at 16, Horton Crescent.

Rupert Brooke excelled academically while at Rugby and was a member of the XV and cricket XI - he also grew his hair long and dressed more flamboyantly than his peers!

1915

HARRY RICARDO

The effectiveness of new-fangled tanks in the Great War was hampered by poor engines which emitted excessive exhaust smoke, giving away their location. A new four-stroke engine designed by Rugbeian **Harry Ricardo** (later Sir Harry) in 1915 improved engine performance to 150bhp and removed the smoke. Engines were Sir Harry's life work. At seventeen, while presumably still at the School, he designed a water pump for the family home in Sussex. After Cambridge he pursued his passion professionally, contributing to major developments in internal combustion engines, octane ratings, diesel engines and sleeve valve designs. Sir Harry was born in 1885 and died in 1974.

Designer, inventor and engineer

1916

A stray bull which wandered into The Close during the First World War, and got stuck in a passageway between two classrooms was eventually persuaded to enter the Quad (presumably New not Old) by a boy called Halford. Halford received a kick in the cheek for his efforts from the ungrateful bull, but received praise for his bravery from Head Master AA David.

1916

THE EASTER RISING

On Monday, April 24, 1916, while war raged across Europe, a rising against the British organised by members of the Irish Republican Brotherhood, the Irish Citizen Army and 200 or so volunteers took over key buildings in Dublin.

During the six-day rebellion, which left 2,000 people dead or injured, the insurgents also mounted attacks on the Royal Irish Constabulary in other parts of Ireland.

The rebels declared an Irish Republic, independent of the British Empire. In the short-term this failed as militarily superior British forces suppressed the rebellion and most of the leaders were executed.

But the incident lit a fuse which led to the Republican party Sinn Fein winning 73 out of 105 Irish seats in the 1918 British General Election, a fresh Declaration of Independence in 1919, and, ultimately, the separation of Ireland and Ulster in 1922.

The creation of the Irish Free State led to a brief civil war in Ireland, while the separation of Ulster led to conflict between Protestant and Catholics during the so-called Troubles.

1916 David Lloyd George

THE RUSSIAN REVOLUTION

Centuries of authoritarian Tsarist rule, military setbacks against Germany, army mutiny, food shortages, working-class unrest and an exiled leader in waiting poised to exploit a power vacuum, all contributed to the 1917 Russian Revolutions.

The first stage took place in spring 1917 when members of the Imperial Parliament, or Duma, forced Tsar Nicholas II to abdicate.

A new, unelected Petrograd-based (then capital of Russia and now called St Petersburg) provisional government took control.

Meanwhile a series of elected workers, councils, or Soviets, had started to emerge, leading to two levels of control - national and local - operating across the country.

In October, the socialist-led Soviets overthrew the provisional government and the Bolsheviks, led by Lenin (returned from exile in Switzerland), seized control.

A peace deal was reached with Germany in March 1918, although this was then replaced by a three-year civil war between the Bolsheviks and anti-Communist 'White Russians'.

King George V refused to give his cousin Emperor Nicholas and his family exile in Britain, fearing revolution at home, leaving them to face bloody assassination by the Bolsheviks.

However, Britain did provide military support for the White Russians, during and after the First World War.

In 1922, five years after the revolution began, the Union of Soviet Socialist Republics was officially established, the first proper Communist state, with Moscow as its capital. Lenin died two years later but the USSR lasted nearly 70 years until the fall of European Communism in the early 1990s.

1917.

STARTING GUN

Rugbeian Robert Collis, as Captain of the XV, in 1918 also had the role of firing the gun to start athletics races.

Enterprising and bold, Collis was unable to find blanks and so apparently used live ammunition from the armoury instead.

According to School historian JB Hope Simpson:

"He nearly shot a master, ELD Cole, and was surprised to see a complete line of spectators fall flat until he realised that he was pointing the gun in their direction while attempting to free the mechanism which had jammed."

1918.
1919.

The Treaty of Versailles was signed on June 28, 1919 to signal the end of the First World War

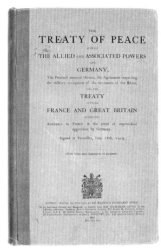

TREATY OF VERSAILLES

Although fighting during the First World War ended at 11am on November 11, 1918, it took more than 200 days for a peace deal to be agreed between the Allies and the Central Powers.

The Treaty of Versailles was signed on June 28, 1919, exactly five years after the assassination of Archduke Franz Ferdinand in Sarajevo by Gavrilo Princip, the event that started the conflict in the first place.

Designed to pacify and weaken Germany, ultimately the treaty did neither. Germany and the other defeated countries were forced to take the blame for the war and ordered to pay 132 billion gold marks (over £280 billion today), as well as surrendering lands to France, Poland and Great Britain. Germany was also excluded from the new League of Nations.

The punitive treaty terms added to hyperinflation in Germany leading to economic collapse, and in the political chaos that followed, Adolf Hitler emerged.

In 1939, 20 years after the treaty was signed, a rejuvenated and rearmed Germany went to war again against, among others, France, Poland and Great Britain.

DICK FRANKS

While Eton and Westminster can lay claim to infamous Cold War double agents Guy Burgess and Kim Philby, Rugby can perhaps do a little better through the quiet achievements of **Sir Arthur 'Dick' Franks** (1920-2008) who headed MI6 and the Secret Intelligence Service from 1978 to 1981. After Rugby and Oxford, Franks served as an intelligence officer in the Western Desert before joining the Special Operations Executive. After a brief post-war stint as a *Daily Mirror* sub-editor, Franks joined British intelligence serving in Cyprus, Iran and Bonn, and headed the service's London station. He became deputy head of SIS in 1977 and then succeeded Sir Maurice Oldfield, serving under two prime ministers, Jim Callaghan and Margaret Thatcher.

Head of MI6 and the Secret Intelligence Service from 1978-1981

1920.

From first class cricket to Chief of the Imperial General Staff

JIM CASSELLS

Jim Cassells, who entered Rugby in 1920, was an accomplished sportsman, representing the School in the 1921 Marlborough Match.

As a right-handed batsman and fast-medium/off spin bowler he played first-class cricket for Cambridge and the Army from 1928 to 1935, appearing in five matches, representing the Egyptian national team, scoring 197 runs, taking 20 wickets and achieving best bowling figures of 6/51.

Alongside his cricket career, Sir Archibald James Cassells (1907-1996) also did well in his military pursuits.

He fought in Normandy, Korea and Malaya and in a 42-year Army career commanded the 51st (Highland) Infantry Division, the 6th Airborne Division, the 1st Commonwealth Division, the I Corps, Eastern Command and the Northern Army Group.

His final post was as Chief of the Imperial General Staff, and during his tenure, he advised the Government on implementing the 1966 Defence White Paper.

1920

PERCIVAL GUILDHOUSE

In 1920 the Old Rugbeian Society raised a fund to perpetuate the memory of Doctor Percival, Head Master from 1887 to 1895, who had died in 1918. He had played a sustained and valuable part in adult education, and was a pioneer of the Free Library Movement as well as a key figure in persuading Rugby to adopt the Library Act.

It was suggested that a foundation be established to become a centre for Adult Education, like the Workers' Education Association and Adult Schools but developing its own philosophy and courses.

At the same time Bloxam House (the present Guildhouse) in the town, came up for sale. It seemed an ideal property in both size and location. A conjunction of name, funds, property and a postwar spirit of wishing to build a better world gave unstoppable impetus to the idea.

A range of bodies and associated bodies paid affiliation fees to fund the Guildhouse, including the Co-operative Women's Guild, National Union of Teachers, Rugby Men's Adult School, Rugby Philharmonic Society, National Union of Foundry Workers and the Rugby Housewives' Committee.

The official opening took place on Tuesday, September 29, 1925, the birth date of Dr Percival, with Rugby Head Master Dr AA David officiating.

The Guildhouse's adult education programme continues today. Eminent visitors to the centre since 1925 have ranged from pianist and conductor Vladimir Ashkenazy to astronomer Sir Patrick Moore and Rugbeian poet Jon Stallworthy. **DH**

1921

WILLIAM VAUGHAN

William Vaughan lacked the academic and clerical standing of his predecessors. He also bore the appearance of a 'shaggy dog' and was the only Rugby Head to die minus a leg.

But his track record at other schools, attention to detail and personal knowledge of every boy in his charge meant his decade as Head from 1921 was a success.

Vaughan was a Rugbeian who read languages at Oxford, where he achieved a double second, and the University of Paris.

He taught for fourteen years at Clifton before taking on the Headmastership of Giggleswick in 1904 and later Wellington College in 1910.

By the time of his return to Rugby, nearly 40 years after leaving as a boy, Vaughan was 57. He was taking on a post which had taxed many younger men but he proved up to the task.

Vaughan swiftly introduced stronger discipline, such as making stiff collars and Sunday evensong compulsory and ignoring the moans of complainers.

In exchange for toughness, Vaughan learnt the name of every boy in the School, visited any boy confined to the sanatorium and encouraged teaching innovations in modern languages and science. And while the activities of boys were watched and tracked, so too were the efforts of the teaching staff.

Vaughan's very individual approach to the boys and staff was captured by EEA Whitworth, a former Rugby master who later became Headmaster of Tonbridge School, in *The Spectator* in 1948.

"He was formidable to young masters or to an unpunctual master; he was formidable, perhaps, to us all as we went about our work, but once inside his study, littered with papers on the desk and books on the floor, with no suggestion of an office, he was to master and to boy a wise and sympathetic friend.

"It was easy to be one of his Housemasters. If a difficult problem arose I took it to Vaughan, and the more difficult the problem, perhaps the failure of a boy which made a stern decision inevitable, the more obvious was the wisdom and the justice of Vaughan's decision, and the Housemaster left confident that with the help of his Head Master the difficulty would be overcome. I believe in such circumstances Vaughan would have been the first to admit what he owed to previous scholastic experience at Clifton, Giggleswick, and Wellington; proved administrative ability without scholastic experience will not enable a headmaster to be the counsellor of his Housemasters.

"But the wisdom of Vaughan's decisions was also due to his knowledge of the individual boy. Vaughan gave little time to administration; otherwise he could not have known the School as he did."

Under Vaughan, the School's estate continued to develop and Rugby also continued its tradition of turning out boys equipped to do useful work, such as Patrick Dean, who became British Ambassador in Washington as well as Chair of Governors, and actor Anthony Quayle.

Vaughan left Rugby a few years short of his 70th birthday in 1931 and fell and broke his leg while visiting the Taj Mahal in December 1937 during a science congress. His leg was amputated and he died two months later, bringing the energy and devotion of a committed and successful Head Master to an end.

William Vaughan: Head Master from 1921 to 1931

HOCKEY

Competitive hockey was played at the School in 1921. In the first fixture, a combined team of masters and boys took on Rugby town, although the match was disrupted by 'a fast-moving flock of sheep, hotly pursued by Mr Lockhart's dog'.

Sheep disrupt a hockey match!

1922

In summer 1922, 92 Rugby boys caught measles and twelve had to have operations. Eleven years later, a boy died when measles broke out again. A subsequent outbreak of influenza and scarlet fever, which also affected two nursing staff, forced the Head Master to close the School.

1921

1922

THE STODGE

The School tuckshop, known to all as the Stodge, opened in January 1922. It had been planned during the war as a source of foodstuffs, without the boys competing with the town for supplies. The School was anxious the town should not feel that the boys were taking advantage of the situation. The Head Master, AA David, put town food shops out of bounds and stopped the boys from receiving food parcels from home. In reality there was little scarcity of food and the desire to provide a school-based shop was largely forgotten until after the war.

The building, which still stands on its original site next to the Temple Reading Room, took its name from the practice of providing a feast for new form mates, when moving up in the School, and laying on a celebratory meal. These were called either a "stodge" or a "guttle". Fortunately, the term guttle passed into obscurity! **RM**

Also called a 'guttle', the 'stodge' still stands on the site where it was opened in 1922

1921 Warren Harding

1922 Andrew Bonar Law

THE BBC

In 1922, the GPO licensed a consortium of British radio manufacturers to operate a single broadcasting company. It was called the British Broadcasting Company Ltd and remained a private company until becoming a public corporation in 1927.

The move to create a single broadcaster followed the first live public broadcast from the Marconi factory in Chelmsford in June 1920, which was sponsored by Lord Northcliffe, owner of the *Daily Mail* and featured opera star Dame Nellie Melba.

Two years later, the burgeoning number of radio societies and licence requests made it sensible to have one broadcasting company, and the first appointed BBC general manager was John Reith. He became Director General when the corporation was formed five years later, and established the BBC as the world's premier broadcaster before leaving in 1938.

His achievements included developing radio broadcasting across the UK and the British Empire and pioneering the world's first television service. Rugbeian Prime Minister Neville Chamberlain used the BBC to broadcast Britain's declaration of war on Germany on September 3, 1939.

THE MEMORIAL CHAPEL

Linked by a passage from the main chapel, the School's Memorial Chapel is in complete contrast to the main chapel.

The passage is not consecrated ground and so the subjects of the windows are not sacred. Among the images of the School motto and house crests are medallions depicting the Retreat from Mons, a naval engagement, the entry of troops into Jerusalem and depictions of tanks and biplanes. This Chapel was designed by **Sir Charles Nicholson** (SH 1881-86), and was consecrated in 1922 with a dedication service held on July 8 that year.

Stone built, again in contrast to the main chapel, it is in the shape of a Greek cross. Each of the four walls is dominated by the large windows which portray the Passion (in the north window), the Crucifixion (to the east), the Resurrection (in the southern window) and the Ascension of Christ (to the west).

Each of the windows, apart from the Crucifixion window, has elements of the School within the painting.

Harry Grylls was the artist responsible for the work. To the bottom left of the north window, a nurse and soldier pray, with the School in the background.

On the walls of the Memorial Chapel, below the windows, Rolls of Honour contain the names of the 686 Rugbeians who gave their lives in the Great War of 1914-18, and of the 350 who fell in the Second World War. In the Memorial lecterns there are commemorative books to these men.

The names of those who died in the two wars are inscribed on three sides of the chapel. The Great War fallen, from the south side, were moved to the east wall, to keep a continuity, with those names from the Second World War placed in the south wall. It took C Stanley, who carved the names from the Great War, over six months to complete his work.

In the floor of the chapel sits the Stone of Remembrance, carved from Hopton Wood stone and Purbeck marble. The inscription is the exact wording from the 'King's Scroll', which was sent to the family of every man who fell.

The lectern, in the north transept, was designed by the architect, and the model of the young soldier was modelled by Esmond Burton. The figure is that of **Wilfred Evelyn Littleboy** (SH 09-14), who was killed in 1917.

The eight drawers contain specially bound volumes of the *Memorials* which record the fallen. The volumes were created by a committee of Masters who worked between 1915 and 1923 to record the lives and deaths of the fallen Rugbeians. The lectern in the south transept is by Fabio Barraclough, a former Art Master at the School, and contains a single volume listing the names of the fallen from the Second World War. Barraclough also created the stone font in the north alcove.

The Bere stone reredos in the sanctuary, by R Moss of Oxford, was part of a single gift, which included the altar, cross and candlesticks. The five figures in the alter niches are by Esmond Burton of London: to the north, St Peter and St Nicholas represent the sailors, and to the south St Alban and St Martin of Tours represent the soldiers. The central group is a Pieta.

In the small ante-chapel are five windows. The window to the south is the founder's window, representing Lawrence Sheriff, who holds a model of the Memorial Chapel. The remaining four windows represent the four great soldier-kings of England: St Oswald, Alfred the Great, St Edmund and King Arthur. The walls are also inscribed with the fallen from other conflicts of the 20th-century.

The organ chamber, which hangs above the body of the chapel itself, was a gift which commemorates the mother and sister of one of the fallen. The case was designed by Nicholson and the organ itself is by Harrison and Harrison of Durham. **RM**

1922.

THE MUSIC SCHOOLS

The decision in 1923 to build a new boarding house on the site of the Hillbrow Prep School with a view to moving Kilbracken House from Hillmorton Road forced the School to consider a proper home for the School's musicians. They had moved around the campus and were currently occupying part of Hillbrow. Although Kilbracken would not be in place until after the war, the plans for Music Schools were quickly moved forward. Designed by Sir Charles Nicholson, a former School House boy, the building was opened in 1926. It was built on the site of the old Physics Schools, the Tin Tabernacle, and conveniently next to the Temple Speech Room. For many years it would not be the exclusive domain of the Music Department as it opened with the Geography schools and three general classrooms also occupying the space. With building developments elsewhere on the campus, Music eventually became the only tenant. In 1939 extensions to the building provided more space but over the years the demand for the subject increased. In 2010 a project was completed which provided nine new practice rooms, two tutorial rooms and a large teaching room, all housed in a striking extension to the original building. **RM**

The Music Schools on Hillmorton Road were opened in 1926

1923

1923 Stanley Baldwin 🇬🇧
1923 Calvin Coolidge 🇬🇷

1924 James Ramsay MacDonald 🇬🇧
1924 Stanley Baldwin 🇬🇧

- 136 -

1925-1938

A QUIET PEACE

1925 THE MOUND SCHEDULED INFLUENZA	**1925** MEIN KAMPF
	1926 LOGIE BAIRD
1927 CHARLES ACTON AND OTHER WRITERS	**1927** JAZZ SINGER
	1928 PENICILLIN
	1929 WALL ST CRASH
1930 SHERIFF	
1931 HUGH LYON BECOMES HEAD	
1934 "THE COMET" NEW SANATORIUM	
1935 CROSS-COUNTRY JON STALLWORTHY DAVID OGLE	**1935** ABYSSINIA
1938 ROBERT HARDY NEVILLE CHAMBERLAIN	

THE MOUND SCHEDULED

In the south-east corner of the original Close lies the Mound. It is understood to be a Bronze-age burial mound, or tumulus, and between the 13th-century and 1847 was surrounded by a wide moat. Spanned by a wooden drawbridge to the north side, it was known as The Island until the 1950s.

It was here that the ending of the Great Rebellion took place in 1797 and where the sixth form held small plots, tended by the 'Island Fags', to provide vegetables and even flowers for Speech Day. This was stopped by Thomas Arnold in 1835, when he had gymnastic equipment (the first in any school), erected here for the senior boys. It was also one of the locations for meetings of the Bigside Levée, the boys who ran the games.

The Mound became a Scheduled Ancient Monument in 1925 and is now protected by law to prevent any disturbance to the site. **RM**

Site of the Great Rebellion in 1797 and a Scheduled Ancient Monument since 1925

1925.

"MEIN KAMPF"

Nazi dictator Adolf Hitler did not actually sit down to write *Mein Kampf* (My Struggle). Fittingly he dictated it instead to Rudolf Hess while serving time as a political prisoner following a failed putsch in Munich.

Published in two volumes in 1925 and 1926, *Mein Kampf* sets out Hitler's vision for a blond-haired, blue-eyed Aryan 'master race', the Third Reich uniting Germany with its neighbour Austria.

"German-Austria must be restored to the great German Motherland. And not indeed on any grounds of economic calculation whatsoever. No, no. Even if the union were a matter of economic indifference, and even if it were to be disadvantageous from the economic standpoint, still it ought to take place. People of the same blood should be in the same REICH."

The copyright ban on the German edition of *Mein Kampf* ran out in 2016 and the book has again been published, 90 years after first appearing.

Rudolf Hess became Deputy Führer and flew over to Britain towards the end of the Second World War to try to negotiate peace. Later he was detained in Spandau prison where he died in 1987.

INFLUENZA

Pressure to build a new sanatorium for the School mounted after a series of outbreaks of illness. In spring 1925, 202 boys were recorded as suffering from flu, and four years later in 1929 the School broke up early after a scarlet fever outbreak.

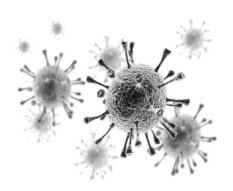

1926

LOGIE BAIRD

TV pioneer John Logie Baird rivals Marconi (telegraph), Bell (telephone), Turing (computer) and Berners Lee (internet) in the field of mass communication inventors.

The Scottish engineer, born in 1888, demonstrated the first working television in London on January 26, 1926 and the first transatlantic TV transmission two years later.

Reporting on Baird's 3½ x 2 inch 'Televisor' screen, *The Times* wrote on January 28, 1926 (on page nine):

The first working television in 1926

"Members of the Royal Institution and other visitors to a laboratory in an upper room in Frith Street, Soho, on Tuesday saw a demonstration of apparatus invented by Mr J.L. Baird, who claims to have solved the problem of television. They were shown a transmitting machine, consisting of a large wooden revolving disc containing lenses, behind which was a revolving shutter and a light sensitive cell. It was explained that by means of the shutter and lens disc an image of articles or persons standing in front of the machine could be made to pass over the light sensitive cell at high speed. The current in the cell varies in proportion to the light falling on it, and this varying current is transmitted to a receiver where it controls a light behind an optical arrangement similar to that at the sending end. By this means a point of light is caused to traverse a ground glass screen. The light is dim at the shadows and bright at the high lights, and crosses the screen so rapidly that the whole image appears simultaneously to the eye."

Today *The Times* publishes several television listings pages every day while its owner Rupert Murdoch also operates satellite TV channels across the globe.

The first full-length 'talkie' feature film

"JAZZ SINGER"

"Wait a minute, wait a minute, you ain't heard nothing yet" were the first words heard by cinemagoers in a full-length 'talkie' feature film.

They appeared in the 1927 American musical film *The Jazz Singer* and were spoken by actor Al Jolson, who was born in 1886.

Producer Darryl F Zanuck won a special Oscar for the film and in 1996, 90 years after Jolson's birth, it was selected to be conserved in the US Library of Congress National Film Registry.

Officially *The Jazz Singer* was not the first sound film or first talkie. But it was the first full feature film with synchronised sound.

It came about after Warner Bros. invested half a million dollars in a new Vitaphone sound system in 1926, a decision which recouped profits of $3.5m dollars for *The Jazz Singer*.

With sad irony Warner co-founder Sam Warner died at the age of 40, just one day before the film's world première in New York on October 6, 1927.

1927.

CHARLES ACTON & OTHER WRITERS

Rugby's famous novelist and poets like Lewis Carroll and Rupert Brooke, have been complemented by a rich seam of historians, journalists and critics following in the tradition of Collingwood, Ransome and Tawney.

Charles Acton (1914-1999) joined Rugby in 1927 and went on to be the music critic at *The Irish Times* for 31 years from 1956.

Hugh Johnson (SF 52-56), who came to Rugby in 1952, is considered to be the world's best-selling wine writer. He has written on the history of wine and an acclaimed book on trees.

Sir Hew Strachan (K 63-67), who was at the School from 1963, is the pre-eminent historian of the First World War as well as being Professor of International Relations at the University of St Andrews, following an earlier post as the Chichele Professor of the History of War at All Souls College, Oxford.

Andrew 'AN' Wilson (M 64-68), who came to Rugby in 1964, has written on Victorian history and biographies of Tolstoy and CS Lewis as well as contributing to national newspapers and magazines.

Andrew Rawnsley (T 75-79), who joined the School in 1975, is a political journalist and broadcaster and has written two books on New Labour.

Tim Butcher (K 80-85) is a former *Daily Telegraph* journalist who has written travel history books including *Blood River* and *The Trigger*.

Writer, photographer and broadcaster **Rob Penn** (SF 80-85) has written books on cycling, the environment and most recently on trees.

PENICILLIN

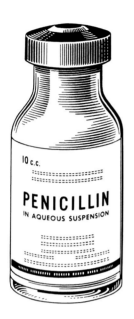

On September 3, 1928, Sir Alexander Fleming, Professor of Bacteriology at St Mary's Hospital, London, returned from holiday to an untidy office full of petri dishes.

The dishes were cultivating Staphylococcus, the bacteria behind boils and abscesses, and on one of them there was a spot of mould surrounded by a clear fluid.

In this dish there was none of the cultivated bacteria, prompting Fleming to think he may have found something that offered natural resistance.

The fluid around the mould turned out to be a strain of penicillin and Fleming had somewhat accidentally discovered an antibiotic which changed the course of medical history and has saved millions of lives.

Although he discovered penicillin, Fleming himself couldn't develop his find successfully and in the early 1930s turned to other things. His work, however, was later carried forward by two scientists called Florey and Chain who showed the effects of penicillin on ill patients.

Once this was realised, penicillin was then produced on an industrial scale to save service personnel during the Second World War.

Fleming, who shared with Florey and Chain a Nobel Prize in 1945, died aged 73 in 1955.

Today penicillin is still used commonly to treat patients and a blue plaque outside St Mary's Hospital, a short distance from Paddington Station, marks the place where Fleming made his accidental discovery.

1929 James Ramsay MacDonald 🇬🇧
1929 Herbert Hoover 🇺🇸

1928.

1929

WALL ST CRASH

The Wall Street Crash began on October 24, 1929.

Stock market prices in the US fell catastrophically and did not regain their 1929 levels for another 25 years.

The crash triggered the Great Depression and its impact was felt around the world for a decade.

Statistics that emerged from the crash included 12m people out of work, 12,000 people unemployed every day, 20,000 company bankruptcies, 1,616 collapsed banks, and a record 23,000 suicides in the US in one year (nearly three an hour).

Describing the event, one observer wrote: *"Anyone who bought stocks in mid-1929 and held onto them saw most of his or her adult life pass by before getting back to even."*

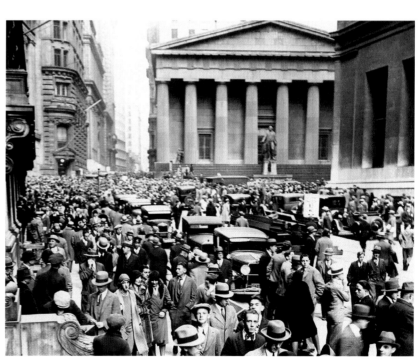

The start of the Great Depression in 1929

SHERIFF ⚖

1922 saw the Governing Body considering options to cope with the rapid rise in school numbers and by 1923 a first report recommended either converting Hillbrow Preparatory School into a boarding house or building a completely new house. The land between Bradley and Hillbrow was not, at this time, owned by the School and a decision was made to purchase this property, Miss Pennington's house and two adjoining fields. Southfield House and the land between Bradley and Hillbrow were thus added to the School's estate. In 1928, Forsyth & Maule were appointed as architects and a year later their plans were accepted with an estimated cost of £45,000. When tenders were submitted, Foster & Dickinson were chosen to build the house, although their revised estimate put the cost at some £48,103. By the time the building was completed, the final cost came to over £52,000. The house opened in September 1930 and was named Sheriff House after the school's founder Lawrence Sheriff. Some 20 boys entered the house at this time and Hugh Johnson, a formidable games player and athlete, became the first Housemaster. The first Head of House was Robert David Gemmell Meek, who was only fourteen years old and for the first year Sheriff was too small to be involved with most house competitions. The opening and naming of the house influenced the decision to give permanent names to the other houses (School House and Town had always retained their original names). From this point on the Houses were no longer named after each succeeding Housemaster.

Sheriff alumini include **David Croft**, writer of *Dad's Army* and *Hi De Hi*… **Walter Moorcroft**, ceramicist and designer… and **Tom King**, Lord King of Bridgwater, former Secretary of State for Defence, and for Environment and Transport. **RM**

1930.

1931 James Ramsay MacDonald 🇬🇧

1931

HUGH LYON

While one of his predecessors as Head steered Rugby through the last year of the First World War, Captain Hugh Lyon recorded his experience of being a German prisoner of war.

"I begin to work out a scheme for my day's work…roughly it runs as follows:- 9.15 to 10, make my bed, sweep and wash up. 10 to 12 or 12.30 work at elementary German or, if inclined at my own writing…. After 'lunch', rest or write till 2 o'clock. Then read till 5, when I change my book. In the evening I generally play bridge or write. As a rough programme it works fairly well. Fortunately Murray has a German grammar, which I share or rather monopolise, as he is not very fit and not inclined for work. The day passes uneventfully, though the unusually good pea soup at lunch is worthy of mention. A few parcels have begun to come in, and great excitement prevails among all who have any hopes of them. At 5 o'clock I change my book for 'Captains Courageous', which I enjoy now (having forgotten it) as much as I did 12 years ago."

As well as being a soldier, prisoner and later a schoolmaster, Lyon was also a poet. And while being held prisoner he wrote *Mulligan, Or Soldier's Stew*, which includes the lines:

There's bits of beef from yesterday and bones as good as new, There's heaps of stuff about would come in handy for a stew; Likewise a brace of rabbits as was 'found' by Pat McGee;- I guess it looks like Mulligan," says Mulligan to me.

In his time as Rugby Head Master for seventeen years from 1931, Lyon concentrated on preparing the School for war and then keeping things afloat during the war years.

A former School scholar, Lyon's studies at Oxford were interrupted by service in the Durham Light Infantry during the Great War when he won the Military Cross.

Afterwards he returned to Oxford, won the Newdigate Prize, secured a first in Greats, taught at Cheltenham and headed the Edinburgh Academy before coming back to Rugby.

Lyon's prewar years were dominated by an extensive building programme, including several boarding houses and the new sanatorium.

The School unsuccessfully invited the then Prince of Wales (later Edward VIII and Duke of Windsor) to open it but he did visit instead on July 3, 1934 – 25 years to the day since his grandfather King Edward VII planted the King's Oak on The Close and opened the TSR.

As Head, Lyon changed aspects of School life, including abolishing early morning school and the School's traditional black coat uniform in favour of grey tweed jackets and flannels.

While Head Master, he was mentor and friend to John Gillespie Magee, author of the famous poem *High Flight*. Magee fell in love with Lyon's daughter Elinor.

Although the School was physically unscathed by bombs during the war of 1939-45 and lost fewer boys than in the First World War, the conflict impacted in many ways.

Numbers dropped at one point to below 500 for the first time in decades, leading to some Houses being used to help the war effort (Cotton became a labour hostel, Stanley a women's hospital and the Ministry of Supply used part of the old sanatorium).

Some staff left the School and were not replaced to help save money and action was also taken to reduce salaries for those who remained.

Other wartime impacts included rationing, blackout, the formation of a Home Guard and Air Raid Patrol units and, once again, boys helped out local farmers who had lost their regular workers to the conflict.

Once the war ended, it took until 1947 for numbers to return to 1930s' level. Lyon left Rugby in 1948 to open the Public Schools Appointment Bureau to find jobs for ex-public school boys. He died in 1986.

Hugh Lyon: Head Master from 1931 to 1948

Cover designed by RB Talbot Kelly

"THE COMET"

In 1934 the last edition of *The Comet*, an unofficial publication within the School, appeared. Lasting for 60 issues *The Comet* poked fun at the School and its staff and was illustrated by PF Stewart and OJW Hunkin.

Editors RCC Hunt and RC Symonds declared in 1933:

"…The Comet has survived fifty-nine numbers. This is remarkable because it is in no way official and does not owe its longevity to the fact that 'it goes on the bill'."

The magazine's longevity was of course based on liberal tolerance by the School which came to an end when it lampooned members of female staff in an article on the 'Rugby-Melbourne Air Race'.

The piece depicted each lady as an aeroplane and *The Comet* came crashing down to earth.

1933 Franklin D. Roosevelt

1934

NEW SANATORIUM

The new sanatorium was opened on Speech Day in 1934 by Sir Michael Sadler. It occupies the site where 'The Firs', a private house, once stood. It consisted of two twelve-bed, three four-bed, and 24 single-bed wards, and also included recreation rooms, a dining room and even an operating theatre. The north-west wing was developed as an out-patients' department, with consulting room, examination cubicles, waiting room and a laboratory. Accommodation was included for nursing and domestic staff. With improvements in health provision locally, the 'school hospital' was less necessary and with the first girls arriving in 1975, the building would largely be converted into a boarding house. The old out-patient department remained and is still in use as the school's medical centre. **RM**

The New Sanatorium opened in 1934, now Dean House

CROSS-COUNTRY

Shrewsbury and Uppingham were the only public schools that competed against the School's cross-country running VIII in the first 40 years after it was founded in 1890. In around 1935, however, competition was doubled when Bromsgrove and Bradfield were added to the list. The captain of the VIII was called the Holder of Bigside Bags and the runners held their first competitive fixture against the Oxford Hare and Hounds Club in 1893.

Cross-country running has featured at Rugby since 1890

1935

1935 Stanley Baldwin 🏴

ABYSSINIA

He was an emperor from Africa, the Lion of Judah and spent the late 1930s and early 1940s in dignified exile in the West Country of England.

Haile Selassie was leader of Abyssinia (now Ethiopia) when Italy's fascist ruler Mussolini signalled he wanted to invade to create an Italian Empire.

Selassie appealed to the League of Nations which vacillated and fudged. Meanwhile the British and French devised a secret pact which proposed some Abyssinian land be given to Mussolini.

When Abyssinia resisted, in October 1935 Mussolini's 100,000-strong army, complete with tanks, poison gas and flame throwers, attacked Selassie's forces and the result was a crushing victory.

Emperor Selassie retreated to exile in south-west England from where he visited local attractions including the newly opened Cheltenham Lido swimming baths.

After returning to Ethiopia in 1941, Selassie continued to rule until his death aged 83 in August 1975 following a coup.

Haile Selassie, the 'Lion of Judah'

JON STALLWORTHY

1935 saw the birth of **Jon Stallworthy** (St 48-53). He began writing poetry at the age of seven and after prep school in Oxford came to Rugby. Following Magdalen College, Oxford, where he won the Newdigate poetry prize, he embarked on a distinguished career as a poet, acknowledged biographer of Wilfred Owen, and later a professor of English at Oxford. In his own words *'my poems all / Are woven out of love's loose ends'*. Stallworthy died in 2014.

1935

DAVID OGLE

Rugbeian **David Ogle** (Tu 35-39), born in 1922, was the man behind two of the most recognisable and respected post-war British designs.

After Rugby from 1935, and Oxford, Ogle flew in the Fleet Air Arm in the Second World War, winning the DSC and MBE.

Following the war he studied design and while working for Bush designed the iconic TR82 radio. With a large burgundy background dial, this was a staple item in households across the UK and retro versions are still made today.

Founding his own consultancy in 1954, Ogle designed the OGLE SX250 sports car, based on the Mini, of which 69 were made.

In 1962, Reliant MD Ray Wiggin saw the SX250 and commissioned Ogle to design a new model for his company.

The result was the legendary Reliant Scimitar GTE, which gained a dedicated following and was a favourite of Princess Anne.

The Scimitar was launched in 1964 at a cost of £1,292 and with a top speed of 117mph.

Sadly Ogle did not live to see the success of the Scimitar, dying while driving one of his own cars on the way to Brands Hatch in May 1962.

The Scimitar launched in 1964 was a David Ogle design

ROBERT HARDY

Actor **Robert Hardy** (M 39-44), who was born in 1925, is the son of a former Headmaster of Cheltenham College.

After serving in the RAF during the Second World War, Hardy completed a degree in English at Oxford, where his tutors included CS Lewis and JRR Tolkein.

As an actor, Hardy appeared in *Coriolanus* at Stratford-upon-Avon opposite Laurence Olivier but became best known for portraying strong characters such as Prince Albert in the 1975 TV series *Edward the Seventh* and vet Siegfried Farnon in *All Creatures Great and Small*.

Hardy is also known for playing Winston Churchill in various productions and Cornelius Fudge in the *Harry Potter* films.

Away from acting, Sir Robert is a renowned expert on the longbows used by medieval archers at Agincourt and has written a book, *The Great Warbow*, on the subject.

1936 Edward VIII 1936 George VI 1937 Neville Chamberlain 1938.

NEVILLE CHAMBERLAIN

At Heston Airport on September 30, 1938, **Neville Chamberlain** (Lee Warner/C 1882-826), the first, and to date the only, Rugbeian to become British Prime Minister, stepped down from the Lockheed aircraft on which he'd flown from Germany following conclusion of the Munich Agreement.

Convinced he had persuaded Hitler not to enlarge the Third Reich, he told an expectant crowd that the German Chancellor had signed a piece of paper that now promised 'peace for our time'.

Feted in London a few hours later, including an appearance with King George VI on the balcony of Buckingham Palace, Chamberlain again reassured the crowds:

"My good friends, for the second time in our history, a British Prime Minister has returned from Germany bringing peace with honour. I believe it is peace for our time. We thank you from the bottom of our hearts. Go home and get a nice quiet sleep."

Everyone knows what happened over the next year: Chamberlain continued to strive for peace while also preparing Britain to face another conflict and Hitler ignored the commitments he never intended to keep.

On the morning of September 3, 1939, Chamberlain again addressed the British people:

"This morning the British Ambassador in Berlin handed the German Government a final Note stating that, unless we heard from them by 11 o'clock that they were prepared at once to withdraw their troops from Poland, a state of war would exist between us.

"I have to tell you now that no such undertaking has been received and that consequently this country is at war with Germany."

Because of the actions of a fanatical dictator, Chamberlain's reputation as Prime Minister has been tarnished and much debated ever since. Some believe he was duped by Hitler and failed to rearm Britain quickly enough, others that by at least talking to Hitler he bought Britain some time to face a war that was inevitable.

Just fourteen months after taking Britain into a second world war, Chamberlain was dead. In-between, he had formed a war cabinet, invited Churchill to take up his old post as First Lord of the Admiralty, been hounded out of Downing Street and had lost his job to Churchill himself.

Viewing Chamberlain through the events of 1938-40 and through the prism of relative failure is inevitable. But it overlooks his role as a politician of honour and peace and his wider contribution to public life.

Chamberlain was born in Birmingham in 1869, the son of the Lord Mayor of Birmingham and cabinet minister Joseph Chamberlain and half-brother of Austen, Conservative party leader and Nobel Prize winner.

After Rugby in the 1880s, he trained as an accountant, working with his father. Later running a metal company in Birmingham, he followed the family tradition of involvement in civic affairs as a governor of the city's general hospital and later as Lord Mayor.

In December 1916, Lloyd George offered Chamberlain the new position of Director of National Service with responsibility for co-ordinating conscription and ensuring essential war industries were able to function with sufficient workforces but the two men clashed and Chamberlain resigned after only eight months.

Marrying at the age of 40, Chamberlain stood for parliament when he was 49, becoming an MP in 1919. Assiduous and hard-working, he was made Chancellor of the Exchequer by Stanley Baldwin in 1923, a post he held for just five months before the Government fell to the first Labour government led by Ramsay MacDonald. When Baldwin returned to office, Chamberlain was offered his old job back but preferred to become minister of health instead. There he drove through a significant reform programme, including the abolition of the elected Poor Law Boards of Guardians which administered relief.

When MacDonald led the National Government, Chamberlain became Chancellor again, managing to control Britain's war debts, achieving a surplus and restoring many of the cuts in unemployment compensation and civil servant salaries.

Having made cuts to rearming Britain in his early budgets, he then reinvested, particularly in the RAF, drawing criticism from deputy Labour leader Arthur Greenwood who described the policy as *"the merest scaremongering; disgraceful in a statesman of Mr. Chamberlain's responsible position, to suggest that more millions of money needed to be spent on armaments"*.

After standing down as Prime Minister, but remaining in Churchill's war cabinet, Chamberlain was severely criticised, along with other public figures, for their part in taking Britain into war in an anonymous book called *The Guilty Men*.

1938

IN WAR,

whichever side may call itself the victor, there are no winners,

BUT ALL ARE LOSERS

NEVILLE CHAMBERLAIN

His reputation was further attacked by Churchill himself in his post-war volume *The Gathering Storm.*

For all the contemporary criticisms of Chamberlain and what he did or did not do to keep Britain out of war, modern commentators tend to take a more sympathetic view.

Historian David Dutton wrote: *"Of course, Chamberlain made mistakes in the 1930s. He overestimated his ability to reach a settlement with the dictators; he probably clung too long to the hope of averting war. But it is doubtful if anyone else would have done much better, Churchill included….he did his best to steer his country safely through the most unpromising situation it faced at any time in the 20th century. Yes, he failed – but could anyone have succeeded?"* The *Independent* in 2009 said to view Chamberlain as *"exemplifying appeasement and nothing else, to see him merely as the historical epitome of spinelessness, ignores two other factors. One is his earlier political career, and what he had done with it. The other is the question of whether or not, in September 1938, he had any choice but to act as he did."*

Chamberlain, who died in November 1940, will forever divide opinion as a politician and peacemaker. His place in Rugby history however is assured – the first to hold two great offices of state, the first to be Chancellor of the Exchequer twice, the first to enter 10 Downing Street, the only Rugbeian to shake the hand of Hitler and the first to lead his country into a world war.

1938

MICKY STEELE-BODGER

After Rugby, **Micky Steele-Bodger** (Tu 39-44) studied at Cambridge and played in the Varsity Match in 1945 and 1946. Gaining nine caps for England from 1946-48, he inaugurated the annual Steele-Bodger XV to play Cambridge as a warm-up to the Varsity Match in 1948.

Alongside his professional career as a vet, Micky has remained deeply involved in rugby all his life. He played as flanker for Harlequins and the Barbarians and is currently President of both the Barbarians Football Club and the East India Club in London.

Micky is a past selector for England and the British and Irish Lions, was RFU President in 1973-74 and is a past chair of the International Rugby Board. In 1990 he received a CBE for his services to rugby.

The Steele-Bodger link with Rugby School continues today as Micky's son Guy, a former Rugbeian himself, is Admissions Registrar.

1939-1945
TO WAR AGAIN

1939 THE SPANISH CIVIL WAR
THE SECOND WORLD WAR

1940 CHURCHILL, DUNKIRK
& THE BATTLE OF BRITAIN

1941 PEARL HARBOR

1942 HEDLEY FOWLER
WILLIAM TEMPLE

1944 D DAY

1945 VE & VJ DAYS

THE SPANISH CIVIL WAR

On March 28, 1939 the three-year Spanish Civil War ended when the victorious Nationalists, led by General Franco, entered Madrid.

The conflict, which cost over a million lives, started after 1931 elections approved a liberal, Second Republic and the end of the Spanish monarchy.

As liberal reforms were introduced, General Francisco Franco led a right-wing revolt. This divided the country into opposing Nationalists and Republicans, triggering civil war.

During the conflict, Franco's fascist movement received substantial military support and resources from Germany and Italy while the USSR aided the Republicans.

Anti-fascist supporters from the US, France and Great Britain also fought with the Republicans in International Brigades, including writer George Orwell. US writer Ernest Hemingway also covered the war as a journalist.

Orwell wrote about his experiences in Spain in *Homage to Catalonia* and Hemingway in *Death in the Afternoon*.

Following the war, General Franco ruled Spain until his death in 1975, after which the monarchy was restored.

The Spanish Civil War cost over a million lives and both George Orwell and Ernest Hemingway wrote about their experiences during the war

Since our School began, Rugbeians have known the roar

OF THE BOMB AND THE CANNON IN THE THEATRES OF WAR

RUGBY

& THE SECOND WORLD WAR

1939.

The history of Rugby School and Rugbeians during the Second World War mirrored the conflict's wider impact on the people of Britain. War has no respect for age, rank or reputation.

Five of the School casualties were eighteen and, at the other end of the spectrum, **Edward Melly** (Elsee 1872-75), who was born in early July 1858, was killed by enemy action (in an air raid) on May 16, 1941. Ordinary Seaman **John Henderson** (St & K 1939-42) RN died on August 26, 1942 and was one of those teenagers. John's brother, Fl. Lt. **Robert Henderson** (St 1935-40) RAFVR, DFC, survived until January 29, 1945. Several sets of brothers can be found on the Memorial Chapel walls. The Pearsons, **Basil** (SF 1938-42) and **Henry** (SF 1933-38) were just 20 and 21 when they were killed. **John** (K 1905-09) and **John David Jardine Mein-Austin** (K 36-40) fell, as father and son, in March 1941 and October 1944.

One of the most poignant stories concerns the Staniland family. Brothers Captain **John Maeburn Staniland** (M 24-28) and Second Lieutenant **Geoffrey Staniland** (M 15-18) lie side by side in Dranoutre cemetery, Belgium. They were killed three months apart in 1915 and, with their Boston background, had become officers in the Lincolnshire Regiment. **Geoffrey** (M 1915-18) junior was a Flight Lieutenant in the Second World War. Maeburn's three sons - oldest **John Staniland** (M 1924-28) had won the Crick in 1928, was a Major and was killed in Normandy in 1944, his twin **Robert William Staniland** (M 1924-28) survived and youngest son **Maeburn Francis Staniland** (M 1927-32) was a Major and wounded during the war. All had been in Michell.

Adrian Stoop (St 1933-38), **Harold Woolley** (SH 1933-38) and **Lewis Masefield** (M 1924-28) died in Italy, Tunisia and Libya. Each had a famous father. **Adrian Stoop** (Steel 1897-1901) **senior** revolutionised the tactics of Rugby Football in the years leading

up to 1914. Rev Geoffrey Woolley joined the Rugby staff in 1920 after being awarded a Victoria Cross and Military Cross on the Western Front. John Masefield OM was Poet Laureate.

The First World War had been primarily a soldier's war. In the second conflict the service casualty figures were far more evenly distributed. The Army again came off worse but nearly 100 airmen were lost as well as close on 40 members of the Royal Navy and Royal Marines. We must also mention fallen Rugbeians in the Merchant Navy as well as several civilians. The first Rugbeian lost Lt. **Patrick Roberts** (C 1925-29) RN died at sea on February 18, 1940 when *HMS Daring* went down. The following day Capt. **Robert Bayly** (SF 1922-28), Royal Artillery was killed. On February 21, Fl. Lt. **Antony Wilson** (M 1920-23) RAF died on operations. From then on not a single month passed without a Rugby casualty.

By August 1945 Rugbeian casualties stretched from Arnhem to Athens, India to Indonesia, Runnymede to the Reichswald Forest and Thailand to Tunisia.

Three hundred and fifty names are in the School's Roll of Honour. Starting at F/O **Harold Adams** (Tu 33-37) RAF in the Western Desert, we end with Lt. Col. **Warren Zambra** (SH 1923-28) RA in Sicily. School House lost 48 former pupils but all eleven Houses made sacrifices. The impact at home was more direct this time round. Total war, including Blitzkrieg and the V weapons, meant no one was immune. **Leonard Smith** (M 1889-93), Mayor of the city of Westminster, was killed on duty by enemy action on May 10, 1941. Sub-Lt. **John Miller** (SH 1933-37) and Lieut. **Robert Armitage** (M 1918-23) were awarded George Crosses. Both were officers in the RNVR and were involved in that most dangerous and unpleasant aspect of warfare, defusing enemy mines: both survived.

Proportionally the number of Rugbeians wounded and prisoners of war was substantially greater in the Second World War. This probably reflects the more fluid nature of that conflict, tactics and the advances in medical science. Despite the 'miracle' at Dunkirk tens of thousands were rounded up in June 1940 and there were surrenders in the Far East. The infamous Colditz Castle held four Rugbeians. One was the Senior British Officer and another made a "home run". SBO Lt. Col. **Guy German's** (SH 1915-20) brother **Raymond** (SH 1922-24) fell at Le Havre in 1944. The successful escaper, Sq. Ldr. **Hedley Fowler** (Tu 1930-33) MC, crashed test flying over Wiltshire in March 1944. Lt. Cdr. **Stephen Beattie** (Tu 1922-25) RN was captured on the St. Nazaire Raid. His Victoria Cross was the only one awarded to a Rugbeian in the Second World War. Major **Esmond Lynn Allen** (B 1917-20) was also a prisoner and became a skilled artist and book illustrator. His cousin, Captain **James Lynn Allen** (K 1925-30), was also captured but that situation only lasted a few hours. The Rugby School Register reads, *"Killed in action, May 29, 1940."* This simple statement hides a war crime. On that day part of the Liebstandarte SS Adolf Hitler Regiment had rounded up a group of British prisoners near Wormhout in France. Driving them into a small barn they proceeded to lob grenades through the open door and shoot those who tried to get away. James Lynn Allen was shot between the eyes as he hid in a nearby pond. Major **John Sanderson Poole** (Steel Stanley 1910-14) DSO, OBE, MC had the misfortune to be a prisoner of the Germans in both wars. **Hugh Lyon** (Steel 1907-12) was a prisoner from May to December 1918 and Head Master from 1931 to 1948. The growing list of Rugbeian casualties for nearly six of those years must have been particularly poignant. Senior servicemen who died included Major General

Philip de Fonblanque, (Brooke 1899-1902) DSO and Air Commodore **Augustus Orlebar** (SH 1910-14) CBE, AFC and Bar. **Ernest Johnson** (Payne-Smith 1895-99) won a Military Cross in the first war and became a master at the School from 1920-1940. He was killed on duty as a Rugby Special Constable on August 14, 1940. Far East prisoners of war endured terrible treatment and conditions. The Roll of Honour lists Lt. **Mark Robertson** (B 1933-38) as *"killed in action, January 11, 1942"*. The detail is that he was wounded and captured by Japanese forces in Malaya on January 10, 1942 but was shot the following morning as he was unable to walk.

Norman Crockatt (W.N. Wilson 1907-12) fought as an officer throughout the Great War, was wounded twice, mentioned in despatches three times and awarded the DSO and MC. During the Second World War he was head of MI9. This secret body assisted prisoners of war in their attempts to return to Britain. Early in the war one of Crockatt's officers drove from London to Rugby with some 50 books on escape from the First World War. Hugh Lyon instructed a group of senior pupils to read them and note all areas that could prove useful to the authorities. The meticulously researched lists proved invaluable and there was no leak in security.

Anthony Quayle CBE (Tu 1927-30) became a most distinguished actor and Royal Shakespeare Company director after the war. He also had a remarkable wartime career seeming to meet everyone of importance. His views on Churchill, Montgomery, Eisenhower, Eden and Noel Coward are refreshingly candid. **Duncan Campbell** (Brooke 1894-99) Argyll and Sutherland Highlanders joined Number 1 Special Force of SOE. He retired in 1949 with the rank of Lieut. Colonel with MBE, MC and Bar.

Capt. Jesse Frank (M 1929-33) joined the US Army as a captain; he was wounded and received the Purple Heart. He fell in the Anzio beach head on May 25, 1944. **Heinz Freund** (SH 1939-42) left England for the USA in January 1943 to join up. His ship went down in the Atlantic. **Stuart Barton** (K 1926-29) joined the US Air Transport Command as a navigator. He died in an air crash in Newfoundland in November 1944. Probably the best-known American of this era was **John Gillespie Magee** (SH 1936-39). Encouraged by his poem-writing Head Master Hugh Lyon, Magee penned the truly beautiful *High Flight*. As a nineteen-year-old American citizen he joined the Royal Canadian Air Force. At that tender age he was killed in a flying accident on December 11, 1941. His words are carved on his Commonwealth War Graves Commission headstone in rural Lincolnshire: *"Oh! I have slipped the surly bonds of earth.......put out my hand and touched the face of God."*

The following casualties reinforce the international element of sacrifices made by Rugbeians. **John Buckley** (Sh 1935-39) Royal Canadian Air Force was the personal assistant to Air Officer Commanding Western Desert. He went missing, presumed killed, on June 3, 1943 and is commemorated at the Runnymede Memorial in Surrey. Major **Ralph Howarth** (W 1929-33) DFC, South African Air Force, died in Italy in 1944. Private **Geoffrey Paddison**, (C 1928-33) 1st. Royal Natal Carbineers was killed in the often forgotten East African campaign in November 1941. **Claude Webster** (M 1924-24), Chaplain, Royal New Zealand Navy died of meningitis in the same month.

Dr David Bradford (SH 1936-40) spent several weeks with the Red Cross tending to the survivors of Belsen Concentration Camp in 1945.

Sq. Ldr. **Charles Lancaster** (SF 1926-30) DFC and Bar was, on November 14, 1944, piloting the aeroplane in which Air Chief Marshal Sir Trafford Leigh-Mallory was flying to take up the post of Air Commander-in-Chief, South East Asia Command. The plane disappeared and there were no survivors. **John Lewis** (Tu 1939-43) was a corporal in the Wiltshire Home Guard. He died of a sudden heart attack in 1943. He was eighteen. Midshipman **Trevor Seaward** (St 1939-40) RN lost his life during the invasion of Normandy on D-Day plus one. Wg Cdr **Uel Titley** (St 1920-24) survived and after the war became the chief rugby football correspondent of *The Times*. Not surprisingly, several Rugbeians changed their surname before or at the outbreak of war. One was **Richard Oppenheim** (SH 1933-38). As Oppenheim he captained the XV and won a RF Blue for Oxford in 1939. As Osborne with the rank of Captain he was part of 6th Airborne Division in Normandy and took up school mastering after the war. Major **Thomas Howarth** (K 1928-32) MC was personal liaison officer to Field Marshal Montgomery, and became High Master of St Paul's after the war.

Marmaduke Hussey (C and Tu 1937-41) was captain of the XV in 1940-41. As an officer in the Grenadier Guards he was wounded, lost a leg and became a prisoner. Post war he became Director General of the BBC.

Despite the number of Rugbeians who lost their lives during both world wars, we must be grateful that the majority of those who served, survived. **DR**

Field Marshall Montgomery

Anthony Quayle

The Book of Honour in the Memorial Chapel

Marmaduke Hussey

Rugbeiams commemorated in the Memorial Chapel

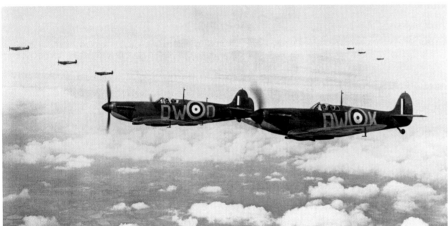

CHURCHILL, DUNKIRK & THE BATTLE OF BRITAIN

In 1940 a Prime Minister who was widely discredited was replaced by one who was widely distrusted. Rugbeian Neville Chamberlain was forced from office in May 1940.

His successor was Winston Churchill, the man who had warned the nation about German rearmament during his 'Wilderness Years' on the backbenches.

Churchill told the House of Commons that he had nothing to offer except blood, toil, tears and sweat.

Within weeks of assuming office, he presided over the mass evacuation of British forces from Dunkirk.

Then, in summer 1940, came the Battle of Britain in which a tiny number of British planes, piloted by young men with a tragically short life expectancy, faced up to the might of Goering's Luftwaffe.

While Churchill knew the country had only just avoided mortal peril twice in just a few months, he carried the trust and faith of the nation with some well-chosen words.

His remarks after the heroics of the RAF, that

"never in the field of human conflict has so much been owed by so many to so few"

struck a chord at the time and are still widely quoted today.

1941

PEARL HARBOR

December 7, 1941 was, according to President Roosevelt, a day 'which will live in infamy'.

His comment followed a surprise attack by the ships and planes of the Imperial Japanese Navy against the United States naval base at Pearl Harbor, Hawaii.

The attack, which left eight US battleships damaged and four sunk, brought America into the Second World War.

Ironically it took America's surprise dropping of atomic bombs on Nagasaki and Hiroshima four years later to defeat Japan and bring the war to an end. Japan launched the attack to stop the US implementing its planned action against the British, American and Dutch bases in south-east Asia.

The Pearl Harbor attack killed 2,403 Americans and injured another 1,178 others. In contrast Japan lost 64 servicemen.

Pearl Harbor: The day that brought America into the Second World War

1942

HEDLEY FOWLER

The tried and tested Rugbeians' qualities of cunning, originality, simplicity and a fine disregard for the rules served RAF POW **Hedley 'Bill' Fowler** well when he decided to escape from Colditz.

While others built gliders and dreamed up complex ways to freedom, Fowler took the more direct approach in 1942 by electing to walk out of the main gates in broad daylight.

The ruse worked and Fowler eventually made his way back to England, only to perish in an air crash in 1944 aged just 27.

Fowler, the great-grandson of Sir Harry Ayers of Ayers Rock fame, was born in London. His family moved to Australia in 1920 but returned a few years later so Bill could go to Rugby.

He returned down under in 1933, studied mechanical engineering at the University of Adelaide and joined the Royal Australian Air Force and then transferred to the RAF.

On 14 May, 1940, while flying a Hurricane in France, Fowler shot down a Dornier Do 17 and the next day an Me 109, but was then shot down himself and taken prisoner.

Fowler wrote an account of the circumstances of his capture:

"On 15 May 1940, I was pilot of a Hurricane which took-off about 1100 hours from Vitry-en-Artois, escorting bombers over Dinant. At approximately 1145 hours I was shot down by Messerschmitt fighters about five miles north of Fumay, on the west bank of the River Meuse. My aircraft was on fire so I baled out and landed in a wood. I left my parachute in the middle of a bush and cut one of the panels out to bind round my head, which was bleeding. I had dropped my helmet on the way down and I was not wearing flying kit. My clothes were standard dress uniform, a khaki 'sidcot suit', and black flying boots.

"After landing I destroyed my pay book and personal letters, but kept my identity disc and a B.E.F. identity card. I threw away my pistol, which was of German make. I then started to walk west through thick woods. My aircraft had fallen in the forest on the east bank of the River Meuse. I walked for about five hours. Going was very rough and I took off my Sidcot suit and carried it. About 1700 hours I was resting by a tree when a French soldier jumped out of a bush and pointed a rifle at me. I speak a little French and he asked me whether I was a German. I showed him my B.E.F. identity card and convinced him that I was a British pilot. This Frenchman was one of six French sappers trying to rejoin their unit. With them I walked through woods to Focroi. Here I left them and joined the remnants of a company of French infantry, commanded by a Sub. Lieutenant. They were much disorganised, and were retreating west ... "

Taken to Stalag Luft 1 prisoner camp, Fowler managed to escape in a fake German uniform and made his way to the coast, before being arrested and transferred to Colditz in December 1941.

Once there, he joined legless RAF air ace Douglas Bader in doing everything they could to annoy the Germans, which included catching wasps and recruiting them to spread anti-German propaganda. Fowler was among a group which plotted to escape, a feat successfully accomplished on September 9, 1942 when he joined a group dressed in false uniforms and managed to leave the castle unchecked.

The party walked about 30km to Penig, then made their way to Switzerland via Stuttgart.

From there Fowler and another officer crossed unoccupied France into Spain and, after a month in a military prison reached Gibraltar and then got back to the UK.

Fowler won the Military Cross for his escape. On being promoted to Squadron Leader he joined the Armament Test Squadron at Boscombe Down but perished in March 1944, test-flying a Hawker Typhoon.

1942

Denys Watkins-Pitchford taught art at the School for seventeen years from 1926. In 1942, under the pseudonym 'BB', he published the children's book *The Little Grey Men*, which won the Carnegie Medal. Watkins-Pitchford was awarded the MBE in 1989 and died a year later.

Headley 'Bill' Fowler was one of very few to have escaped from Colditz Castle

WILLIAM TEMPLE

The son of *'the greatest schoolmaster of his day'* **William Temple** is described as *'the most significant Anglican churchman of the twentieth century'*.

In a unique combination he followed his father Frederick, who became Head Master of Rugby in 1857, as Archbishop of Canterbury in 1942.

At Rugby (SH 1894-1900) William excelled intellectually. His relentless work ethic emerged early and is captured in a letter to his father from school: *"How could any intelligent boy who was able to get through two hours work in thirty minutes spend the remaining ninety minutes except by adding to his store of knowledge?"*

Temple's lively sense of humour and even temper outweighed any expression of priggish superiority. In addition to singing and oboe playing, his was a particular presence on The Close where 'his duty to the side was merely to lean against the scrum which thereupon swept forward' and he was known as 'the boy who had never been known to fall down at football'.

Going up to Balliol in 1900 he took a double first and became a Fellow of Queen's. Temple was a philosopher before he was theologian and never lost his love of English Literature for its own sake.

His substantial volumes *Mens Creatrix* and *Christus Veritas* trace his journey towards a convinced Christian framework for life. In the true sense an amateur theologian, *'for him, everything was related to God to be cherished and studied in that revelation'*.

William Temple's themes for life were moulded and developed by active engagement, not simply by academic study. He was committed deeply to the Workers' Educational Association with his life-long Rugbeian friend RH Tawney and involved himself in the Coal and General Strikes of 1925 and 1926.

Temple's calling to ordination in the Church of England was not smooth. He was ordained priest in 1909 and the following year, aged 29, was appointed Headmaster of Repton. He moved to the living of St James's Piccadilly in 1914, and after a Canonry at Westminster Abbey became Bishop of Manchester in 1921.

In addition to reorganising a diocese with a population of over 3.5 million people by creating the new Diocese of Blackburn, Temple continued with his commitment to improving the condition of the disadvantaged, chairing a pivotal Conference on Christian Politics, Economics and Citizenship in Birmingham in 1924. At the same time he gave himself tirelessly to Christian Unity and Mission and chaired the main Protestant movements that led to the 1948 World Council of Churches. Temple was translated to York in 1929 and to Canterbury in the middle of the Second World War.

Best known today for his pamphlet *Christianity and Social Order* (Penguin 1942), Temple's principles for Christian engagement with the challenges of inequality still resonate.

Perhaps the best testimony to a life cut short by over-work at 63 comes from a soldier serving overseas, who had heard one of the Archbishop's many wartime wireless broadcasts: *'now we understand what Christianity really is'*. **DU**

William Temple, Archbishop of Canterbury and 'the most significant Anglican Churchman of the twentieth century'

1942.

In June 1944 Allied forces started the largest military operation in history.

Called D-Day, June 6 launched Operation Overlord, landing 156,000 American, British and Canadian on five Normandy beaches.

The campaign, involving 5,000 ships and 11,000 aircraft, began the liberation of Europe. Facing stiff German resistance, Allied losses were high, with 4,000 dead and 10,000 wounded.

But years of planning and co-ordination meant beachheads were established and thousands of pieces of equipment brought in on floating Mulberry Harbours.

As the invasion began, supreme commander General Dwight D Eisenhower issued the following message:

"You are about to embark upon the Great Crusade, toward which we have striven these many months. The eyes of the world are upon you. The hopes and prayers of liberty-loving people everywhere march with you. In company with our brave Allies and brothers-in-arms on other Fronts, you will bring about the destruction of the German war machine, the elimination of Nazi tyranny over the oppressed peoples of Europe, and security for ourselves in a free world."

1944.

1945 Harry S. Truman 🇺🇸   1945 Clement Attlee 🇬🇧

1945

Celebrations in London at the end of the war in Europe

VE & VJ DAYS

On May 8, 1945 Victory in Europe Day marked the moment when the combined efforts of Western capitalism and Soviet communism defeated German fascism.

A week earlier, on April 30, 1945, Nazi leader Adolf Hitler committed suicide in his Berlin bunker. His successor, Admiral Dönitz surrendered in Reims on May 7 and a day later in the German capital.

Joining countless others across the world, a million people celebrated VE day in the streets of London.

In London, Prime Minister Winston Churchill appeared before the crowds with King George VI and Queen Elizabeth (later the Queen Mother) on the balcony on Buckingham Palace. The King and Queen's daughters, Princesses Elizabeth and Margaret, did an early version of the Royal Walkabout by mixing with the jubilant throng.

VE Day did not bring the Second World War to a close. That required the combined work of two different forces in the form of the world's first atomic bombs.

At 8.15 am on August 6, 1945 a United States Air Force aircraft called Enola Gay dropped an atomic bomb called, with tragic understatement, 'Little Boy', on the Japanese city of Hiroshima.

Three days later, at 11.02 am on August 9, a second bomb called 'Fat Man' was dropped on Nagasaki, from a Boeing B-29 Superfortress.

The bomb dropped on Hiroshima, which destroyed 70% of the city, killed 80,000 people directly and up to 160,000 by the end of the year from radiation. The Nagasaki bomb killed around 40,000 directly and about the same number over the next few months.

On August 15, 1945 the Japanese announced their surrender and this became known as VJ Day (Victory over Japan).

1946-1966
THE ROCK AND ROLL YEARS

1946 ROBIN COLLINGWOOD		**1946**	THE UNITED NATIONS
1947 TOM KING			
1948 ERNEST GOWERS SIR ARTHUR ffORDE		**1948**	GANDHI ASSASSINATION THE NHS
		1949	NATO
1951 DR SPARKS			
1952 HUGH JOHNSON		**1953**	THE CORONATION OF QUEEN ELIZABETH II DNA EVEREST
1954 GOVERNANCE & CO-EDUCATION		**1954**	BANNISTER & BRASHER BILL HALEY
		1955	THE WARSAW PACT
1957 WALTER HAMILTON NICK MONTAGU			
1960 SALMAN RUSHDIE			
1962 NUMBERS		**1962**	CUBAN MISSILE CRISIS
1963 ROBERT AKENHEAD CHRISTOPHER ORLEBAR HEW STRACHAN		**1963**	"PLEASE PLEASE ME" JFK
1965 DAVID URQUHART		**1965**	DEATH OF SIR WINSTON CHURCHILL
		1966	CHINESE CULTURAL REVOLUTION 1966 WORLD CUP

ROBIN COLLINGWOOD

Robin 'RG' Collingwood (WN Wilson / C 1903-08), whose name is remembered today at the Collingwood Centre, wrote the seminal book *The Idea of History*, published in 1946.

Born in Lancashire, Collingwood entered Rugby in 1902 and later shone in Greats at Oxford where he then became a Fellow of Pembroke College.

In parallel to being a philosopher of history, Collingwood was an historian and archaeologist, his most famous excavation being a circular ring ditch near Penrith known as King Arthur's Round Table.

After his death from a stroke in 1943, Collingwood's pupil TM Knox (later Sir Malcolm Knox, the eminent Anglo-Scottish philosopher) collated his writing and published *The Idea of History*.

This influential work centred on the idea of history being about recalling the thinking of people from the past.

Historian Dr Ian St John described Collingwood's influence on the teaching of history.

Commemorated at the School today through the Collingwood Centre

"Anyone studying history today will be familiar with the historical ideas of R.G Collingwood. The notion that every well-constructed history lesson should commence with a question; the emphasis upon thinking oneself into the mind of the historical actors; the insistence that all sources be interrogated to assess their authority: all are doctrines featuring prominently in Collingwood's work."

1946

When **Antony Wing** (SF 1946-52) audibly broke his leg playing rugby against Uppingham, subsequent physiotherapy at St Cross Hospital interested him so much that he switched from classics to science and later entered the medical profession.

1947

Gilbert Roberts (Sh 1947-52) was among boys who used silver nitrate from the School's science labs to blow up desk lamps in House studies. The loud explosion would plunge the victim's study and surrounding rooms into darkness and deafen the owner of the lamp.

1946.

THE UNITED NATIONS

Central Hall, Westminster, was the venue for the first meeting of the General Assembly of the United Nations on January 10, 1946.

Haileybury old boy Clement Attlee, the Labour leader who ousted Winston Churchill in the 1945 landslide General Election, welcomed delegates to 'this ancient home of liberty and order'.

At the first meeting, Zuleta Angel of Colombia called delegates to order. Then Paul-Henri Spaak of Belgium was elected President of the General Assembly by 28 votes to 23, beating Trygve Lie of Norway. Lie's consultation prize was to become UN Secretary General.

Today a plaque on the side of Central Hall commemorates the first gathering, which was attended by among others Eleanor Roosevelt, former First Lady, widow of FD Roosevelt and US delegate to the UN from 1945 to 1952.

TOM KING

Tom King (SH 47-52), now Lord King of Bridgwater, is the best known from a strong bench of post-war Rugbeian government ministers.

Entering parliament in 1971, King served in Mrs Thatcher's government as Energy Secretary, Employment Secretary and Northern Ireland Secretary.

He was also Defence Secretary for three years from 1989, first under Thatcher and later under John Major, overseeing Britain's military commitments during the 1991 Gulf War.

Following Lord King, **Ian Lang** (St 54-58), now Lord Lang of Monkton, was at Rugby before studying at Cambridge, where he was a member of Footlights.

Lang also held cabinet posts under John Major, as Secretary of State for Scotland and President of the Board of Trade.

Alan Howarth (K 57-62), now Lord Howarth of Newport, served as a junior employment minister under Margaret Thatcher and, defecting to New Labour in 1995, was later a junior minister for media, culture and sport.

Andrew Mitchell (Tu 69-74) served as International Development Secretary and Chief Whip in the 2010 coalition government, before standing down after an alleged argument with a police officer in Downing Street.

Although not serving as a minister, **Sir Nicolas Winterton** (ST 51-56) served as a backbench MP from 1971 to 2010, and chaired the Health Select Committee from 1990 to 1992.

Lord King of Bridgwater

1947.

1948

ERNEST GOWERS

Rugbeian **Sir Ernest Gowers** (M 1894-1899) made a lasting contribution to good writing through his 1948 book *Plain Words*. This best-seller explained how the worst linguistic crimes of civil servants could be avoided through clear, simple English. Now called *The Complete Plain Words*, it is still in print and just as good today. Gowers was born in 1880 and at Rugby combined sporting and academic success. He won a scholarship to Cambridge and achieved a first in classics. Entering the Civil Service, Gowers was a high-flyer, holding a wide range of senior public posts, including running London's civil defence during the Second World War and later chairing a commission on the death penalty. He died aged 85 in 1966.

Improving communication through clear, simple English!

SIR ARTHUR ffORDE

A 1961 British Pathé newsreel shows Queen Elizabeth II being greeted at the new BBC Television Centre by the Corporation's Chairman **Sir Arthur fforde**.

fforde's time overseeing the BBC was the second unexpected step in his career. After Rugby from 1914 to 1919, fforde was a scholar of Trinity College, Oxford. Then he became a solicitor and partner at Linklaters (where he helped create the Unit Trust) and during the Second World War was Deputy Director-General in the Ministry of Supply.

Unsurprisingly, the announcement of his appointment as Head Master of Rugby in 1948 raised eyebrows, including an exchange in *The Spectator*:

> *"I would suggest to your correspondent...that there are solicitors, Sir Arthur among them, whose work covers a somewhat wider range than "drafting leases, wills and pleadings in a stuffy office." It is presumably Sir Arthur fforde's professional experience in advising on the administrative and financial problems of undertakings big and small, in addition to his qualifications as a public servant during the war, that have commended themselves to the Governing Body."*

Whatever fforde's perceived qualifications to be Head, chair of governors Sir Will Spens felt he had the qualities and practical experience to steer Rugby through an important post-War period.

Inheriting a strong Common

Room, fforde was able to concentrate on wider issues, including modernisation, material shortages and finance.

Areas tackled by fforde during his time as Head included repairs to buildings, improved heating, the appointment of a Second Master to share the burden of running the School, increasing fees to more than £400 a year by 1956 to meet rising costs and expanding numbers to more than 700.

At the lighter end of the scale, boys enjoyed being presented with top hats when *Tom Brown's Schooldays* was filmed on site and later when the BBC filmed a live programme on life at the School.

Swapping Rugby for the BBC in 1957, fforde admitted to a press conference at the GPO that he did not actually own a TV set.

Aside from the law, government and leading great institutions, fforde, like James and Lyon before him, was a published poet. After leaving the BBC in 1964, he died in 1985, just a year before Lyon.

1948.

Sir Arthur fforde: Head Master form 1948 to 1957

GANDHI ASSASSINATION

Mahatma Gandhi, leader of the non-violent protest movement which contributed to India gaining independence in August 1947, was assassinated five months later on January 30, 1948.

At 5.15pm militant Hindu nationalist Nathurum Godse approached Gandhi as he stood on the steps of Birla House in New Delhi where a prayer meeting was about to take place.

Godse shot Gandhi three times in the chest at close range. Gandhi, who had survived four previous attempts on his life, was taken inside Birla House where he later died.

As Godse approached Gandhi, one of the girls flanking him explained that he was already late. Godse brushed her aside and fired. Gandhi apparently invoked God by saying 'Hey Ram' when he was shot.

Godse, working with others, carried out the assassination in protest at a fast Gandhi had started against the Indian Government's decision to withhold the second instalment of money from Pakistan following partition.

Mahatma Gandhi led the non-violent movement which contributed to India gaining independence

THE NHS

Sir William Beveridge's report recommending Britain introduce a 'welfare state' set in motion the launch of the NHS on July 5, 1948.

If Beveridge was technically the father of the NHS, Welsh radical firebrand health minister Aneurin 'Nye' Bevan was definitely the midwife.

Aside from the sheer logistics and complexity of the task, the biggest hurdle to overcome was the intransigent resistance of the medical profession itself.

Bevan took on the medics and won, although admitting he had to 'stuff their mouths with gold' to persuade consultants to participate.

Before the NHS, many people suffered in silence with poor health or even died early because they could not afford to pay doctors' bills.

Following the launch, health care became free, including, in the early days items such as glasses and dentures.

NATO

On April 4, 1949, the treaty setting up the North Atlantic Treaty Organisation was signed in Washington DC by twelve founding members.

Enshrining the principle of collective security among independent nations belonging to the UN, the North Atlantic Treaty contains to this day only fourteen articles.

NATO is based in Brussels and today has 28 members, the most recent being Albania and Croatia which joined in 2009.

Spending on defence by NATO countries represents 70% of the total spent on defence globally each year.

The treaty requires NATO countries to help fellow members which are attacked. This happened for the first and only time after the World Trade Center bombing on September 11, 2001 in New York.

Britain has held the post of Secretary General of Nato three times.

Nato's first Secretary General was General 'Pug' Ismay from 1952 to 1957 (previously Winston Churchill's chief military advisor during the Second World War). Lord Carrington, who resigned as Foreign Secretary following Argentina's invasion of the Falkland Islands in 1982, was Secretary General from 1984 to 1988, and former Labour Defence Secretary Lord Robinson held the post from 1999 to 2003.

1950s

A Michell Head of House in the early 1950s was found in bed with one of the maids. The Head Master punished him by withdrawing his right to be Head of House on alternate days.

1949

1951

1950

Town House pupil **Tony Barson** helped organise extras for the filming of *Tom Brown's Schooldays* in the summer of 1950, with shoots in Rugby and the Nettlefold Studios in Walton-on-Thames. His reward was an invitation to attend the film's world première at the Odeon, Haymarket in spring the following year.

DR SPARKS

Dr JP Sparks, a Rugbeian who succeeded RE Smith as School Medical Officer in 1950, alerted the Governing Body to an alarming decline in the resistance of the School's boys to sports injuries.

Reporting to the governors in 1951, Sparks recorded that there had been 450 injuries reported as a result of playing rugby in 1951, compared to just 183 in 1940.

The suspected cause, he suggested, was that *"conditions during and after the war had reduced boys' resistance to infection and injury"*.

HUGH JOHNSON

Rugbeian **Hugh Johnson** (SF 52-56) is one of the leading wine writers in the world. Entering Rugby in 1952, Johnson became involved in wine after being asked his opinion on two different red Burgundy wines in 1961, later writing *"one was magic and one was ordinary. This caught my imagination."*

Johnson published *Wine* in 1966, the seminal *The World Atlas of Wine* in 1971, and *The Story of Wine* in 1989. He has also written widely on trees and horticulture.

President of the Sunday Times Wine Club since 1973, Johnson was selected *Decanter* Man of the Year in 1995, was promoted Officer in the French Ordre National du Mérite in 2004 and Officer of the Order of the British Empire (OBE) in 2007 *'for services to wine-making and horticulture'*.

1951 Winston Churchill

1952 Elizabeth II

1952.

THE CORONATION OF QUEEN ELIZABETH II

Queen Elizabeth II was crowned in Westminster Abbey on June 2, 1953 as the world watched.

Despite opposition from Prime Minister Winston Churchill, the Queen insisted that live pictures of the coronation service should be broadcast across the globe.

Millions clamboured to watch it which, givin a huge boost to television set makers.

When the service got underway, Her Majesty was temporarily immobilised when she could not step forward because the pile on the carpet in the Abbey had been brushed in the opposite direction, catching the metal fringe of her robes.

The temporary impasse was resolved when she asked the Archbishop of Canterbury to provide a small push to 'get me started'.

During the ceremony the Queen was anointed with holy oil. The original oil had been destroyed during the war and the firm which made it had gone out of business. Fortunately, however, an elderly relative of the company had a few ounces of the base left and a new batch was produced.

1953

1953 Dwight D. Eisenhower

DNA

The molecular structure of DNA was discovered by Francis Crick and James Watson at a Cambridge laboratory in 1953.

Crick and Watson met at Cambridge in 1951 and, although DNA had been isolated by Friedrich Miescher in 1869, it was the pair's model building using X-ray diffraction data that led to the historic breakthrough.

Publishing their findings in *Nature* magazine in April 1953, Crick and Watson later shared the 1962 Nobel Prize for Medicine along with another DNA scientist called Maurice Wilkins.

The DNA's 'double helix' structure is regarded as one of the great scientific discoveries, made in one of the world's greatest science cities.

Crick's contribution to the understanding of life science is remarkable given that he obtained a second class degree in physics from University College, London.

Crick and Watson (right) shared the 1962 Nobel Prize for Medicine

1953.

EVEREST

New Zealand beekeeper, explorer and philanthropist Sir Edmund Hillary was the first man to reach the summit of Everest in the company of Sherpa Tenzing Norgay.

Born in 1919, Hillary served as an aviator during the Second World War, before taking up mountaineering. He was part of a reconnaissance expedition to Everest in 1951 and a member of a British team led by Colonel John Hunt when he reached the top at 11.30am on May 29, 1953.

Hillary and Tenzing spent fifteen minutes at the top of Everest which Hillary later described as a *"beautiful snow cone summit"*.

News of Hillary's success, a triumph by a man from an outpost of the British Empire, was greeted enthusiastically in the UK as people prepared for the coronation of Queen Elizabeth II a few days later.

After Everest, Hillary, who followed in his father's footsteps as a beekeeper, added the double achievement of reaching both the North and South poles.

He also set up the Himalayan Trust to support the people of Nepal which has helped build schools and hospitals in the region.

The news of Hillary's ascent of Everest with Tenzing Norgay arrived in London just before the Coronation of Queen Elizabeth II

GOVERNANCE & CO-EDUCATION

The Governing Body steered Rugby through the trauma of two world wars. A characteristic of this period was the remarkable (and perhaps with hindsight, undesirable) longevity in office of some members. Frederick Temple served from 1874 to 1902, Lord Kilbracken 1890 to 1932, Sir Will Spens 1930 to 1959, Terence Maxwell 1936 to 1973 and Sir Patrick Dean 1939 to 1983.

The 1960s and 1970s brought new financial problems. Years of depression, war, inadequate maintenance of 300-year-old jerry-built houses, listed properties and rent controls combined to dire effect on the London Estate, for 350 years a source of wealth. The Estate was showing every sign of becoming a burden rather than a benefit. The Governing Body's solution in 1972 was to recruit Sir Oliver Chesterton to chair the London Estate Committee as a full Governing Body member. Sir Oliver started by persuading all who had to be persuaded that Estate income had to be held back to create a fund for refurbishment. He then led negotiations with the local authority to cope with some of the most intractable properties. Finally he ensured the Estate was managed to the highest standards. By the time Sir Oliver retired in 1988 the Estate was once again income-earning in full measure.

The appointment of Sir Alan McLintock as chairman in 1988 after a fifteen-year apprenticeship as finance Governor moved Rugby's governance squarely into the late 20th-century. Term limits were set for members 'with some flexibility for the Chairman and Deputy Chairman'. The size of the Governing Body was increased to allow for more effective resourcing of committees. Statutes were revised, recognising girls as pupils (20 years after the event) and removing the requirement for the Head to be a communicant member of the Church of England.

Sir Alan's style was masterly. There is no better illustration than the decision to make Rugby fully co-educational. Richard Bull, the Head Master, wanted to do

Today the objects of Rugby School are:

The provision of a broad liberal Christian education at a boarding and day school at Rugby for children from Rugby and neighbourhood and elsewhere, and by ancillary or incidental activities and other associated activities for the benefit of the community.

this but initial discussions with the Common Room led to huge controversy. The Governing Body wanted to do it, but calmly.

Alan McLintock asked Sir Campbell Adamson, a senior Governor, to chair a working party of staff and Governors to consider the future of the School, co-education being but one of many topics. Hew Strachan and Michael Fowle, two junior Governors, were members, as were Richard Bull, the Bursar and three from the Common Room. Many sensible conclusions were reached but one conclusion firmly reached was kept *in pectore* – full co-education. The Governing Body was determined but discreet and cautious.

Richard Bull was approaching 60 and wanted to retire. Who was to replace him? The best candidate was Michael Mavor whose track record at Gordonstoun included the introduction of full co-education. Mavor was left in no doubt what the Governing Body wanted him to do – and it was what he wanted to do. How and when, even whether, were left entirely to him but he knew that he would have total Governing Body support to do what he wanted to do. And he did it brilliantly.

Finally in 2010, the Statutes were revised again. The Royal Society, Lord Chancellor and University appointments were abolished, but, more importantly, a new objects clause was enacted. This replaced the simple words in the Founder's Will and Intent which had stood unchanged, while the Founder's School had changed enormously, as reflected by many Acts of Parliament, and the Clarendon Commission's innumerable Orders.

1954.

BANNISTER & BRASHER

Supported by Rugbeian pacemaker **Chris Brasher** (SH 42-46), Roger Bannister became the first man to run a mile in under four minutes on May 6, 1954.

Bannister, Brasher and Chris Chataway ran together on the track at Iffley Road, Oxford before a crowd of around 3,000 spectators. Brasher was the first pacemaker before handing over to Chataway.

A 25-year-old medical student, Bannister took the lead with 200 yards to go and finished the race in three minutes and 59.4 seconds.

Bannister's record lasted just 46 days, and has been lowered by seventeen seconds over 60 years but is still regarded as a landmark feat.

After retiring from athletics Bannister became a distinguished neurologist, Master of Pembroke College, Oxford and a Knight of the Realm.

His pacemaker, Chris Brasher, went on to win a steeplechase Olympic gold medal in 1956 and co-founded the London Marathon in 1981.

Chris Brasher acted as a pacemaker on this famous occasion

Roger Bannister, the first man to run a mile in under four minutes

1954.

A Rugby athlete started a famous movement

BY RUNNING 26 MILES FOR SOCIETY'S IMPROVEMENT

FINISH

BILL HALEY

Rock Around the Clock, by Bill Haley and The Comets, was recorded on April 12, 1954.

Widely regarded as the first, or one of the first, recognised rock and roll songs it was a number one single in the UK and US, and charted again in the UK in the 1960s and 1970s.

Around 40 million copies of the record have been sold worldwide and it is ranked number 158 in the *Rolling Stone* magazine's list of *The 500 Greatest Songs of All Time*.

The two-minutes and eight-seconds song took 35 minutes to record but Haley's vocals were almost inaudible on the first take.

This was resolved by a Decca Records engineer splicing together segments from the only two takes that had been recorded. This included Danny Cedrone's guitar solo as there was no time to record a new one.

Cedrone was paid $21 for playing on the track but sadly fell down a staircase a month after the song was released and died of a broken neck at the age of 33.

Bill Haley, one of the first 'Rock and Rollers'!

1954

1955 Anthony Eden 🇬🇧

1955

THE WARSAW PACT

After West Germany joined NATO, 'The Treaty of Friendship, Co-operation and Mutual Assistance' was signed between Albania, Bulgaria, Czechoslovakia, East Germany, Hungary, Poland, Romania, and the Soviet Union.

The Treaty, called The Warsaw Pact after the city where it was signed, was a mutual defence agreement with each country pledging to aid the other if attacked. It was also an opportunity for Soviet influence and military hardware to be positioned across Eastern Bloc countries as a counter to the military threat of US-backed Western Europe.

In 1956 Hungary tried to leave the Treaty, prompting Soviet forces to crush the uprising. Twelve years later the Soviets, backed by other Pact members, invaded Czechoslovakia.

After the Berlin Wall came down, Communism fell and the USSR broke up in the early 1990s, the Pact no longer served any purpose and was officially terminated in Prague in 1991.

The Warsaw Pact was signed as a defence agreement in answer to NATO

1957

WALTER HAMILTON

Walter Hamilton is most remembered for leading two major English public schools, Westminster and Rugby, and a Cambridge college.

Less well known are his thoughts on Russian education, which, according to the news agency Tass quoted in *The Glasgow Herald* in February 1962, were highly favourable.

"Dr Walter Hamilton…was quoted today as saying that the Soviet educational system was the 'best in the world'….Dr Hamilton, head of a delegation of British head masters and head mistresses…had noted the successes achieved by Russian boarding schools in their five years' existence and emphasised they were open to broad sections of the population. He had been particularly impressed by the organisation of vocational, physical and aesthetic education and had said that British teachers could learn much from their Russian colleagues."

Hamilton's comments were not his first on boarding behind the Iron Curtain, as the *Daily Mail* reported in November 1960 when two Russian schoolmasters visited Rugby and called the practice of caning boys 'an affront to human dignity'.

According to the report, Hamilton, who admitted caning 'about once a term', 'listened intently' to his visitors before declaring 'their attitude is all bosh'.

And in response to caning being degrading he retorted: *"Do my boys look degraded?"*

Born in 1908, Hamilton was a scholar and multiple prize winner at Trinity College, Cambridge in the late 1920s and a fellow for four years from 1931.

After a stint at Eton, and then back at Trinity, he became Headmaster of Westminster School in 1950 before arriving at Rugby in 1957, the first Cambridge Head since Henry Ingles in 1794.

In his time at Rugby, the School continued to expand in numbers, learning and teaching modernised and developed, and new alternatives to traditional games, such as social services and the Duke of Edinburgh Award, were introduced.

Reflecting on progress under Hamilton, historian JB Hope Simpson commented: *"…Rugby has kept abreast of – and in some respects led – the advances demanded by modern trends in education…. But…making possible all the changes of these later years there yet remains the rock-foundation of a tradition laid by former generations of boys and masters…a tradition difficult to lay hold of or define, but fundamentally demanding a habit of industry and of service, showing itself in varying ways at different times, but with a basic character which is unchanging."*

After leaving Rugby in 1966, Hamilton was elected Master of Magdalene College, Cambridge in 1967 until retiring in 1978. He died in 1988.

Walter Hamilton: Head Master from 1957 to 1966

1957

NICK MONTAGU

Retired civil servant **Sir Nicholas Montagu** (Sh 57-62) made his mark in the world of academia and taxation. Born in 1944, Montagu entered Rugby in 1957 before gaining a double first at Oxford in classics, ancient history and philosophy. From 1966 to 1974 he lectured in philosophy at Reading University before entering the civil service, working in health and social security, the Cabinet Office and transport. In 1997 he was appointed Chairman of the Inland Revenue. Since his retirement in 2004, Montagu's public service posts have included Chairman of the Financial Ombudsman Service and Chairman of the Council at Queen Mary, University of London. He holds honorary doctorates from Middlesex, Bradford and Reading Universities, and was appointed Knight Commander of the Order of the Bath (KCB) in 2001.

SALMAN RUSHDIE

Writer **Sir Salman Rushdie** (B 61-65) was born in Mumbai to a Muslim family, and came to Rugby in 1960 before reading history at Cambridge. After a stint working in television in Pakistan, Rushdie joined an advertising agency in Britain. His second novel, *Midnight's Children*, which won the Booker Prize in 1981.

It was his fourth novel, *The Satanic Verses*, published in 1988, which thrust Rushdie into perhaps unwonted prominence worldwide. In 1989, the Supreme Leader of Iran, Ayatollah Khomeini, issued a *fatwa* – or death sentence – against the author, asserting the book offended Islamic law making Rushdie an apostate. This prompted widespread demonstrations, including public burnings of the book. Rushdie was forced into hiding for the next nine years during which he assumed the alias Joseph Anton. The *fatwa* remains in place: whilst Iran's stance may have softened a little, that adopted by the likes of Hezbollah and Al Qaeda remains obdurate.

Rushdie has won awards across the world and in 2007 was knighted for his services to literature.

1960.

1961 John F. Kennedy

Numbers at the School peaked at 771 in 1962

NUMBERS

While maintaining and increasing pupil numbers has always been one of the key expectations of all Heads, a spike upwards caused some difficulty for Rugby in 1962.

The School reached a peak of 771 pupils in that year, a number which according to Head Master Walter Hamilton *"pleased no one but the bursar"*.

Accommodating so many boarders was not made any easier when a fire in Tudor destroyed the dormitories just a week before the start of the autumn term.

1961

Two weeks before a visit to the School in 1961 the Queen Mother broke a bone in her foot. Wearing a special raised clog, Her Majesty was ferried across the School's two quads in a wheelchair pushed by **Peter Berners-Price** (St 56-61), who later became President of the Rugbeian Society and Chairman of the School's 450th Anniversary Year.

1962

CUBAN MISSILE CRISIS

For thirteen days from October 16 to 28, 1962, the world stood on the brink of nuclear war. The cause was a standoff between the United States and the USSR over the siting of Soviet ballistic missiles in Cuba.

A year earlier the US had been involved in a failed invasion of Cuba, known as the Bay of Pigs, and had since placed missiles within range of Moscow in Italy and Turkey. In response Soviet leader Nikita Kruschev allowed missiles to be placed in Cuba, in direct reach of the US.

Speaking to the American people on television on October 22, 1962, President Kennedy confirmed the US had set up a military blockade to prevent delivery of further weapons and demanded withdrawal of the missiles in Cuba. For nearly two weeks neither side backed down, leading to genuine fears of nuclear war between the USA and the USSR.

After fraught negotiation, the Soviets agreed to withdraw their missiles in exchange for the US agreeing never to invade Cuba and to take away their missiles in Turkey. Both sides also agreed to establish a telephone hotline to avoid future escalations.

President Kennedy died just one year after the crisis and Kruschev died in 1971.

The world on the brink…..

ROBERT AKENHEAD

Former High Court Judge **Sir Robert Akenhead** (SF 63-67) came to Rugby in 1963 before going to Exeter University. He was called to the Bar in 1972 and served as an Assistant Recorder and Recorder before being appointed a Judge of the High Court in 2007, when he was also knighted. For three years from 2010 he oversaw the Technology and Construction Court. Akenhead retired from the Bench in 2015 and has now returned to working as an arbitrator, mediator and adjudicator.

1963.

1963 Alec Douglas-Home 🇬🇧

CHRISTOPHER ORLEBAR

Christopher Orlebar (SH 58-63) left Rugby in 1963, the year Boeing introduced the Mach 0.9 727. Just thirteen years later he was flying supersonic when he took the controls of Concorde.

Orlebar was born in February 1945 and after Rugby went to Southampton University, followed by the College of Air Training at Hamble. Joining BOAC in 1969, he was assigned to VC10s before becoming a Concorde pilot and instructor in 1976.

After a decade with Concorde, Orlebar was appointed training captain for the Boeing 737 and retired from BA in 2000.

Orlebar's best-selling book, *The Concorde Story*, appeared in 1986, charting the development, launch and operation of the Anglo-French project.

Today Orbelar is a liveryman of the Honourable Company of Air Pilots and Air Navigators and a Fellow of the Royal Aeronautical Society.

A Rugbeian pilots Concorde!

HEW STRACHAN

Rugbeian **Sir Hew Strachan** (K 63-67) is one of the leading authorities on the history of conflict, in particular the First World War.

Born in 1949, Sir Hew left Rugby for Cambridge in 1968 where he then later studied for his doctorate. After lecturing at Sandhurst, he became a fellow at Corpus Christi College, Cambridge for thirteen years.

In 1992, he was appointed Professor of Modern History at Glasgow University and Director of the Scottish Centre for War Studies, before becoming Chichele Professor of the History of War, and Academic Fellow at All Souls College, Oxford until 2015. He is now an Emeritus Fellow of the College.

Sir Hew is currently Professor of International Relations at the University of St Andrews, is a Brigadier of the Royal Company of Archers, the Queen's Bodyguard for Scotland, and Lord-Lieutenant of Tweeddale.

Publications by Sir Hew include *The First World War: Volume 1: To Arms* (2001), *Clausewitz's On War: A Biography* (2007) and *The Direction of War* (2013).

Non-academic roles for Sir Hew have ranged from being a member of the Chief of Defence Staff's Strategic Advisory Panel to being a trustee of the Imperial War Museum and a Commonwealth War Graves Commissioner.

In 2014, Sir Hew criticised America and Britain for the strategic direction of their military involvement in Iraq and Afghanistan, which he said had *"left them in a far worse position than they were before".*

> *"Sexual intercourse began*
> *In 1963 (which was rather late for me)*
> *Between the end of the Chatterley ban*
> *And the Beatles' first LP".*

POET PHILIP LARKIN

"PLEASE PLEASE ME"

The LP in question was *Please, Please Me* which was released on March 22, 1963.

The record presented to the world the combined talents of four Liverpool youngsters who went on to become the biggest-selling and most influential pop group in history.

Aside from their music, the Beatles helped to define the 1960s and Britain's place within it. Their popularity led to Beatlemania, hits on both sides of the Atlantic, and opportunistic prime minister Harold Wilson presenting them with MBEs in 1965.

When they tired of touring and traditional three-minute singles, the Beatles moved culture and music on again with their ground-breaking *Sgt Pepper's* album in 1967.

Eventually worn out by more than a decade of making music in the spotlight and riven by personal discord, the Beatles broke up in 1970. Co-founder John Lennon was murdered in New York in 1980 and youngest member George Harrison died from lung cancer in 2001.

Today, drummer Ringo Starr still plays and tours with his own band, while Sir Paul McCartney is recognised as one of the world's most successful popular music artists and composers.

1963.

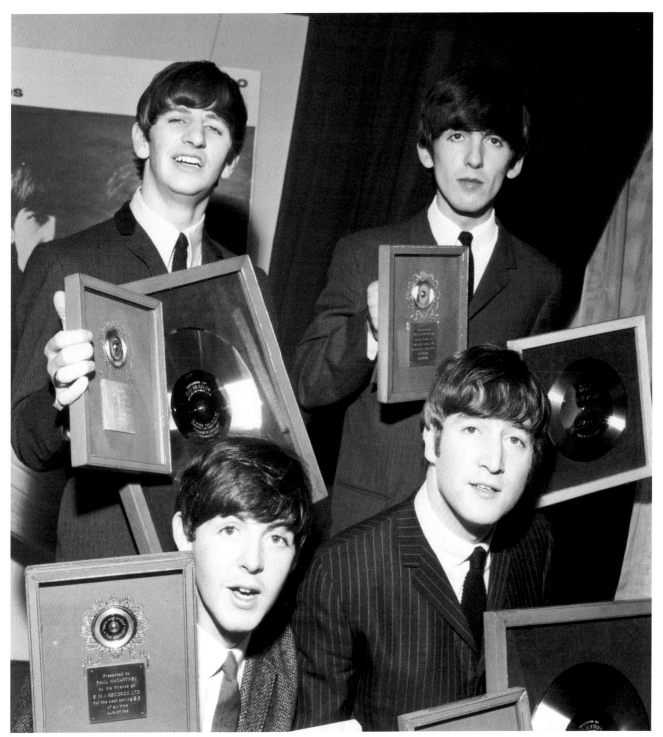

The Beatles helped to define the 1960s

John F. Kennedy: Assassinated November 22, 1963

1964

During cold winters in 1964 and 1965 Kilbracken gardener Ivor Truman flooded the House croquet lawn so it could be used for ice hockey.

1963 Lyndon Johnson

JFK

At 12.30pm Central Standard Time on November 22, 1963, Lee Harvey Oswald shot US President John F Kennedy as he rode through Dallas in an open-top motorcade.

Kennedy's wife Jacqueline tried frantically to save her husband and became a worldwide symbol of dignity in grief when she stood, just over two hours later, in her bloodstained dress, aboard Air Force One where Vice President Lyndon Johnson took the presidential oath.

Her reputation rose further in the days following her husband's assassination and at his public funeral in Washington DC.

Hiding in the Texas School Book Depository, Oswald, a former marine marksman, used a high-powered 6.5×52mm Italian Carcano M91/38 bolt-action rifle. Kennedy was struck several times and lost part of his skull.

The dying President, a practising Catholic, was taken to the Parkland Memorial Hospital where he received the last rites from a priest and was pronounced dead at 1pm.

In his first proclamation as new President, Johnson announced on November 23 that two days later would be a national day of mourning for 46-year-old Kennedy. The assassinated leader was laid to rest at Arlington National Cemetery in Washington DC, where his grave is marked by an eternal flame.

1963.

1965

DEATH OF SIR WINSTON CHURCHILL

Revered by most, distrusted by many, statesman, orator, writer and warrior Sir Winston Churchill passed away at home in London aged 90 on January 24, 1965.

Churchill was born at Blenheim Palace in 1874. He served in India as a cavalry officer in the 1890s, was captured and escaped as a soldier/journalist during the Boer War and entered Parliament in 1901 as a Conservative.

Crossing the floor to the Liberal side, as Home Secretary he let anarchists burn during a siege in Sidney Street, London. And despite preparing the fleet for war, he was forced to resign as First Lord of the Admiralty after the ill-fated Dardanelles campaign, retreating to command men as a colonel in the trenches in France.

During the 1920s he was an undistinguished Chancellor of the Exchequer, crossing back to the Conservatives and during the 1930s a lone voice from the backbenches warning against the rise of Hitler.

Succeeding Chamberlain as Prime Minister in 1940, Churchill's bulldog spirit and strategically good relations with the USA, helped Britain through the Second World War but he was then rejected by his people in the 1945 General Election.

Returning to Downing Street for a second time in 1951, he was made a Knight of the Garter by a young Queen Elizabeth II, before eventually handing over power to Antony Eden. He stayed on as an MP until three months before he died.

The funeral in London of Sir Winston Churchill

DAVID URQUHART

David Urquhart (K 65-70) came to Rugby in 1965 and after studying business at Ealing Technical College followed a commercial management career with BP.

Following ordination in 1984 he started his church career in Hull, later becoming a vicar in Coventry in 1992 and an honorary canon at Coventry Cathedral. In 2000 he became suffragen Bishop of Birkenhead and was appointed Bishop of Birmingham six years later.

Urquhart told the people of Birmingham after his enthronement that he wanted the diocese to engage in *"worship, making disciples and prophetic witness"*.

The Bishop of Birmingham

CHINESE CULTURAL REVOLUTION

China's decade-long 'Cultural Revolution' began in May 1966. Led by chairman Mao Zedong, the socio-political movement tried to impose pure Communist ideology and eliminate capitalist and traditional elements across China.

A campaign of violent struggle, conducted for Zedong by a new, young Red Guard, targeted members of China's bourgeoisie through public humiliation, prison, torture, harassment and property seizure.

Alongside this, relics and artefacts were destroyed, cultural and religious sites damaged, and schools shut.

The Revolution affected China politically and stalled industrial production by more than 12% in 1968.

It continued until 1976 but by 1981 had been rejected by the country's Communist Party which said it had been

"responsible for the most severe setback and the heaviest losses suffered by the Party, the country, and the people since the founding of the People's Republic".

Bobby Moore receiving the World Cup trophy from Queen Elizabeth II for England in 1966

1966 WORLD CUP

Like so many occasions involving England, the match was against tough opponents from Germany and had to be decided in extra time.

But on July 30, 1966, the England football team, led on the pitch by the quietly brilliant Bobby Moore and off it by quietly imperious Alf Ramsey, actually won the World Cup.

The match, held in the Wembley sunshine in front of 90,000 spectators, including the Queen and Prince Philip, was perhaps never in doubt given Geoff Hurst scored three times, the only hat trick in a World Cup Final.

Yet it was not without controversy, with Hurst's third effort hitting the goal line and only being called good after consultation between the referee and a Soviet linesman.

Despite this moment of tension, England, who were hosting the tournament, won the match 4-2 and completed their only victory, before or since, in their only World Cup Final.

Following their win against West Germany, Bobby Moore cemented his reputation as one of the greatest players of his generation, again leading England in a classic encounter against Pele's Brazil during the World Cup four years later, which, inevitably, Brazil won.

Alf Ramsey was knighted for his efforts but later gave up his managerial duties after England failed to qualify for the 1974 competition.

1966

A Bradley boy believed Housemaster Geoff Helliwell had unwittingly signed off a note for the purchase of a 'haystack', according to **Tim Hale** (B 66-71). When the boy tried to get the purchase of a tractor approved a short while later, Helliwell asked if the machine was required to move the haystack.

1966.

1967-1999
HERE COME THE GIRLS

1967 JIM WOODHOUSE BECOMES HEAD			
1968 ANTHONY HOROWITZ		**1968** LUTHER KING	
		1969 MOON LANDING	
1972 CLIVE SCHLEE		**1972** BLOODY SUNDAY THE MUNICH MASSACRE	
		1973 BRITAIN ENTERS THE EEC YOM KIPPUR WAR ABBA "WATERLOO"	
		1974 NIXON RESIGNS	
		1975 END OF VIETNAM WAR	
1976 ANDREW RAWNSLEY JOHN GIMLETTE CRESCENT		**1977** ELVIS DIES	
1978 DEAN ISABEL WOLFF			
1979 DAVE BARK-JONES ROGER RINGROSE PETER KEMBER GARETH LLOYD-JONES		**1979** MRS THATCHER FALL OF THE SHAH	
1980 ROB PENN TIM BUTCHER FRANCESCA HUNT CHRISTOPHER HINGLEY		**1980** JOHN LENNON ZIMBABWE	
		1981 REAGAN & POPE JOHN PAUL DAVID OWEN & THE SDP	
1982 RICHARD MONTGOMERIE FIONA HUGHES D'AETH		**1982** THE FALKLANDS	

1998 APPLE
THE GOOD FRIDAY AGREEMENT

1997 NATHAN WILLIAMSON

1997 DEATH OF DIANA
TONY BLAIR

1995 ANDY KEELING
LOUISE HARRISON

1994 THE CHANNEL TUNNEL

1993 SOUTHFIELD

1991-2001 THE YUGOSLAV WARS

1990 MARSHALL

1990 MANDELA RELEASED

1989 THE SPORTS CENTRE
THE DESIGN & TECHNOLOGY CENTRE
MICHAEL MAVOR BECOMES HEAD

1989 FALL OF THE BERLIN WALL
MASSACRE IN TIANANMEN SQUARE
THE INTERNET
INVASION OF KUWAIT

1988 RUPERT BROOKE

1986 JOHN GILLESPIE MAGEE JR

1985-9 DISASTERS

1985 RICHARD BULL BECOMES HEAD

1985 LIVE AID
MIKHAIL GORBACHEV

1984 JOHN ATTWATER

1982 RICHARD MONTGOMERIE

When Armstrong took a small step onto the moon

GIRLS CAME TO RUGBY, NONE TOO SOON

1967

JIM WOODHOUSE

Jim Woodhouse was just 33 when he arrived as Rugby's new Head from Westminster in 1967, inheriting detailed plans for a Royal visit to mark the School's 400th birthday.

It was fitting Queen Elizabeth II honoured the School with her presence that historic year, given the patronage shown by her forebear Elizabeth I to Rugby's founder, Lawrence Sheriff.

Although young for a Head and new in post, Woodhouse stepped up to the challenge of welcoming the Queen and Prince Philip.

Planning for the visit was led by Philip Snow, the School's assistant bursar, who was a former colonial administrator, former captain of the Fiji cricket team, and brother of CP Snow.

Recalling the event, Snow wrote:

"He was just as kindly as Walter and had an innate dignity. At that age the job was not going to be easy but he carried it off…Coming half way through the preparations for the Royal visit, which was to be in May and the quartercentenary proper two months later, he readily accepted what had been planned… Each time we went over the route, checking the time of each leg of the programme…The Queen asked to see as many of the boys' activities as possible."

The day of the Royal visit was rain sodden and every man on parade got a wet head as only Prince Phillip, wearing a raincoat and trilby, was allowed a hat.

Meeting Snow, Prince Philip asked: *"So you are the chap who fixes the fees like those I get from Gordonstoun? Do you manage to balance the books?"*

During the visit, the Queen was asked to open the new gates at the edge of The Close erected in her honour, an event which in the great tradition of ceremonial occasions did not go smoothly.

Asked to insert a key and turn it anticlockwise:

"The Queen duly inserted the key and turned it anticlockwise without being reminded. Of course it happened. The gate refused to open. She tried three times. Being gold, the metal now twisted. Something had providentially prompted the imperturbable architect to carry an ordinary steel key in his pocket. With extreme difficulty, while the assembled school, masters, parents and public were locked inside awaiting the royal entrance, the architect extricated the bent key and offered the substitute… This was making the Queen's day…"

Aside from successfully presiding over a 400th birthday and a Sovereign's visit, Woodhouse was responsible for two lasting decisions during his time at the School.

Shortly after becoming Head, he persuaded the Governors that the role of Head and Housemaster of School House could no longer be combined. So the first dedicated Housemaster was appointed, the job going to a Rugbeian, staff member and former Scotland fullback John Marshall, who continued in the post until 1983. The other even bigger step was to admit Rugby's first girls in 1976, changing for ever four centuries of masculine history.

Given the scale of this leap for the School, the introduction of girls and their gradual increase in number each year happened more smoothly than some might have predicted but not without some challenges.

The first girls were sixth formers accommodated in a converted wing of the School sanatorium. From this small start, Dean, the first official girls' House was opened in 1978 for thirteen girls.

One of this baker's dozen, Lucinda Holmes, the School's current Chair of Governors, recalled the experience in *Floreat* in 2016.

"We were a mixed bunch from as far afield as Toronto, Scotland, London, Dorset and the Midlands.

"Some had fathers or brothers who were Rugbeians, others had brothers still in the School, but most (like me) had no previous connection at all.

"Dean House was run by a Housemaster, the Rev Gerald Hughes, and his wonderful wife, Sylvia. They were helped by eager female tutors who were wives of Masters. I'm not sure in retrospect that they were ready for the massive task that lay ahead of them.

"Looking back now, being in such a minority in still a chauvinistic environment was not easy. We knew we were discussed, rated, watched, laughed at and more. Who wouldn't remember with dread our notorious arrival in Chapel on the first morning – inspected as we were by the entire School as we walked the length of the nave to our seats."

Although many aspects about Rugby altered little under Woodhouse, his change of the management of School House and starting the School on the road to becoming co-educational were far-reaching decisions.

While still in his mid-forties, Woodhouse, a keen sailor, departed for Lancing College on the south coast in 1980 taking with him his leaving gift from Rugby - a wind sail board presented in front of staff, parents and pupils in the Temple Speech Room.

ANTHONY HOROWITZ

Rugbeian **Anthony Horowitz** (SF 68-73) is a prolific creator of mystery and suspense dramas in print and on screen.

Discovering his love of writing at Rugby in the late 1960s, Horowitz read English at the University of York and published his first novel, a humorous adventure story for children called *The Sinister Secret of Frederick K Bower* in 1979. Horowitz's work since then has encompassed the *Alex Rider* series for young readers, two Sherlock Holmes novels and a 2015 James Bond novel called *Trigger Mortis*.

On television, Horowitz was the creator and writer of *Foyle's War*, and has also written scripts for *Poirot* and *Midsomer Murders*.

1967

Head of School **JCB Boyes** (St 62-67) was in charge of the two gold fountain pens furnished for the Queen to sign the School's visitors' book on her visit in 1967. The Queen and Prince Philip were amused when the first one refused to work, but fortunately the second one proved more reliable.

1968

Jim Woodhouse: Head Master from 1967 to 1980

LUTHER KING

Dr Martin Luther King's vision for a peaceful, racially equal America ended when he was shot dead just after 6pm on April 4, 1968. But with tragic irony his death brought in new civil rights laws for America just one week later.

The acknowledged leader of the American black Civil Rights movement, 39-year-old Dr King, who won the 1964 Nobel Peace Prize, was killed in Memphis, Tennessee, as he prepared to lead a march of sanitation workers protesting against low wages and poor working conditions.

He was standing with the Reverend Jesse Jackson on the balcony of the Lorraine Motel when he was hit in the neck by a single shot and died in St Joseph's hospital soon afterwards.

US President Lyndon Johnson said he was 'shocked and saddened' by Dr King's death.

"I ask every citizen to reject the blind violence that has taken Dr King who lived by non-violence."

Riots and looting broke out in over 100 cities across America following Dr King's death. This prompted President Johnson to urge Congress to pass Civil Rights legislation, known as the Fair Housing Act, which was achieved on April 11, just a week after the assassination.

The man who shot King was James Earl Ray, who was on the run from Missouri state prison. He was arrested at Heathrow Airport on June 8, 1968 and in March 1969 sentenced to 99 years in prison. He died aged 70 on April 23, 1998.

1969 Richard Nixon

The death of Martin Luther King in 1968 heralded a new civil rights law for America

1968.

1969

SPECIAL EDITION

LIFE

TO THE MOON AND BACK

$1.50

MOON LANDING

As Neil Armstrong said, the landing of Apollo 11 on July 20, 1969 was a 'small step for a man' but a 'giant leap for mankind'.

If the East-West military standoff was the 'cold war' on planet Earth, the race between the USSR and the USA to reach the moon was played out in the even colder atmosphere of space.

The Russians took the lead when they landed a human-made object, but no human, on the surface of the moon in 1959. This led to President Kennedy's pledge in 1961 *"before this decade is out, of landing a man on the Moon and returning him safely to the Earth"*.

Armstrong and Buzz Aldrin landed their lunar module at 20.18 and at 02.56 Armstrong became the first man to plant a footstep on the moon's surface.

A US flag was planted on the surface of the moon during the lunar walkabout, along with a plaque signed by President Nixon reading:

"Here men from the planet Earth first set foot upon the Moon July 1969 AD. We came in peace for all mankind."

"BLOODY SUNDAY"

On January 30, 1972, soldiers from the 1st Battalion, Parachute Regiment shot 26 unarmed civilians in Derry, Northern Ireland, killing fourteen, in an incident known as 'Bloody Sunday'.

The soldiers' actions were cleared in a tribunal headed by British Lord Chief Justice Lord Widgery because they had, allegedly, been shot at and faced bomb throwers.

In the summary of his report, Lord Widgery wrote:

"None of the deceased or wounded is proved to have been shot whilst handling a firearm or bomb. Some are wholly acquitted of complicity in such action; but there is a strong suspicion that some others had been firing weapons or handling bombs in the course of the afternoon..."

However, Major Hubert O'Neill, the coroner who investigated the deaths of those killed, wrote in 1973:

"This Sunday became known as Bloody Sunday and bloody it was. It was quite unnecessary. It strikes me that the Army ran amok that day and shot without thinking what they were doing."

A subsequent inquiry, led over twelve years by Lord Saville, declared in 2010 that the killings were in fact unjustified, the soldiers had not been attacked and Prime Minister David Cameron issued a formal apology.

Bloody Sunday happened when around 10,000 marchers gathered to protest against the British government's policy of internment.

During the march in the Bogside area of the city, some local youths threw stones at soldiers who responded with water cannon, CS gas and rubber bullets. Soldiers sent in to arrest rioters then opened fire, killing thirteen men and injuring thirteen others (including a fifteen-year-old boy and a woman), one of whom later died.

The British Government issued a formal apology for 'Bloody Sunday' in 2010

1970s

The School purchased its first calculator in the early 1970s – a Hewlett Packard costing £170. In the early 1980s twelve BBC microcomputers were networked in a basement of the Science department.

1970 Edward Heath 🇬🇧

1972

In his time at Sheriff from 1972 to 1976, **Chris Boot** and other boys filled the outlet pipe of the House washing machine with shampoo, causing a 'mountain of foam'.

CLIVE SCHLEE

Clive Schlee (C 72-76) entered the School in 1972 before reading history at Oxford. After seventeen years with Jardine Matheson, he joined the Pret A Manger chain as Chief Executive. Today he also owns 50% of the Itsu sushi restaurant chain.

THE MUNICH MASSACRE

The 1972 Olympic Games in Munich were supposed to reflect peaceful, modern post-war Germany.

The event is remembered, however, for the capture and murder of eleven Israeli athletes by Palestinian terrorists and the failed efforts of German police to rescue them.

The athletes were taken hostage by the Palestinian group Black September, supported by German neo-Nazis. The two groups wanted the release of over 200 prisoners in Israel and two founders of the Red Army Faction held in Germany.

The terrorists demanded helicopters to escape, a move which was granted by the German authorities. This led to a subsequent gun battle at Fürstenfeldbruck military airbase, near Munich, in which nine Israeli athletes were killed, along with five Black September members and a German policeman.

The incident started when the terrorists broke into the Israeli team quarters on Tuesday, September 5, 1972, killed two athletes, including wrestling coach Moshe Weinberg, and took nine others hostage.

Following the massacre German police were widely criticised for mishandling the situation and blamed for the gun fight in which the hostages were killed.

A dark day in 1972 when 11 Israeli Athletes were killed by 'Black September'

1973

BRITAIN ENTERS THE EEC

President de Gaulle twice vetoed the UK's application to join the EEC in 1961 and 1969, fearing a decline in France's voice in the Europe and too much US influence. But for Conservative Prime Minister Edward Heath it was third time lucky in January 1973 when finally Britain was allowed to join the European club, along with Ireland.

Heath was clear about the benefits of EEC membership for the UK, saying:

"It is going to be a gradual development and obviously things are not going to happen overnight.

"But from the point of view of our everyday lives we will find there is a great cross-fertilisation of knowledge and information, not only in business but in every other sphere."

Britain and Ireland took membership to nine countries, compared with over 20 today.

In opposition, the Labour Party voted against the UK joining, even though Harold Wilson had applied as Prime Minister in 1969. Labour deputy leader Roy Jenkins defied the party whip, voted with the Conservative government and resigned his position.

A year after joining the EEC, Wilson replaced Heath and returned to Downing Street. In 1975, following Foreign Secretary Jim Callaghan negotiating better terms for the UK, a referendum was held on whether to stay in or leave.

The referendum voted to stay in the EEC, although this was reveresed in a second referendum in 2016. In 1977 Roy Jenkins left the Government to serve as President of the European Commission, before returning to the UK in the early 1980s to help found a new breakaway, pro-Europe political party, the SDP.

YOM KIPPUR WAR

The Yom Kippur Arab-Israeli War lasted from October 6 to 25, 1973 and one of its impacts on the world was the pushing up of the price of oil.

The war started when a coalition of Arab states, led by Egypt and Syria, entered the Sinai and the Golan Heights to win back land taken by Israel during the Six-Day War of 1967, and reopened the Suez Canal.

The surprise attack started on Yom Kippur, Judaism's holiest day. As the conflict unfolded, the US supplied its ally Israel, and the Soviet Union did the same for its ally Egypt.

This led to renewed nuclear tension between the USA and USSR for the first time since the Cuban Missile Crisis of 1962 and at one point President Nixon put all American nuclear stations on 24-hour alert.

A UN-brokered ceasefire on October 22 did not work but a successful settlement was reached three days later after intense shuttle diplomacy, with US Secretary of State Henry Kissinger, a central figure between Washington and Moscow.

The conflict led to the 1978 Camp David Accords which returned Sinai to Egypt and was the first peaceful recognition of Israel by an Arab country.

However, it also pushed up the price of world oil after Arab oil producers embargoed exports to the US and Western Europe following America's massive airlift of armaments to Israel during the conflict.

ABBA "WATERLOO"

Dressed to the nines in flares, with voices like angels and clean-cut Scandinavian good looks to match, Swedish supergroup Abba started their journey as one of the biggest bands of the 1970s in Brighton on April 6, 1974.

Agnetha, Benny, Björn and Anni-frid sang their own composition *Waterloo* with verve and enthusiasm as Sweden's entry in the Eurovision Song Contest.

The song, which somewhat incongruously celebrated the defeat of Napoleon by the Duke of Wellington and General Blücher in 1815, won hands down with 24 points. It achieved number one in several countries and sold over 10 million copies.

Although winning the Eurovision Song Contest is not a passport for success for most artists, Abba proved the exception, enjoying huge popularity in the late 1970s and early 1980s.

By the 1990s Abba were regarded by many as 'uncool'. But a catalogue of well-crafted songs saw them come back into fashion in the new millennium, helped by the hit musical and film *Mamma Mia!*, named after one of their hits.

Despite current popularity and continued commercial success, Abba have not reformed and played together since officially splitting up in the 1980s.

The 'Yom Kippur' war in 1973 again raised East/West tensions

NIXON RESIGNS

On the wall of the editorial conference room of the *Washington Post* hangs a hot metal page bearing the reverse headline 'Nixon Resigns'.

The two words relate Nixon's decision to stand down as President on August 9, 1974, following the Watergate Crisis which *Washington Post* reporters Woodward and Bernstein had doggedly and bravely reported.

Watergate was named after the Watergate complex in the city, where in January 1972 a group of burglars, including a salaried worker from Nixon's re-election campaign, were caught breaking in to the offices of the Democratic National Committee headquarters.

Nixon untruthfully denied any knowledge of the break-in and promised there would be 'no whitewash' at the White House. A range of people were arrested, charged and imprisoned with the trail eventually leading to the Oval Office itself.

Faced with impeachment, Nixon decided to resign. He was then pardoned by his successor Gerald Ford, who was previously Vice President.

Although respected as something of an 'elder statesman' in later years, Nixon never shook off his 'Tricky Dickie' reputation. He died aged 81 in 1994.

Woodward and Bernstein's part in Nixon's downfall was told in the film *All the President's Men*, starring Dustin Hoffman and Robert Redford.

Watergate led to Nixon's resignation in 1974

1974.

1974 Gerald Ford 🏳

1974 Harold Wilson 🇬🇧

1975

END OF VIETNAM WAR

The fall of Saigon on April 30, 1975, brought to an end a war which had started 20 years before.

The Vietnam War pitted North Vietnam, supported by the USSR, China and other communist allies, against South Vietnam, supported by the USA, Australia and other allies.

The US, which entered the war in 1961, lost 58,282 soldiers, another 303,644 were wounded and 1,626 were missing in action. More than 400,000 South Vietnamese were killed and more than 900,000 Viet Cong and North Vietnamese.

A Paris Peace Accord in January 1973 was agreed by all sides and supposedly ended the conflict, but fighting continued. It took the fall of Saigon for the war to stop completely, and north and south Vietnam were reunified the following year.

The key figure behind the drive for a united Vietnam was communist leader Ho Chi Minh. In his early life it is claimed Minh worked as a pastry chef at the Carlton Hotel in Haymarket, Central London, now the site of the New Zealand High Commission.

CRESCENT ☾

In September 1975, three day girls were admitted to Stanley House and were provided with a study on the private side, where they were the responsibility of Peter Hare, the housemaster. Two stayed for only one year and were daughters of members of staff. The third was Jill Rogers, the daughter of a local GP, who moved to Crescent House when it opened in September 1976 and became our first head of house.

In January 1975, Jim Woodhouse, the Head Master, asked me if I would, with Fiona my wife, take on responsibility for the first girls' house; this was to open in September at 6 Horton Crescent. The next, rather frantic, nine months were spent in planning both how the girls would fit into the School and how the building would be adapted – basically by our moving to occupy the original family accommodation nearest to Horton Crescent and the girls occupying what must have been the smaller servants' rooms and kitchen at the other end.

The key decision was that the girls would be wholly our responsibility – I was to be their housemaster with all that implies at Rugby, and Crescent would be their 'home'. In addition, they would have lunch and tea in Stanley, Bradley or Town Houses, thus having a link with boys'

houses; this was valuable but not always easy, especially at tea. The girls got their own breakfast in Crescent and, unlike boys, were expected to do their own laundry, in preparation for life at college. We provided for ten boarders in five double rooms and up to eleven day girls in two shared downstairs studies, strongly encouraging day girls to stay the night from time to time so the two groups were well integrated. Tutors were recruited and with our small team of dailies, played a crucial role over the next sixteen years.

So it was, that in September 1976, Crescent House opened and the first, intrepid, group of twelve girls arrived to join Jill Rogers. Perhaps inevitably, given the time scale, the house wasn't quite ready and the girls lived on the top floor of the San for half a term. A late-night meeting for coffee with boy patients went deliberately unnoticed by the housemaster in case the house became the shortest surviving house in history.

From 1978, other girls' houses followed in Dean, Southfield and Rupert Brooke. As in Crescent, the girls were under the oversight of their own housemaster, with each house working with a number of boys' houses for lunch and tea. Girls wore their own 'smart business clothes', not an easy thing

to oversee but, as numbers grew, they gradually became a more familiar part of the school, able to enjoy a wider range of sporting, musical, dramatic and other activities as well as working hard for their A levels.

Before Richard Bull retired, the Governors decided that the school would go completely coeducational but that the new Head Master Michael Mavor would implement this. On that basis we agreed to extend our term to sixteen years, as it was obvious that Crescent would be too small to be an all-through girls' house. Bradley became a girls' house and our older girls moved there for their second year. Thus Crescent House closed after 16 years in which there were 161 members of the house, but only one housemaster and wife. Each girl was given a drawing of the house by the then chaplain, Keith Lanyon-Jones, as a memento and a service and lunch were held to mark its closure.

In Bradley and as the number of girls' houses grew, housemistresses were appointed instead of housemasters but in 1976, when Crescent opened, the full-time staff had been almost all men. Returning to Rugby only a few years later, when Fiona became lay chaplain, it was very striking how well girls had become integrated throughout the school. **IN**

1975.

ANDREW RAWNSLEY

Journalist, writer and broadcaster **Andrew Rawnsley** (T 75-79) studied at Lawrence Sheriff School before winning a scholarship to Rugby. After gaining a first in history at Cambridge, where he edited the university newsaper and won *The Guardian* Student Journalist of the Year award, he joined the BBC in 1983.

In 1985 he joined *The Guardian* and later moved to *The Observer* as Chief Political Commentator and Associate Editor. Rawnsley has presented programmes on politics for Channel 4 and the BBC and published two books on the creation and fall of New Labour.

1976 James Callaghan 🇬🇧

1976

JOHN GIMLETTE

John Gimlette (Sh 76-81) won the prestigious Shiva Naipaul Prize for travel writing in 1997 for his book *Pink Pigs in Paraguay*. Born in 1963, he entered Rugby in 1976. Gimlette's books have included… *At the Tomb of the Inflatable Pig: Travels in Paraguay… Theatre of Fish: Travels in Newfoundland and Labrador… Panther Soup: A European Journey in War and Peace…* and *Wild Coast: Travels on South America's Untamed Edge*, which was awarded the Dolman Travel Book Prize in 2012. As well as travel writing, Gimlette has worked as a ranch hand, taught English, manned a frontier-post for Bolivian customs and now practises as a barrister in London, specialising in clinical negligence and personal injury.

The death of Elvis Presley in 1977 reverberated around the world

ELVIS DIES

By the late 1970s the early deaths of pop stars like Buddy Holly, Brian Jones of the Rolling Stones, Jimi Hendrix and Marc Bolan of T Rex were sad but no longer shocking.

The announcement on August 16, 1977 that Elvis Presley had died, however, was news that reverberated around the world.

Presley returned to his Graceland home from the dentist at around 7pm on that day and went to rest before an evening flight. He was later found dead in his bathroom from heart failure having supposedly taken a range of prescription drugs including morphine, Valium and codeine.

Elvis was mourned widely in 1977 and still is today. Some ardent fans believe he did not really die at all and there is a charity website dedicated to recording 'sightings' of the singer.

After Elvis died, Frank Sinatra said he would *"miss him dearly as a friend. He was a warm, considerate and generous man."*

US President Jimmy Carter added:

"Elvis Presley's death deprives our country of a part of itself. He was unique and irreplaceable. More than 20 years ago, he burst upon the scene with an impact that was unprecedented and will probably never be equalled. His music and his personality, fusing the styles of white country and black rhythm and blues, permanently changed the face of American popular culture. His following was immense, and he was a symbol to people the world over of the vitality, rebelliousness, and good humour of his country."

1977 Jimmy Carter

1977.

MARK & ED BODDINGTON

Despite hailing from a famous brewing dynasty, Rugbeian cousins Mark and Ed Boddington have forged successful careers away from ale making and pubs.

Mark (W 77-82) trained with eminent furniture maker John Makepeace and now produces hand-built, custom-made furniture for royalty, Hollywood actors and billionaires.

Mark's first distinguished customer was the Duchess of Westminster. Since then his client list has grown to include the Rothschilds, the late David Bowie and Madonna.

Ed (K 78-83) is Group Chief Executive of Harvest Media, which specialises in audience participation services, including managing the voting for *Pop Idol*, *American Idol* and *The X Factor* in the US, Asia and the UK.

After a marketing background, Ed is now also a partner at Bosham Capital Advisors, chairman of marketing agency One Big Idea Ltd, and is chair of governors at Wallingford Preparatory School in Wallingford.

Edward 'Bod' Boddington

1977.

1978.

DEAN

Dean was originally a private house called 'The Firs' which was bought by the school in the early 1930s and opened as the school infirmary on Speech Day 1934. Dean House itself was opened in September 1978 for around thirteen girls. It was the second girls' house, Crescent House having been opened in 1976. It is named after Sir Patrick Dean, (SH 1922-28), who was Chair of the Governing Body 1972-1984. Dean was known as the 'posh hotel' by the original intake of girls. Its Art Deco architecture and its previous role as the school San meant the building had a feeling of space in some areas, in contrast to other boarding houses. The Common Room was so small and the popularity of the girls so great that on occasion visitors were being turned away as there was no room for them.

The first House Master from 1978 to 1980 was the Rev. Gerald Thomas Hughes (Assistant Master 1971-80), who later became Vicar of Dunchurch and Rural Dean of Rugby. The longest-serving House Master was Michael Pattinson, who was at Dean from 1984-1996. Michael joined the Rugby staff in 1969 and was Head of Biology from 1972-1984. Michael's other claim to fame was membership of the Great Britain Shooting team. **RM**

ISABEL WOLFF

Author **Isabel Wolff** (CR 76-78) left Rugby in December 1978 and taught in India for six months before reading English at Cambridge, where she acted with fellow student Stephen Fry. After university she worked at the BBC as a producer and documentary presenter, while writing features for the *Spectator*, *Independent* and *Daily Telegraph*.

She has written more than fifteen novels, her first being the romantic comedy *The Trials of Tiffany Trott*.

"If I've been successful it's due to the two years I spent in the sixth form at Rugby. I look back on that time with inexpressible gratitude, and with a nostalgic ache."

1979

DAVE BARK-JONES

Actor **David Bark-Jones** (M 79-83) joined the School in 1979. After Newcastle University he made his stage debut in 1992. He has appeared at the National Theatre and won an award for his portrayal of Richard Hannay in *The 39 Steps*. On television he played Lt Denny in the Colin Firth production of *Pride and Prejudice* and appeared opposite Keira Knightley in *Oliver Twist*. Bark-Jones' film roles have included Bertie in Guy Richie's *RocknRolla*.

1979

Rugby's shooting team beat 65 other schools to win the Bisley Shield in the summer holiday of 1979. The team's captain, **Peter Temperley** (K 74-79), returned the following term to sit for Oxbridge, during which time the editor of this book served as his House fag. Also during this term, Head Master Jim Woodhouse awarded the School a half holiday in recognition of the shooting team's success.

MRS THATCHER

On May 4, 1979, Margaret Thatcher brought to an end 258 years of men holding the office of Prime Minister.

The former Education Secretary under Ted Heath, who defeated him for the leadership of the Conservative Party in 1975, had sometimes looked shrill and unsure in opposition against the formidably experienced older figure of Jim Callaghan.

But rising inflation and a series of public strikes over pay during the 'Winter of Discontent' in 1978-79 swung things against Labour, and after losing a vote of no confidence on devolution, Callaghan triggered the General Election.

Thatcher's reign started badly, with recession caused by her tough economic policies. But her decision to send a Task Force to regain the Falkland Islands in 1982 helped to see her return to office again in 1983 and 1987, seeing off challenges from Michael Foot and Neil Kinnock.

By 1989-90, Mrs Thatcher began to lose her popularity and control. The ill-fated poll tax led to riots, and cabinet conflict led to the resignations of Chancellor Nigel Lawson and Deputy Prime Minister Sir Geoffrey Howe.

When Michael Heseltine challenged her for the leadership of the Conservative Party in November 1990 she stood firm, but eventually resigned, allowing newly promoted John Major to take over as Prime Minister.

Elevated to the House of Lords, Lady Thatcher died in 2013.

Bringing to an end 258 years of male Prime Ministerialship

1979 Margaret Thatcher 🇬🇧

1979

ROGER RINGROSE

Actor **Roger Ringrose** (SH 79-85) has appeared at the National Theatre and in TV programmes including *Waking the Dead, Silent Witness, Coronation Street, EastEnders, The Hour, Broadchurch, Spooks, Call the Midwife* and *Mr Selfridge*. After Rugby, Ringrose studied modern languages at Nottingham University. His 2016 portrayal of Alan Bennett at the Newbury Playhouse was very well received, with one reviewer writing: "Roger Ringrose IS Bennett, but not in some sort of superficial tribute act way. His performance is so convincing that he achieves the impossible, and we have Alan Bennett in the room."

FALL OF THE SHAH

The last Shah of Persia fled his country for exile on January 16, 1979, during the Iranian Revolution. He left behind a regency council which fell to rebel troops on February 11, ending monarchical rule and bringing Ayatollah Khomeini into power.

Shah Mohammed Reza Pahlevi and his wife, Empress Farah, had faced increasing opposition to their US-supported rule and lavish lifestyle. A campaign of civil resistance began and there were strikes and demonstrations in the late months of 1978.

The Shah and the Empress left Tehran on January 16, and flew to Aswan in Egypt. The couple's three youngest children had been flown to the US a day earlier.

Following the collapse of the monarchy, Iran voted to become an Islamic Republic on April 1, 1979. Khomeini, who had returned to Iran after living in exile in Paris, became Supreme Leader in December.

After leaving Iran, the former Shah lived temporarily in Egypt, Morocco, the Bahamas and Mexico. In October 1979 President Carter allowed the Shah into the US for medical treatment. He eventually settled in Egypt, where he died in July 1980.

Ayatollah Khomeini appointed Supreme Leader of Iran in 1979

PETER KEMBER

Peter Kember (Tu 79-82) entered Rugby in 1979. Today he is a musician and producer, known most widely by the name Sonic Boom, and co-founder of the band Spaceman 3.

GARETH LLOYD-JONES

At Rugby, **Gareth Lloyd-Jones** (M 80-84) become Holder of Bigside Bags and Deputy Head of School. In 1984 he joined the Tie Rack retail chain and later owned many of its key London stores. In the mid-1990s, Lloyd-Jones moved into the food and drink sector, founding the Madison coffee shop chain and expanding the Bel and the Dragon gastro pub business. In the past ten years he has successfully developed London pubs and restaurants and is now involved in a new steak house restaurant chain. Gareth became President of the Rugbeian Society in November 2016 for a term of three years.

JOHN LENNON

Former Beatle John Lennon escaped the goldfish bowl of Liverpool and London in the 1970s and settled in New York, becoming a house husband after the birth of his second son Sean in 1975.

In 1980 he emerged to record a new album with his wife Yoko Ono. *Double Fantasy* was released in November and on December 8, 1980, Lennon went back into the Record Plant Studio to work on a single track called *Walking on Thin Ice*, sung by Yoko.

Returning to his apartment in the Dakota building, Lennon was shot at five times by Mark David Chapman, a fan from Hawaii who earlier that day had had his copy of the new album signed by Lennon. Four bullets struck Lennon in the back and, despite efforts to save him, he passed away at New York's Roosevelt Hospital.

Within days thousands of fans held a candlelit silent vigil for Lennon and news of his death, like that of Elvis only three years earlier, sent shockwaves around the world.

Chapman, whose defence team claimed he was insane at the time of shooting, was sentenced to between 20 years and life for shooting Lennon and only recently emerged from the Wende Correctional Facility in Erie County, New York.

1980

ROB PENN

Rob Penn (SF 80-85) was born in Iraq in 1967 and grew up in Russia and the Isle of Man. Penn became a solicitor after leaving Rugby and studying history at Bristol University. He then decided to cycle around the world.

Since then he has worked as a writer, photographer and broadcaster on topics including cycling, travel and British woodlands. Penn's book *It's All About the Bike* was a *Sunday Times* bestseller in the UK and has been translated into thirteen languages. His most recent book, *The Man Who Made Things Out of Trees* was BBC Radio Four's 'Book of the Week' in December 2015.

In 2013, Penn cycled 1,200 km through the heart of the Amazon rainforest with former England cricket captain Andrew Flintoff for a Sky television programme.

TIM BUTCHER

The 2007 best-selling book *Blood River* by **Tim Butcher** (K 80-85) recounted his perilous crossing of the Congo in the footsteps of Victorian explorer HM Stanley. Born in 1967, Butcher won an exhibition to Oxford and later joined the *Daily Telegraph* where he worked for nearly 20 years as a leader writer, defence correspondent, Middle East correspondent and Africa bureau chief. Butcher's most recent book, *Trigger* (2014), traced the life of Gavrilo Princip, the man whose assassination of Archduke Franz Ferdinand sparked the First World War. In 2013, he was awarded the Mungo Park Medal by the Royal Scottish Geographical Society for his achievements as an explorer and educator.

ZIMBABWE

On Friday, April 18, 1980, Zimbabwe, formerly known as Rhodesia, was granted independence from the United Kingdom.

The transition from colonial to self-rule happened 90 years after a pioneer column belonging to Cecil Rhodes had entered Mashonaland, established Fort Salisbury and created the colony in his own name.

The first Prime Minister of independent Zimbabwe was Robert Mugabe, who then became President in 1987, a position he still holds.

In 1965 Rhodesia made a unilateral declaration of independence from the UK and established a white, segregationist government led by Ian Smith.

Smith's Republic of Southern Rhodesia did not have international recognition. In June 1979 the republic was replaced by Zimbabwe-Rhodesia after Abel Tendekayi Muzorewa won the first majority elections.

Again without international recognition, the republic reverted to British control called Rhodesia under governor Lord Soames, until Robert Mugabe's Zimbabwe African National Union (Zanu) won a majority, and independence for Zimbabwe.

Mugabe's Zimbabwe has earned a reputation for aggressively displacing white minority farmers, violently suppressing political opposition and rigging election results, but despite repeated calls for him to stand down, he has stayed in power.

In March 2015, Mugabe told Japanese journalists:

"You just go to Zimbabwe now and ask the people whether I should stand down. They will be angry with you.

"If they don't like my long stay in power they should criticise my people – I do not vote for myself into power."

FRANCESCA HUNT

After sixth form at Rugby, actress **Francesca Hunt** (Cr 80-82) studied at Oxford and then joined the Bristol Old Vic Theatre School from 1987-9 and the Moscow Arts Theatre School from 1989. As well as stage and television work, Hunt appeared in the films *A Prince Among Men* in 1997 and *Charlie and the Chocolate Factory* in 2005.

CHRISTOPHER HINGLEY

After Trinity College, Oxford, the **Rev Christopher Hingley** (SF 62-67) has dedicated his life to teaching in Zimbabwe, for many years as Principal of Petra High School under extraordinarily difficult conditions.

"There has been a great feeling of fear, which has particularly affected young people… messages warn people that if they go to work or take their children to school, their lives will be in danger.

"Our Aslan Camp as a refuge for children and teenagers from the stresses and fears of ordinary life has become more necessary than ever. All the complexity involved in the organisation is made worthwhile when you see the smiles of pure joy on the children's faces when you tell them their parents have agreed they can go on camp… and won't need to pay anything."

1980

REAGAN & POPE JOHN PAUL

Just months after singer John Lennon was shot and murdered in New York, assassination attempts were made on a US President and a Pope within six weeks of each other.

Ronald Reagan, who had regularly played a gun-toting cowboy as a Hollywood actor, had been President just 69 days when he was shot by John Hinkley Jr while leaving a speaking engagement at the Washington Hilton Hotel in Washington DC on March 30, 1981.

Shot in the chest and below the left arm, Reagan famously said to his wife Nancy: *"Sorry honey, I forgot to duck."* He made a full recovery and went on to win a second term of office in 1984.

At 5.19pm on May 13th, 1981, Pope John Paul II was travelling in his 'Popemobile' in St Peter's Square in Rome when he was shot in the chest.

The Pope's would-be assassin was Mehmet Ali Agca, a Turk who had previously been jailed for shooting dead a newspaper editor but escaped from prison.

Like Reagan, the Pope recovered and continued in office until he died in 2005. He visited Agca in prison, they became friends and the Pope's request for him to be pardoned and released was granted in 2000.

Agca returned to Turkey where he served the remainder of his original sentence before being released in 2010. In December 2014 he laid two dozen white roses at the tomb of Pope John Paul II in Rome.

The Fiat vehicle that carried the Pope on the day he was shot is now in the 'carriage museum' within Vatican City.

Both Ronald Reagan and Pope John Paul were both the target of assassination attempts in 1981

1981

DAVID OWEN & THE SDP

The election of a Conservative government in 1979 sent the Labour Party, still then led by defeated former Prime Minister Jim Callaghan, into turmoil.

As the Party lurched to the left, four prominent former Labour cabinet ministers decided to break away and launch a new, moderate centre-ground movement.

The Social Democrat Party was launched on March 26, 1981, by former Education Secretary Shirley Williams, former Defence Secretary Bill Rogers, former Foreign Secretary David Owen and former Home Secretary, Chancellor and European Commission President Roy Jenkins.

The new party gained a considerable following among voters who felt they were not served by the traditional Conservative, Labour and Liberal parties.

Roy Jenkins returned to the House of Commons as the SDP's first MP, representing Hillhead in Glasgow. In the 1983 General Election, an SDP-Liberal Alliance polled only 700,000 fewer votes than Labour, but this translated into only six SDP MPs.

In the 1987 election, the SDP and the Liberals campaigned jointly under their leaders, David Owen and David Steel, a stance which confused the electorate and they fared less well than four years earlier.

By the end of the 1980s, early enthusiasm for the SDP as a stand-alone political force had waned and the party merged with the Liberals to form the Liberal Democrat Party.

Roy Jenkins, who became Lord Jenkins of Hillhead and Liberal Leader in the House of Lords, died in 2003, while the other three founding members of the SDP are current members of the Upper House.

David Owen, leader of the Social Democrat Party formed in 1981

1981 Ronald Reagan 🇺🇸

THE FALKLANDS

The 1982 Falklands War started on April 2, 1982, and ended on June 14. In that time, just over 900 people died, including 255 British service personnel and three Falkland islanders.

In January 1982 the UK government had scrapped its only warship in the region (a survey ship although a Royal Navy vessel), believing Argentina would never fight for the Falklands. However, Argentina's struggling military junta, led by General Galtieri, saw an opportunity to boost its domestic popularity and sent an invasion party.

While America urged diplomacy, UK Prime Minister Margaret Thatcher dispatched a Task Force on April 5 to retake the islands.

Although British forces regained the islands, there were major setbacks, including the loss of six Royal Navy ships. The first was *HMS Sheffield* which was hit above the waterline by an Exocet missile, causing a fire that killed 20 crew.

Colonel H Jones, who died leading his unit during the battle for Goose Green, famously received a posthumous Victoria Cross for bravery, and Welsh Guardsman Simon Weston became a symbol of courage in adversity after being badly burned when his landing craft was bombed.

When Argentina invaded the Falkland Islands in 1982, Margaret Thatcher dispatched a Task Force to retake it… which they did in 73 days!

FIONA HUGHES D'AETH

Former Rugbeian Society President **Fiona Hughes-D'Aeth** (D 80-82) was among the first girls to attend the School. In Floreat in 2016, Fiona looked back on her time at Rugby.

"As a loyal Rugbeian what was my father to do, with three daughters, there was no chance to send them to follow in the family footsteps… until one bright day Rugby announced they were taking girls into the 6th form. We were signed up on the spot. Little did he realise the long-term consequences of this bold move, three Rugbeian daughters later, a son-in-law gained along the way and then a granddaughter joining the ranks too! We were told on arrival at Rugby in 1980 that we needed to be the three 'Bs: brainy, brawny and beautiful, well I am not sure that any of us met those criteria, but as one of 50 girls among over 700 boys it was hard not to stand out. Contrary to expectations we were not marked out of 10 as we walked into chapel on that first day but it was still daunting. Facing those challenges together meant the girls formed a tight, mutually supportive unit and many of my closest friendships today were forged in that two years at Rugby. Stand out memories? The smell of toasting white bread in the Dean kitchen at break, post Saturday night bar talking long into the night, dissecting the night's adventures, proudly watching the 1st XV on The Close. I vividly remember calling home from the trusty payphone in Dean and telling my father what a wonderful time I was having, blithely saying it was like a holiday camp – "bloody expensive holiday camp" was his reply but he would agree it was one of the best decisions he made to give his girls the chance to be ORs too."

Today Fiona is director of Gabbitas Education in the Middle East and is married to Jonathan Hughes-D'Aeth, Headmaster of Repton, Dubai and a former geography teacher and housemaster at Rugby.

1982.

RICHARD MONTGOMERIE

Son of former Michell Housemaster and classics teacher Bob Montgomerie, **Richard Montgomerie** (T 84-89) played first-class cricket for Sussex, Northamptonshire and Oxford University. On gaining a Blue in cricket at Oxford, Montgomerie made his first-class debut for Northamptonshire in 1994, staying for eight seasons. Joining Sussex in 1999, he was a member of the county championship winning side in 2003. At the end of the 2007 season, during which Sussex won their third championship in five years and he scored 1,000 runs at an average of 40, Montgomerie retired to go into teaching. Today he is a Housemaster at Eton where he also teaches chemistry and was master-in-charge of the XI for nine years. In total Montgomerie played 251 first class matches, scored 14,337 runs (average 35.84), and achieved 29 first class centuries with a highest score of 196.

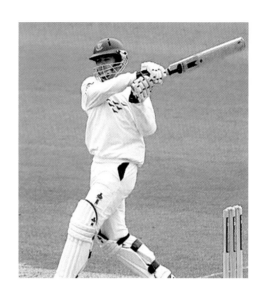

1984

JOHN ATTWATER

John Attwater (K 85-90) won a scholarship to Rugby in 1984 from the Prebendal School in Chichester, where he was a cathedral chorister. After a gap teaching in a prep school and studying PPE at Oxford, he worked for ten years at Wells Cathedral School. In 2005 he joined Sevenoaks School, where he became deputy head, and in 2010 he was appointed Headmaster of King Edward's School, Witley.

Attwater sits on on the advisory board of the The SpringBoard Bursary Foundation, which developed from Rugby School's Arnold Foundation.

RICHARD BULL

After thirteen years with one Head at the helm, Rugby then faced the unsettling experience of four in a decade.

Brian Rees, former Head of Merchant Taylors and Charterhouse, succeeded Woodhouse in 1980 and over three years managed to increase numbers to more than 800, their highest ever.

He left the School in difficult personal circumstances in 1984, and Rugby then turned to **John Marshall**, the long-serving first Housemaster of School House, to steady the ship.

With the support of other senior masters, Marshall ably led the School during this challenging time before the arrival of fellow Rugbeian **Richard Bull** from Oakham in 1985.

After his first stint at Rugby as a pupil, Bull completed his National Service in the Bedfordshire and Hertfordshire Regiment, before taking a First in Greats at Brasenose College, Oxford, where he gained a golf Blue.

He joined Eton as an assistant master in 1955, teaching Latin and Greek, and after thirteen years became a Housemaster known, with the support of his wife Anne, for his humane, caring approach and liberal outlook.

After 22 years at Eton, the Bulls moved to Oakham in 1977, where Richard successfully helped the school move to co-education. Bull recalled being 'summoned' by Rugby's Governors but, expecting not to be offered the job, spoke strongly about what he thought the School needed from its new Head.

Later he remarked:

Richard Bull: Head Master from 1985 to 1990

1985.

"I looked the other day at the coats of arms of Rugby Head Masters [displayed in School House] and decided that I am easily the least distinguished person ever to have been Head Master."

One of Bull's main missions at Rugby was to continue the process started by Jim Woodhouse and take the School into full co-education.

A year after arriving he submitted a plan to do this to the Governing Body, however it was rejected pending a fuller review of the School's future. The Governing Body adopted a wider package of reforms, which were carried through by Bull's successor after he resigned in 1990.

He retired to Radnorshire where he pursued his love of music, particularly the clarinet, and died in 2015.

Guy Ayling, who was Head of School at Rugby and went on to become Warden of Llandovery College, recalled Bull in *Floreat* in 2016.

"When Richard arrived…in 1985 it was a place in need of change. It seemed somehow to have stalled on a bridge in time, caught between its Tom Brown heritage and future of modern progressive educational thinking….into this maelstrom came a schoolmaster of rare calm, sensitivity and civilising potential.

"Our meetings were always conducted courteously, with Richard listening sympathetically and genuinely batting away wild and unrealistic demands for, amongst much else, a nightly pupil bar. He was therefore a man of forbearance, guiding me through discussion in which I demonstrated an over-confidence and naivety so typical of that age. It is for that kindness and compassion for which Richard should be best remembered."

On July 13, 1985, 1.9 billion people around the world watched 'Live Aid'

"LIVE AID"

On October 23, 1984 BBC reporter Michael Buerk reported on famine facing the people of Ethiopia.

Seeing the report, Irish singer Bob Geldof from the Boomtown Rats decided to act, working with fellow singer Midge Ure from Ultravox. By the end of the year the pair had marshalled a host of pop stars to record a charity single called *Do they know it's Christmas,* which became one of the biggest-selling records of all time.

While their first efforts were badged *Band Aid,* Geldof went one better on July 13, 1985, when he again persuaded stars to perform in key live concerts at Wembley Stadium in London and the John F Kennedy Stadium in Philadelphia, and called them *Live Aid.* The concerts featured a galaxy of stars, including in the UK, Queen, Status Quo, David Bowie, Dire Straits and Paul McCartney. Singer Phil Collins performed in London and then flew over on Concorde to take part in the Philadelphia event on the same day too.

An estimated 1.9 billion people watched the broadcasts, the biggest ever known, across 150 nations.

The events raised an estimated £150m for famine relief, fundraising helped by emotive appeals by Geldof during the London concert, including the words:

"Don't go to the pub tonight. Please stay in and give us your money. There are people dying now."

Geldof later received an honorary knighthood for his work.

1985
Andrew Beardon (Sh 85-90) and colleague **Simon Harwood** crept into Kilbracken one night and stole a silver sword from the dining room wall. They quickly returned the sword on discovering it was worth thousands of pounds.

MIKHAIL GORBACHEV

Leonid Brezhnev led the Soviet Union from 1964 to 1982, lending a degree of constancy to one of the nuclear world superpowers, while the other was led by five Presidents, only three of whom were elected.

Over the next three years his two successors, Yuri Andropov and Konstantin Chernenko, died in office.

When Mikhail Gorbachev, aged 54, was appointed in 1985 to become the USSR's fourth leader in three years, few imagined what would happen next.

Instead of continuing the unbending, anti-Western stance of the USSR, Gorbachev oversaw a revolution as seismic, but less violent, as the overthrow of Tsarist rule in 1917.

During his time as Soviet leader, Gorbachev's 'glasnost' (openness) and 'perestroika' (restructuring) policies started domestic reform. He built strong relationships with key Western leaders like Margaret Thatcher and Ronald Reagan and agreed to cut the USSR's stockpile of nuclear weapons.

By the time he left office in 1991, Communism had all but ended, the Berlin Wall had fallen and long-serving Eastern Bloc dictators like Romania's Nicolae Ceausescu had been overthrown.

Gorbachev received the Nobel Peace Prize in 1990 and later founded the International Foundation for Socio-Economic and Political Studies (The Gorbachev Foundation).

Gorbachev's 'glasnost' and 'perestroika' led to domestic reform in the USSR

1985.
1985-9 .

DISASTERS

A series of seemingly unending large-scale tragedies in the UK claimed the lives of more than 700 people in the second half of the 1980s.

A fire at Bradford City football ground on May 11, 1985 killed 56 and injured at least 265.

On March 6, 1987, the ferry *Herald of Free Enterprise* capsized just after leaving the Belgian port of Zeebrugge, killing 193 passengers and crew.

Eight months later, on November 18, a fire at King's Cross St Pancras tube station killed 31 people and injured 100.

On December 21, 1988, 243 passengers and sixteen crew were killed when a terrorist bomb blew apart Pan Am Flight 103 in the skies above Lockerbie in Scotland.

Just 18 days later, a Boeing 737-400 crashed on the embankment of the M1 motorway near Kegworth while attempting to land at East Midlands

Airport, killing 47 people and injuring 74 others.

Four months later, on April 15, 1989, 96 people were crushed to death and 766 injured, at a football match between Liverpool and Nottingham Forest at Hillsborough Stadium, Sheffield.

And four months later, 51 people were drowned when the party pleasure boat *Marchioness* collided with the dredger *Bowbelle* on the River Thames on August 20, 1989.

Bradford City Stadium   *Herald of Free Enterprise*   *Fire at King's Cross*   *Locke*

JOHN GILLESPIE MAGEE JR

In January 1986, President Reagan quoted *High Flight* by Rugbeian poet **John Gillespie Magee Jr** (9 June 1922 – 11 December 1941) in his address to the American people after the Challenger space disaster. The opening lines are…
'Oh! I have slipped the surly bonds of Earth/And danced the skies on laughter-silvered wings'
They speak of Magee's airborne exhilaration, but it was the last…

'Put out my hand, and touched the face of God'
which Reagan borrowed to express the sorrow of his nation. Magee (1935-39) had won the School poetry prize in 1938. He visited the US in 1939 but because of the outbreak of war did not return for his final year. He served in the Royal Canadian Air Force and died in a mid-air collision over Lincolnshire in 1941.

1986

1986

In 1986 **Camilla Dyson** (D 84-86), a keen orienteer, was the first and only female entrant of the Crick, posting a remarkable time of 1:14:16, ahead of most of the male runners. In 1988, the 150th anniversary of the first Crick Run was marked by 88 Rugbeian individuals taking part, as well as seventeen older ORs who covered the course as a relay!

Rugbeians have also been invited to run the Crick with the School since 2004 and over 50 now regularly do so each year.

Am 103

Plane crash on the M1

Hillsborough

The 'Marchioness' disaster

GEOFF FOXCROFT

For more than 40 years Geoff Foxcroft OBE was a leading figure in science education. He taught physics at Rugby from 1958 to 1986 and was a most distinguished head of science for 21 years. He played a major part in introducing modern physics into schools and was a key member of the team which developed the Nuffield A-level physics course, changing for a generation the teaching of post-sixteen physics.

The son of a bookstall manager at Lime Street station, he gained a first at Cambridge and communicated his enthusiasm for physics to generations of pupils, many of whom enjoyed successful scientific careers. In retirement, he brought his wisdom and humanity to his membership of the Governing Body. **IN**

Foxcroft, a leading figure in science education

1986.

1988.

RUPERT BROOKE

Rupert Brooke House developed from a row of four houses built in the mid-19th century. For many years, the building which forms the private side was home to Kenneth Stubbs, Director of Music for a quarter of a century. A keen plantsman, Stubbs created a garden for many years known as Stubbs's Piece, now occupied by the new Modern Languages Centre. In 1988 the four houses became one sixth-form boarding house named after Rupert Brooke. The first Housemaster from 1989 to 1994 was Stephen Drew. In its first year, the house had 38 girls. In 1993, with full co-education increasing the number of girls, the decision was made to convert the staff bar and dining room, which took up part of the building, into facilities for the girls (minus bar). In 2000 the Sunnyside building, next to the Estates Department, was annexed to Brooke to accommodate the increased number of girls, before Tudor House was converted to a girls' boarding house in 2002. The result was that for two years Brooke had 50 girls, with a further 26 in Sunnyside. In 2002 the Sunnyside girls moved across the road to Tudor. **RM**

A 27-mile concrete barrier divided East from West Germany for 29 years, before it was pulled down in 1989

FALL OF THE BERLIN WALL

On August 13, 1961 the German Democratic Republic (GDR) began to build a concrete barrier separating East and West Berlin.

The Berlin Wall symbolised the divide between capitalist West and communist East Germany. The GDR decided to build it to protect its people against 'fascists' wanting to stop a socialist state being built in East Germany.

The 27-mile barrier consisted of two concrete walls with a 160-yard 'death strip' in between, containing watchtowers, anti-vehicle trenches, guard dog runs, floodlights and machine guns.

During the time it stood, around 5,000 people attempted to escape over the wall into West Berlin of whom around 200 died trying.

The barrier lasted until November 9, 1989, when East German officials decided to open up the wall following a build-up of political unrest and erosion of Communist power in Eastern Bloc countries. Official demolition of the wall began on June 13, 1990, and took two years.

The fall of the Berlin Wall paved the way for East and West Germany to be reunited, which took place formally on October 3, 1990.

MASSACRE IN TIANANMEN SQUARE

A people's protest movement for less state corruption and increased democracy was bloodily crushed in Tiananmen Square, Beijing, on June 3, 1989.

Student-led demonstrators took up residence in the square for seven weeks, demanding reform. Eventually the Chinese authorities lost patience and sent in soldiers with guns and tanks to suppress the protest.

Hundreds of protestors were shot or crushed by vehicles but the official death count is unknown. Operating theatres at a nearby children's hospital were filled by casualties with gunshot wounds, many of them uninvolved local residents.

One eyewitness said:

"We took the wounded on stretchers and went down [Tiananmen] Square. As we went down the side of the Square, we saw soldiers with large plastic bags. They were putting people in the bags. I could not tell how many people...

US President George Bush said he deeply deplored the use of force and UK Prime Minister Margaret Thatcher said she was *"shocked and appalled by the shootings"*.

In 2004, the *New York Times* wrote:

"It's often said that an impoverished, poorly educated, agrarian country like China cannot sustain democracy. Yet my most powerful memory of that night 15 years ago is of the peasants who had come to Beijing to work as rickshaw drivers. During each lull in the firing, we could see the injured, caught in a no-man's-land between us and the troops. We wanted to rescue them but didn't have the guts. While most of us in the crowd cowered and sought cover, it was those uneducated rickshaw drivers who pedalled out directly toward the troops to pick up the bodies of the dead and wounded."

A brave demonstration for more democracy in China that was brutally crushed

1989.

THE SPORTS CENTRE

In 1989 the decision was made to consolidate and develop the sports facilities into a new purpose-built centre. The magnificent outdoor 'Tosh' would provide the foundation, being used as the basis for a new indoor heated pool. The first phase would include the 25-metre pool, a multi-use sports hall and three squash courts. A second phase was to include more squash courts, two Rugby Fives courts, a weights room and expanded changing facilities. The building was opened in April 1991 by the Duchess of Kent.

After refurbishment work in 2003, the fitness centre was added and opened in 2005. The addition of the cafeteria and meeting room offered welcome additions to the centre and in 2010 the long planned Rugby Fives courts were added to the complex. **RM**

The Sports Centre swimming pool

The Design Centre

The Lewis Gallery

THE DESIGN & TECHNOLOGY CENTRE

Announced at the same time as the Sports Centre, the Craft, Design and Technology Centre, now known just as the Design Centre, was built to bring together Art, Art History, Ceramics and Design Technology (CDT). The 11,000 square-foot complex also houses a major Media Centre, which includes a broadcast-quality television studio and three editing suites. A first-floor bridge links the centre to the Science Schools. Graphic Design and Photography are also part of the complex with the main Photography room taking up residence in one third of the old fives courts.

In 2006, with generous funding from a former Rugbeian, the new art gallery, The Lewis Gallery, was opened in what had been two of the three fives courts built in 1860. **RM**

THE INTERNET

If the inventions of the telephone in 1876 and television in 1926 were the first steps in the development of modern mass communication, it took another 63 years for perhaps the biggest leap of all.

While working at the CERN particle physics laboratory in Geneva, Tim-Berners Lee devised an electronic based communication system using hypertext. He called it the World Wide Web.

Having established the idea and concept, Lee went a step further and on August 6, 1991, created the first web site, called http://info.cern.ch. This explained the concept of the web and guided users on setting up websites.

Today, four out of every ten people on earth has an internet connection compared to one in every 100 in 1995. The number of internet users reached a billion in 2005 and in 2016 was nearly three and a half billion.

Berners-Lee, who was born in 1955 and knighted by the Queen in 2004, is quoted as saying:

"The Web as I envisaged it, we have not seen yet. The future is still so much bigger than the past."

'The future is still so much bigger than the past'....and it still is !

1989.

INVASION OF KUWAIT

On August 2, 1990, Saddam Hussein's Iraqi Army entered and occupied neighbouring Kuwait. In response a coalition of 34 nations, led by the United States, embarked on the Gulf War which lasted until February 28, 1991.

Iraq entered Kuwait to obtain oil reserves and expand its power in the region.

The coalition formed to remove Iraq troops, the largest since the Second World War, launched Operation Desert Storm on January 16, 1991, with a massive air and naval bombardment. This was followed by a successful ground assault on February 24.

Coalition forces lost around 150 troops in the conflict against 20,000 to 30,000 on the Iraqi side.

A key personality during the conflict, apart from Saddam Hussein and US President George Bush, was US General Norman Schwarzkopf.

Commenting on the effectiveness of the coalition's ground forces, Schwarzkopf said:

"Yesterday at the beginning of the ground war Iraq had the fourth largest army in the world. Today they have the second largest army in Iraq."

1990

A coalition of 34 nations launched 'Desert Storm' in 1990 to force Iraq from Kuwait

MICHAEL MAVOR

Described by *The Scotsman* as *"probably the most talented all-round schoolmaster of his generation"*, Michael Mavor was not the first man from north of Hadrian's Wall to lead Rugby.

But he was the first to play bagpipes in the New Quad, the first to make Rugby fully co-educational, and the first to appoint a girl, Louise Woolcock, as Head of School.

As a golf enthusiast all his life, Mavor possessed every type of club needed to be a good teacher and school leader.

Born in Malaysia in 1947 he won an exhibition to read English at Cambridge, via Loretto, where he had been captain of cricket, hockey and golf, editor of the school paper, Head Boy and pipe major.

In 1969 he headed to Illinois for four years on a university teaching fellowship before returning to Tonbridge School, where he taught English and drama, coached sport and became director of studies.

At just 31, in 1979, Mavor was appointed headmaster of Gordonstoun. There he oversaw schooling for Princes Andrew and Edward, raised academic standards and proved adept at dealing with local difficulties, such as expelling nine pupils a year after his arrival for possessing cannabis.

Returning south to Rugby in 1990 he arrived with bold plans for the School.

Mavor was not backward in his reforms, taking the School fully co-educational and appointing its first head girl, despite banner-waving protests and boys boycotting a chapel service marking the 200th anniversary of the birth of fellow Rugby reformer Thomas Arnold.

Mavor was lured back to his old school, Loretto, in 2001 which he led until retirement in 2008.

Michael Mavor: Head Master from 1990 to 2001 took the School fully co-educational

An accomplished speaker and a stickler for accuracy and standards, Mavor also possessed a sense of spirit that appealed to pupils and a strong pastoral touch.

At Rugby he liked to stand on the Chapel steps and greet pupils by name. He also took pupils who were ill a bag of Maltesers, believing they were the best medicine.

More adventurously, he was not afraid to play his bagpipes in public, or skateboard or strike golfballs down the chapel aisles of the schools he led.

Passing away suddenly aged 62 in 2009, Mavor's contribution to Rugby was recalled in the *Daily Telegraph*.

"The transformation of Rugby into a great co-educational boarding school was his lasting achievement, but colleagues and old pupils will remember principally a headmaster who, through all his administrative trials and tribulations, remained a schoolmaster; he had a cheerful word for each of them and a real interest in what they were doing, which continued long after they had left school. It helped that he was widely gifted – 'the nearest thing to a Renaissance man,' said a former colleague, 'that you are likely to meet'.

The same article added: *"Rugby was a [tougher] proposition. Numbers were declining, and the School was in danger of losing its reputation as one of England's pre-eminent schools. With the support of his governors but opposition from a sizeable minority of masters and boys, Mavor embarked immediately on making the school co-educational.*

"A boys' school with girls was not good enough: as soon as possible there were to be equal numbers of boys and girls. It was a brave decision for a proudly masculine school, birthplace of the most manly form of football. Boys proclaimed on posters that they were 'Not Sexist. Just traditionalist.'

"Mavor responded with good humour and quiet determination. His insistence that the girls must have excellent facilities, but so must the boys, helped. He was brave, too, in insisting on higher entry standards, even if that meant vacancies for a time. Few headmasters transform the tone and atmosphere of the school they inherit – but Mavor did – and Rugby's present standing owes much to his vision and to the refurbishment and rebuilding to which he committed the school."

LUKE PEBODY

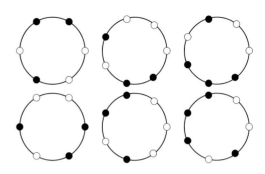

Born in 1977, Rugbeian **Luke Pebody** (Tu 90-93) contributed to solving the mathematical 'necklace problem'. After leaving Rugby in 1993 he went to Cambridge to study maths at the age of sixteen. During a doctoral degree at the University of Memphis, Luke presented a possible solution for a maths question concerning the number of stages needed to reassemble black and white beads in a necklace. He showed that six stages were sufficient, regardless of the number of beads.

1990.

MARSHALL

Warwickshire's decision to change the age of transfer to secondary school had led to a falling off in the numbers of boys moving from Lawrence Sheriff to Rugby. The alteration meant boys would have to make two changes of school, at twelve+ and thirteen+. The decision was made to provide entry for local boys at 12, and in January 1990 the first entrance examination was held. September of that year saw the first eleven boys arriving at the newly converted 'Stables' in the south-west corner of The Close. The

Head Master's stables had been built in 1878, when the original site became part of New Quad. The Junior Department, so named, was the day house and feeder for Town and Southfield. John Marshall, a former pupil, member of staff and Scottish international rugby player, ran the Junior Department from its creation until 1994. By 1996 numbers had increased and the demand for a second year group meant there were nine members of JD1 and eight members of JD2. Accommodation for the second year was provided

by the refurbishment of the old Butterfield cricket pavilion which looks out on to New Bigside. After much discussion it was decided that the Junior Department was in truth another day house and should have a name and a house emblem. The name was obvious after John Marshall had taken on and developed the group. The house emblem proved to be more problematic with several images rejected. The final emblem is the rowan, a symbol of good luck and protection, a good Scottish tree. The design is from an illustration by George Barnard who had been Drawing Master at Rugby from the 1840s. In September 1997, the newly-named Marshall House boasted some 30 pupils. The house was officially re-named and opened on May 17, 1997. This occasion saw the re-naming of the year-groups in Marshall House, from JD1 and 2 to G1 and G2 (it was decided that H-Block might not be the best name). Whilst most Marshall House pupils move up into Town and Southfield, there have been occasional exceptions who have moved up into boarding. **RM**

MANDELA RELEASED

At nearly quarter past four in the afternoon on February 11, 1990, Nelson Mandela was released from prison. The symbol of resistance to South Africa's apartheid regime had spent 27 years locked up for his beliefs.

Born in July 1918, Mandela studied law at university and then became a founding member of the African National Congress's youth league. In 1961 he led a sabotage campaign against the government and was sentenced to life imprisonment a year later for trying to overthrow the state.

Mandela was held in three prisons, most famously in solitary confinement on Robben Island. International protests for his release led eventually to President FW de Klerk relaxing apartheid laws and allowing Mandela to go free.

On his release from prison, Mandela told a crowd of thousands at City Hall in Cape Town: *"I greet you all in the name of peace, democracy and freedom for all."*

In 1994 Mandela became South Africa's first black president, creating a Truth and Reconciliation Commission to look at past human rights issues and endeavouring to lead a reforming government.

In 1995 he famously appeared at the Rugby World Cup Final at Ellis Park Stadium in Johannesburg where South Africa, the host nation, faced New Zealand. Wearing a green Springbok jersey and cap, Mandela handed the Webb Ellis trophy to South Africa's victorious captain, Francois Pienaar, at the end of the match. The game was later made into a film called *Invictus* with Morgan Freeman playing Mandela.

Mandela won the 1993 Nobel Peace Prize and died in December 2013.

After 27 years in prison, Nelson Mandela was released in 1990, and in 1994 became South Africa's first black President

1990s

School classics' teachers Ian Barlow and Keith Maclennan discovered a 1903 entrance scholarship paper to Rugby in a cupboard and could not answer the Latin questions. They found some, but not all, the answers in a Latin Primer text book.

THE YUGOSLAV WARS

While the break-up of the Eastern Bloc following the fall of the Soviet Union ended the East-West Cold War, the demise of communism triggered a decade of brutal and bloody nationalist conflict in former Yugoslav territories which started in 1991.

Yugoslavia was formed officially in 1918 and then recreated after the Second World War. It encompassed Bosnia-Herzegovina, Croatia, Macedonia, Montenegro, Serbia and Slovenia, and two autonomous Serbian provinces, Kosovo and Vojvodina.

Under Marshal Tito, Yugoslavia was a stable region but after the fall of communism deep nationalist divisions re-emerged.

A series of separate conflicts over ten years, collectively known as the Yugoslav Wars, included the 1991 War in Slovenia, the 1991-95 Croatian War of Independence, the 1992-5 Bosnian War and the 1998-99 Kosovo War.

Violent ethnic cleansing, crimes against humanity and rape were common, with opposing military leaders from different sides later facing genocide charges.

Although an estimated 140,000 people lost their lives during the Yugoslav Wars, the conflict was largely ignored by many other European countries, including those who had fought against German nationalism from 1939-45.

The late journalist Christopher Hitchens criticised Western indifference to the conflict:

"That war [Bosnian war] in the early 1990s changed a lot for me. I never thought I would see, in Europe, a full-dress reprise of internment camps, the mass murder of civilians, the reinstitution of torture and rape as acts of policy. And I didn't expect so many of my comrades to be indifferent – or even take the side of the fascists."

Largely ignored by the rest of Europe, 140,000 people lost their lives in the 'Yugoslav Wars' between 1991 and 1999

1991-2001.

SOUTHFIELD

Southfield House was bought by the School in 1923, along with adjoining land, to enable the building of Sheriff House. It first appears in the Blue Books of 1984 as a sixth form girls' boarding house, under Tony Tiffin, but with the advent of full co-education in 1993, it became the first house for day girls. The first cohort of boarders in Southfield numbered about twelve, rising to eighteen by 1992. Just before the change, it had been proposed that Sunnyside, then staff accommodation, would become the new day house. In the event, Southfield became the day house. The lack of dining facilities meant Southfield girls continued to lunch in other houses, particularly Town House. The house was taken over, in 1996, by Frances Myers who was the first female scientist and member of the Biology Department. Christmas Suppers were held in OBS, as the continued lack of a Southfield dining room prevented 'home dining'. 2003 saw the first Southfield-only house play. In previous years this had been a joint venture with Town House. The play was *The Ash Girl*, by Timberlake Wertenbaker. With the need for a new girls' boarding house identified by 2003, the Southfield building was chosen as the most suitable location. In April 2005 Southfield house moved across the road, to Sunnyside. The original proposal of Sunnyside as the day house for girls had finally been completed and a new extension with room for some 57 day girls was created. **RM**

1993.

1993 Bill Clinton

1994.

31.5 miles long, the tunnel between England and France took six years to build

THE CHANNEL TUNNEL

In 1802 the idea of building an underwater tunnel between England and France was first mooted. But it was nearly 200 years before the concept became reality.

The Channel Tunnel was formally opened by the Queen and France's President Mitterand on May 6, 1994. The tunnel is 31.5 miles long, and its 23.5 mile stretch under water is the longest undersea section of any tunnel in the world.

The tunnel cost £4.65 billion (eight times higher than expected), took six years to build, and involved 13,000 people, ten of whom died (eight of them British) during the construction.

Boring machines used to dig the tunnel together weighed 12,000 tonnes (more than the Eiffel Tower) and each was as long as two football pitches. One from the British side remains buried under the Channel and another was sold on eBay for £39,999 in 2004.

The American Society of Civil Engineers has recognised the Channel Tunnel as one of the 'Seven Wonders of the Modern World'. Others include the Empire State Building in New York and the Panama Canal.

1995

ANDREW KEELING

Major General **Andy Keeling** CB CBE (T 56-61) joined the Royal Marines in September 1961 and served for 34 years during which he served in Borneo, Aden, Cyprus, the Falklands, Northern Ireland and North Iraq. He played hockey and squash for the Royal Navy. He commanded at all levels, including 45 Commando and 3rd Commando Brigade. He was Representative Colonel Commandant from 1998-2002.

Since retiring he has been closely involved with several military charities including Blind Veterans UK (Chairman) and the Special Boat Service Association (President).

In August 2014 Andy completed a South Downs Yomp, walking 100 miles of the South Downs Way for The Royal Marines Charitable Trust Fund.

LOUISE HARRISON

In 1995, **Louise Harrison**, née Woolcock (B 94-96), became the School's first female Head of School. Her appointment caused uproar and among some boys who objected to being led by a girl. Recalling the moment, Louise wrote:

"In the summer term of 1995 I was in the LXX of Bradley House. I had been at Rugby for only ten months, but was enjoying it enormously. I was relieved to have got through the first lot of A level exams, had made a fantastic group of friends and was enjoying the fast-paced life...boarding school offers. Around this time of year the Levée are chosen for the forthcoming year. I knew that my Housemistress had put me forward to be interviewed by the Headmaster for, I thought, the job of Deputy Head of School and there was lots of talk around the School as to who would get what. No one was more surprised than me when the Headmaster called myself and Huw Brown to be Joint Heads of School! A week before my appointment I had posed for the press holding a portrait of Thomas Arnold as part of a story The Times were running on Arnold's life. I thought nothing more about it...until one of the journalists came

back a few days later and asked to take some more photos. Early the next morning, however, my housemate Ella came running down the corridor and banged on my door. Apparently the photos had made it to the front page of The Times, *with a headline about the boys revolting, soon to be a common theme. By then my parents had already been warned by a cousin who had seen the front page on her early morning commute. They were all bemused by the strength of the boys' reaction and the press excitement. The boys had revolted a few days beforehand. The rebels had missed Chapel, put up posters, and, of course, called the papers. This might sound minor in this age of freedom, but then, it was a reasonably big deal for us. Especially a big deal as it was because of me! Huw Brown was in Whitelaw, so many of the Whitelaw boys ignored the boycott. Huw and I were Chemistry Lab partners and got on well. One night around that time one of the boys, from my year in Michell (I think), decided to scale the Chapel in order to put up the posters. I remember one of them: 'Girls don't play rugby, boys don't play netball – don't mix us up.' Of course, even then girls did play rugby and boys (certainly Aussie boys) did play netball with true masculine vigour,*

but the point was made. Another time he also scaled the Chapel to put a girl's bra on the roof. I liked him and I think he was probably just having fun! The press arrived en masse, or so it seemed to me. They asked lots of questions and tried to get me to say something negative about the boys. I have no idea what I did say, I just made it up as I went along. They also interviewed my friends and other pupils and door-stepped my mother when she got home from work. It was a crazy time. During the school year it was my girl friends in my house and the other girls' houses who kept me going. They had a tough time in lessons to support me, I know. I also got letters from girls in other schools wishing me well. As the year went by the boys realised I wasn't going to change their lives so radically that they would have to give up playing rugby or change the uniform to pink. They got used to me and by the time the next Joint HOS was appointed it had no effect on the School at all. By then, the first girls to join the lower school were about to enter the LXX and there were no single sex years left."

Continuing her connection with the School, Louise is now Honorary Secretary of the Rugbeian Society.

NATHAN WILLIAMSON

Nathan Williamson (Tu 92-97) was greatly influenced at Rugby by the then Head of Music, Peter Crook, and his piano teacher, Anthony Herschel Hill. After studies at the Guildhall School of Music and Drama, and Yale University, Nathan taught at the Yehudi Menuhin School before pursuing his career as a composer and concert pianist full time. He founded the Southwold Concert Series in 2008 which continues to grow in stature year on year.

Nathan has been commissioned to compose the '450th Overture' to celebrate the School's anniversary year.

1997.

DEATH OF DIANA

In the first week of September 1997 the world mourned Diana, Princess of Wales.

Killed on August 31 in a car crash in Paris with her boyfriend Dodi Al Fayed, Princess Diana was one of the most famous and photographed women in the world.

Diana's death produced a tidal wave of shock and grief in Britain and around the world. A mountain of flowers was placed outside Kensington Palace, her London home, and tributes poured in from world leaders.

The Queen was at her summer residence, Balmoral Castle, at the time of Diana's death and wanted to stay there to protect her grandsons, William and Harry.

However, she faced mounting public and media criticism for not returning to Buckingham Palace and also for not flying the Royal Standard at half mast. Listening to advice, the Queen came to London, lowered the flag and made a moving television broadcast.

Diana's funeral at Westminster Abbey on September 6 attracted around three million mourners and onlookers to London. It was broadcast to 200 countries in 44 languages and watched by 2.5 billion people.

As the Princess's coffin made its way to the Abbey, Princes William and Harry walked behind it with their grandfather Prince Philip.

Inside the Abbey, singer Elton John, a friend of the Princess, performed a new version of his song *Candle in the Wind*. The song, produced by former Beatles' producer Sir George Martin, was released on September 13, 1997, and sold over 33 million copies, the most for any single in history.

1997 Tony Blair 🇬🇧

TONY BLAIR

Nearly 20 years of Conservative rule came to a crashing end on May 2, 1997, when New Labour, led by a youthful Tony Blair, swept to power.

At 43, Blair was the century's youngest Prime Minister, gaining an incredible 179-seat overall majority, the biggest for any party since 1935.

Commenting on his victory, Blair said:

"Today, we are charged with the deep responsibility of government. Today, enough of talking - it is time now to do."

Speaking after his defeat, John Major said:

"When the curtain falls it's time to get off the stage and that is what I propose to do."

Tony Blair served as Prime Minister until 2007 when he handed over to his arch rival Gordon Brown

1997

As Chairman of Spectrum Communications, **Peter Berners-Price** (St 56-61) worked with **Hugh Davies** (St 55-60) to organise the 'Hong Kong Farewell' ceremony, which signalled the end of 150 years of British rule. Hugh was Chairman of the Joint Liaison Group responsible for negotiating the handover with the Chinese on behalf of Governor, Christopher Patten, and the Foreign and Commonwealth Office.

1998

A British designer created the 'Apple' icon

APPLE

Although Steve Jobs is credited as the man who created and rescued consumer electronics company Apple, it was British designer Jonathan Ive who first brought the company's design icon products to the market.

On August 15, 1998, Apple introduced a new all-in-one computer, designed by Ive, called the iMac, and sold nearly 800,000 in the first five months.

Apple followed up the iMac with the iPod in 2001, which sold 350 million units by 2012. Alongside this was the iPhone which was launched in June 2007 and sold more than 700 million units by 2015.

In 2012 Ive received a knighthood for his global design work. Steve Jobs (who once said *"What we're doing here will send a giant ripple through the universe"*) died in 2011 and a film about his life, with Michael Fassbender in the lead role, was released in 2015.

THE GOOD FRIDAY AGREEMENT

On Friday, April 10, 1988, the Good Friday Agreement was signed in Belfast. The historic document consisted of a multi-party agreement by most of Northern Ireland's political parties and an international agreement between the British and Irish governments.

Central to the agreement were key areas such as decommissioning of weapons by terrorist groups and implementing full civil and cultural rights.

Two referendums were held on the agreement in Britain and Ireland on May 22, 1998, and the agreement came into force on December 2, 1999.

The Good Friday Agreement effectively ended The Troubles in Northern Ireland, but at a price. The IRA eventually renounced its campaign of violence and gave up its weapons but the British government controversially agreed in return to release convicted IRA terrorists.

The late Mo Mowlam, as Northern Ireland Secretary, was a key figure behind the agreement, along with Prime Minister Tony Blair.

Arriving for the talks on April 8, Blair said:

"A day like today is not a day for soundbites, really. But I feel the hand of history upon our shoulders. I really do."

In contrast, blunt-speaking Mrs Mowlam was heard to say to Sinn Fein's Gerry Adams:

"Bloody well get on and do it, otherwise I'll head-butt you!"

Prime Minister Tony Blair signs the Good Friday Agreement with Irish Taoiseach Bertie Ahern

1998.

2000-2013
ARNOLD RELOADED

2000   THE NEW MILLENNIUM

2001 MICHAEL FOWLE
PATRICK DERHAM BECOMES HEAD

2001 9/11 & THE TWIN TOWERS

2002 POLLY STENHAM
EWEN FERGUSSON

2003 GRIFFIN
THE ARNOLD FOUNDATION FOR RUGBY SCHOOL

2003 ENGLAND WIN RUGBY WORLD CUP

2004 BOXING DAY TSUNAMI

2006 SAM RUDDOCK

2009 ROBERT SWANNELL

2009 BARACK OBAMA

2012 JUBILEE & THE OLYMPICS

MICHAEL FOWLE

Michael Fowle (St 53-58), chaired the School's Governing Body from 2002 to 2009, a period which covered the successful launch of the Arnold Foundation.

After leaving Rugby in 1958, Michael went to Clare College, Cambridge, and later qualified as an accountant with Peat Marwick (now KPMG). He spent 38 years with KPMG, 22 years as a Partner and held a range of senior positions, including Chairman of the company's London and South division. In addition to numerous directorships, Michael has been a Trustee of Place2Be, the Prince's School of Traditional Arts, the Prince's Drawing School, the Penguin Collectors' Society and a Director of the Independent Schools Council.

Michael and Margaret Fowle

2001 George Bush Jnr

2001

2000

THE NEW MILLENNIUM

The world saw in the Third Millennium on January 1, 2000, in spectacular style. Australia's Sydney Harbour hosted a fireworks extravaganza and in New York visitors were bombarded by four tonnes of confetti. In London, Prime Minister Tony Blair linked hands with the Queen to sing *Auld Lang Syne* in the controversial Millennium Dome, and two million people lined the banks of the River Thames to watch fireworks.

PATRICK DERHAM

Michael Mavor's call back to Loretto was urgent and therefore John Allen led the School ably for a term (as John Marshall had done 20 years before) until Patrick Derham was free to move from Solihull to take on the task.

Derham is a rarity amongst Rugby Heads. From a working-class background, he was born in 1959 to an Irish Catholic father and a Dutch mother. His early years were muddled – seven schools before he was twelve, then TS Arethusa, a Shaftesbury home training boys for the Merchant Marine. But after two years Arethusa closed and private philanthropy sent young Derham to Pangbourne. At Pangbourne he was Head of School before going to Cambridge for a First in History. He

is clear that it was his Pangbourne experience that convinced him of the benefits of independent school education and in particular the benefits of boarding education to children from unsettled homes.

Therefore, it was no surprise that after Cambridge Derham became a teacher in independent schools. Three years at Cheam were followed by fourteen at Radley, being Head of History twice and a housemaster, before going to Solihull as Headmaster in 1996. Five successful years at Solihull led him to Rugby at age 42 in 2001.

It is too early to assess Patrick's impact on Rugby. Certainly Rugby soon learnt that Patrick is not a patient man. It was clear from the beginning that Rugby in his time would be a School where innovation thrived, a School which was a leader and was seen to be a leader, a School which always emphasised service to others. There was no delay in leading – even though Patrick sometimes forgot that the Governing Body were not necessarily impressed by a Head who drummed his fingers on the table while they reflected upon his ideas.

It was probably at his first Governing Body meeting that Patrick declared, defying opposition (though there was none), that Rugby must have a fundraising foundation and that its task must be to provide means-tested boarding bursaries for children whose home backgrounds made boarding education crucial for their wellbeing.

Much work and two years later, the Arnold Foundation was born, setting the ambition that soon 10% of Rugby pupils would be funded either through the Lawrence Sheriff Bequest (day pupils) or through the Arnold Foundation (boarding pupils). Towards the end of 2016 nearly £20m had been raised, allowing 115 pupils to benefit from a Rugby education.

The Arnold Foundation led to a number of successful partnerships with organisations which could help Rugby recruit potential pupils – **Into**University, Eastside Young Leaders' Academy, Clarion Voice, Hawick High School, George Greens School on the Isle of Dogs and others – a model followed by other schools as they sought to widen access.

Next it was decided that the non-means-tested quantum of all academic and other scholarships (including awards to day foundationers) should be limited to 10% for fees, but all being augmentable to over 100% depending on family means, a lead followed by many other independent schools.

The Cambridge Pre-U was born in Patrick's Rugby study, when he discovered that a number of other independent school Heads shared his concern that many schools were shifting to the International Baccalaureate for the wrong reasons and that a strong alternative was needed to modular A levels. Patrick and Rugby took a leading role in the immensely stimulating work with Cambridge Assessment, going back to first principles in drawing up an exam system. Rugby also led the way with the ground-breaking Extended Project.

From early in Patrick's time, Rugby had partnered in several ways with Bishop Wulstan, the Roman Catholic secondary school on the Barby Road, opposite Hillbrow. Sadly the Church decided that Bishop Wulstan had to close. After the premises had been unoccupied for several years the School was able to acquire them on the open market, to form the superb facilities of the Collingwood Centre – another assembly hall / performance venue, a second sports hall and a Sixth Form Centre, as well as fine teaching facilities and considerable free land.

Finally, the SpringBoard Bursary Foundation. Six years after the beginnings of the Arnold Foundation, Patrick led the Arnold Foundation Board and the Governing Body to consider how the Arnold Foundation experience could benefit many more pupils in many more schools.

In 2012, Rugby commissioned an extensive evaluation of the scalability of the Arnold Foundation's model to a national level, undertaken *pro bono* by McKinseys. There was scope and demand for a national roll out: the SpringBoard Bursary Foundation was born from Rugby's experience, driven by Patrick, with its own chief executive and staff, its own distinguished board of trustees and its own fundraising.

In terms of day to day life, Patrick and Alison made Rugby's Common Room and all staff feel they were part of a community. He knew everyone by name, or certainly by reputation, whether they were teaching or in Operations and Admin. He and Alison never failed to have a smile or word for everybody; they loved and valued that sense of belonging to the Rugby School community. Their Friday night Advent term suppers for teaching staff were a valuable part of the integration process and Patrick's competitive spirit on the table tennis table reduced many almost to tears!

In terms of the wider community, both Patrick and Alison were great supporters of the Bradby Club, always hosting the annual Garden Party at Rokeby and running the annual Quiz Night – Patrick loves quizzes and, of course, must win!

Patrick was no soft touch, but yet, as Common Room members can attest, when things had gone wrong (as they do), he was always a great support. Even though his impatience was sometimes as apparent to staff as it was to the Governing Body, there was huge respect for Patrick as a Head.

Patrick Derham: Head Master from 2001 to 2014

2001

9/11 &
THE TWIN TOWERS

On the morning of September 11, 2001, nineteen al-Quaeda terrorists hijacked four planes heading for the United States.

They crashed two into the twin towers of the World Trade Center in New York, and one on to the Pentagon in Washington DC. A fourth crash landed in a field in Arlingon County, Virginia, after the hijackers were overpowered by passengers.

The world watched live on television the planes flying into the World Trade Center and within two hours both 110-storey buildings had collapsed.

The terrorist attacks on America killed 2,996 people (including nineteen highjackers, 343 firefighters and 72 law enforcement officers) of whom 67 were British. They also caused billions of pounds in infrastructure damage.

After several months, Osama Bin Laden, leader of al-Qaeda, claimed responsibility for the attacks. The action prompted widespread retaliation by the West including the invasion of Afghanistan, the ill-fated second war in Iraq in 2003 and the setting up of the US-run Guantanamo Bay prison camp in Cuba.

It took US Special Forces until May 2, 2011, to hunt down and kill Bin Laden. Meanwhile the site of the twin towers, known as Ground Zero, is marked by pools in memory of those who died, their names engraved in stones surrounding the water.

9/11….a moment in history that shocked the world

POLLY STENHAM

Playwright **Polly Stenham** (St 02-04) joined the School in the sixth form in 2002.

Daughter of Channel Four founder and Royal College of Art Chairman 'Cob' Stenham, Polly showed her early talent with an adaptation of *Alice in Wonderland* as a Stanley House play. This involved a montage of film and acting in which the Cheshire Cat appeared in a tree outside the School bookshop.

Despite dyslexia, Stenham began an English degree at UCL but left aged 20 after one year, when her first play *That Face* was premiered at the Royal Court Theatre in London in 2007.

The play won the Evening Standard's Charles Wintour Award, a Critics' award for the Most Promising Playwright of that season and the Theatrical Management Association's Award for Best New Play. Sadly her father died in 2006 and did not live to see the play.

Stenham's 2009 play *Tusk Tusk*, directed by Jeremey Herrin, was also staged at the Royal Court, followed by *No Quarter* in 2013. Her 2014 play *Hotel* was performed at the National Theatre.

Lizzie Beesley, who taught Stenham English at Rugby, described her as

"One of the most dynamic and entertaining playwrights in the UK today. Polly is a real tour de force and is clearly only at the beginning of what should be a very lengthy and prodigious career. I hope…Rugbeians will be as inspired by her work as she was by Tennessee Williams and Edward Albee and become the muse for future writers. That Face *has already been set as an A level text so Polly is already inspiring students to think about, and to analyse, some of the most difficult sociological problems an artist can confront."*

EWEN FERGUSSON

Former British Ambassador to France **Sir Ewen Fergusson** (SH 45-51) was chair of the Governing Body from 1995 to 2002.

Born in 1932, after leaving Rugby Sir Ewen went to Oriel College, Oxford. He played rugby for the university and gained five caps for Scotland as lock making his debut against France at Murrayfield on January 9, 1954.

Following two years with the King's Royal Rifle Corps, Sir Ewen became a diplomat in 1956 and over the next 35 years served in senior posts including British Ambassador to South Africa from 1982-4 and to France from 1987-92.

Alongside his work on the Governing Body, he was Chairman of Coutts and the Savoy Group in the 1990s and a trustee of the National Gallery from 1995-2002.

An honorary fellow of his old Oxford college, Sir Ewen was appointed KCMG in 1987, GCVO in 1992 and GCMG in 1993.

2002.

GRIFFIN

Rugby's ten-year co-education programme was completed with the creation of Griffin House in September 2003. The house takes its name from the three Griffin heads on the School's coat of arms.

The first seven Griffin girls started the F Block in 2003. In September 2004, they were joined by a new F Block year of six and ten LXX girls. They were based at 5-7 Horton Crescent in one of the staff houses while the new boarding house was built. This brought the total number of girls' houses to six. This new thirteen-eighteen boarding house, which accommodates 44 girls, is on the site of the old Southfield House, next to the Sports Centre. Isabel Wolff, one of the first girls to enter Rugby in 1976, officially opened Griffin House in September 2005.

2003.

ENGLAND WIN RUGBY WORLD CUP

On November 22, 2003, Jonny Wilkinson, fly-half for the England rugby team, kicked a last-gasp injury time drop goal.

His effort gave England a 20-17 victory over their arch rivals Australia who hosted the match in their own back yard.

Going into the event, the England team, led by the imperious Leicester lock Martin Johnson and coached by Clive (now Sir Clive) Woodward, were the number one team in the world.

Earlier the same year, England had won the Six Nations Grand Slam, their first for eight years and their ranks included a galaxy of world-class players including Jason Robinson, Jason Leonard, Richard Hill, Matt Dawson and Will Greenwood.

Also in the team was winger Ben Cohen, nephew of 1966 England football World Cup winner George Cohen.

After England won the 2003 final, Martin Johnson was handed the Webb Ellis Cup, named after the Rugbeian who created the game.

Martin Johnson raises the Webb Ellis Cup…
but it was Jonny Wilkinson who kicked the winner!

2003

THE ARNOLD FOUNDATION FOR RUGBY SCHOOL

The Arnold Foundation was set up in 2003 to offer full bursaries to talented students with a need for boarding. Alongside the day places funded by Lawrence Sheriff's bequest, this programme has transformed the lives of many young people and enriched the life and culture of the School as well.

Rugby was one of the first independent schools in the country to offer such a programme. Its success is distinguished by a genuine desire by Rugby School to transform the lives of young people, a proven commitment to finding the right pupils in the first place and a commitment to ensuring long-term pastoral support. Sitting alongside Rugby School's academic tutors, the Arnold Foundation tutor team provides additional guidance, support and encouragement to the young boys and girls in its care, and also reaches out to their families through the Parent Liaison team. This dedicated pastoral engagement lies at the very heart of the Arnold Foundation and has contributed to its success.

Finding the right students, those who have a need for boarding and stand to gain most from a boarding education at Rugby, is crucial. Candidates are identified largely through our work with partner organisations which themselves are working with children in some of the UK's most disadvantaged communities. These organisations provide support through the recruitment process and afterwards with mentoring, guidance and space to study during the school holidays.

In its 450th anniversary year, Rugby School is celebrating its charitable ethos and Lawrence Sheriff's founding bequest in 1567, as well as the inclusive education of Thomas Arnold. The Arnold Foundation is very much an integral part of this ethos and culture; pupils benefit from the high standard of academic education at Rugby and participate in the vast range of sport, music, drama, art, visiting lectures and trips. In turn, the School community benefits from the diverse experience, background, energy and commitment that these talented young people bring to Rugby. Former Foundation pupils are now at university or have now graduated and embarked upon worthwhile careers; among them a TV journalist, actors, a doctor, accountants and a vet.

Arnold Foundation awards are funded entirely through voluntary donations. Our ability to help so many young people would not be possible without the huge commitment of our generous donors. During our anniversary year we will build on this commitment long into the future and through our legacy campaign *"if you will, they can"*. The Foundation currently has 35 pupils across all five year groups at the School and 115 young people who have benefited to date. Our 100th pupil funded by the Arnold Foundation joined the School in September 2015, a very special milestone.

Our regular events provide a platform for all those involved in the Foundation to gather together, and over the years we have offered a programme with fabulous speakers, committed advocates and an annual lecture which has attracted inspirational leaders from the Rugbeian community and beyond. At these events former Arnold Foundation pupils, the Ambassadors, reflect so eloquently on the transformational opportunity of a Rugby boarding education and their commitment to giving back.

Many schools have sought to emulate the success of the Arnold Foundation. It is testimony to this success that the national SpringBoard Bursary Foundation, which offers boarding opportunities across both independent and state boarding schools, was established on, and inspired by the Arnold Foundation.

"Before I went to Rugby I did not have the confidence to even apply for medicine as I felt I was 'not the kind of person' who applies to train as a doctor. Rugby taught me that actually nothing is out of bounds if one has the ability to do it well. I now apply this attitude to everything I do in life…..carrying out research at Oxford University, presenting my work at national medical conferences and being accepted on an exchange programme to research epilepsy at one of the USA's top hospitals. I cannot express how life-changing my time at Rugby was. Of course, the School helped me achieve good A level results, but I believe the true value of Rugby is not just the high grades, but more intrinsically in the values it instils. The Arnold Foundation does not just fund a few years at an exceptional boarding school, it profoundly changes the mindset of ambitious young people to give them the opportunity to transform their lives for the better."

Dr Michael Mather (C 06-08) is currently a junior doctor in Newcastle.

BOXING DAY TSUNAMI

2004

It had the energy equivalent to 23,000 atomic bombs, shook the earth by 1cm, spread across 600 miles and killed 230,000 people in fourteen countries.

The 2004 Boxing Day Tsunami took place in the Indian Ocean. Tectonic plates that had been pushing together for thousands of years caused a 9.0 magnitude earthquake, shifting the seabed by ten yards and moving trillions of tons of rock.

The third largest earthquake ever recorded lasted nearly ten minutes and caused waves up to 100ft high. Of the countries affected, the biggest impact was on Indonesia, Sri Lanka, India and Thailand.

In some places, the ocean retreated a huge distance before the waves came back in, prompting some tourists to wander the exposed sea bed and take pictures.

The tsunami prompted an enormous humanitarian reaction across the world.

UN Secretary General Kofi Annan said at the time:
"This is an unprecedented global catastrophe and it requires an unprecedented global response."

US President George Bush added:
"We join the world in feeling enormous sadness over a great human tragedy... The carnage is of a scale that defies comprehension."

Nigel Willgrass, a survivor who lost his wife in the tragedy, said:
"I wanted to take her wedding ring and they wouldn't let me. There was nobody there for me. It was just awful."

Petra Nemcova, a Czech model who survived, recalled:
"People were screaming and kids were screaming all over the place, screaming 'help, help'. And after a few minutes you didn't hear the kids any more."

230,000 people died on Boxing Day 2004 as a result of the Tsunami caused by a massive earthquake in the Indian Ocean

SAM RUDDOCK

Paralympic athlete **Sam Ruddock** (T 06-08), who suffers from cerebral palsy, joined the School in the sixth form in 1990 in Town House and later studied international relations at Loughborough University where he gained a first. He made his debut for the Great Britain Paralympic Athletics Team in 2012 and is the current British record holder in the F35 shot put.

Alongside his competitive career, Sam works as an Athlete Mentor for the Youth Sport Trust, working with secondary schools in the UK to encourage pupils to use the values and lessons learnt through sport.

2006.

2007 Gordon Brown

2009.

BARACK OBAMA

Barack Obama became the first black President of the United States on January 20, 2009. He saw off a strong bid from former First Lady Hillary Clinton to become the Democratic contender in the race for the White House and then defeated Republican Vietnam War veteran Senator John McCain.

Before taking office, Obama delivered his famous 'Yes we can' speech before a crowd in his home city of Chicago.

In the speech, he mentioned 106-year-old Ann Nixon Cooper from Atlanta who had voted in the election.

"…Tonight, I think about all that she's seen throughout her century in America - the heartache and the hope; the struggle and the progress; the times we were told that we can't, and the people who pressed on with that American creed: Yes, we can.

"At a time when women's voices were silenced and their hopes dismissed, she lived to see them stand up and speak out and reach for the ballot. Yes, we can. When there was despair in the dust bowl and depression across the land, she saw a nation conquer fear itself with a New Deal, new jobs and a new sense of common purpose. Yes, we can.

"When the bombs fell on our harbour and tyranny threatened the world, she was there to witness a generation rise to greatness and a democracy was saved. Yes, we can. She was there for the buses in Montgomery, the hoses in Birmingham, a bridge in Selma, and a preacher from Atlanta who told a people that 'we shall overcome'. Yes, we can.

"A man touched down on the Moon, a wall came down in Berlin, a world was connected by our own science and imagination. And this year, in this election, she touched her finger to a screen, and cast her vote, because after 106 years in America, through the best of times and the darkest of hours, she knows how America can change. Yes, we can."

Obama, who won a second term in 2012, introduced a universal health insurance package, stabilised the US economy and gave the order for US special forces to hunt and kill Osama Bin Laden.

ROBERT SWANNELL

Qualified accountant and barrister, **Robert Swannell** (Tu 63-68) left Rugby in 1968 and later chaired the Governing Body for five years from 2009. After a 30-year career with Schroders/Citi Group, where he chaired Citi Group's European Investment Bank, Robert became Chairman of HMV and a senior independent director of both The British Land Company and 3i Group plc. He is currently Chairman of Marks & Spencer. Robert's non-corporate roles have ranged from chairing the Government's Shareholder Executive Board to involvement with the FSA's Regulatory Decisions Panel and the Takeover Panel Appeal Board. He joined the School's Governing Body in 2004 and is a founder and Trustee of the SpringBoard Bursary Foundation.

2009 Barack Obama

2010 David Cameron

"Yes we can"… but perhaps it's been more difficult…

DIAMOND JUBILEE & THE OLYMPICS

On June 3, 2012, the Queen and other members of the royal family travelled aboard the barge *MV Spirit of Chartwell* along the River Thames to mark her Diamond Jubilee as part of a series of jubilee events.

The celebration, which came only a year after the public wedding of Prince William to Kate Middleton at Westminster Abbey, was followed a month later by the opening of the 2012 Summer Olympic Games in London.

As part of the spectacular opening ceremony directed by Danny Boyle, the crowd watched a video supposedly showing the Queen meeting fictional spy James Bond, played by Daniel Craig, in Buckingham Palace.

Shortly later a body double of the Queen was seen parachuting out of a plane before the real monarch took her seat in the Olympic Stadium.

The Olympics proved to be a huge success for the host nation with Great Britain winning 29 gold medals. British stars of the games included gold medallists Bradley Wiggins, Jessica Ennis, Greg Rutherford and Mo Farah.

The success of the London Olympics and the patriotic fervour of the Queen's Diamond Jubilee made 2012 a very special year

2012.

2014-2016
NEW WORLD

2014 PETER GREEN BECOMES HEAD

2016 AMBITIOUS PLANS APPROVED
TO CELEBRATE THE SCHOOL'S
450TH ANNIVERSARY IN 2017

FROM PAST TO FUTURE – PETER GREEN

One wonders what Elizabeth I's grocer, Lawrence Sheriff, would make of the School he founded in 1567. Would he take satisfaction from the fact that in nearly every sphere of life Rugbeians have made their mark on the world?

We have produced Prime Ministers of European nations, an Archbishop of Canterbury, and a Nobel Peace Prize winner. Thanks to one Rugbeian we have Alice in her Wonderland; to another, some of the most poignant lines of war poetry; and to another, young Tom Brown and his tormentor, Flashman. The men and women across the world who have taken an oval ball in their arms and run have a Rugbeian to thank for the game they play. Rugbeians have contributed to stage and screen, to politics, the arts, philosophy, medicine, and public life. They have upheld justice as judges and law makers; helped run governments, schools, universities; founded businesses; won Olympic gold medals. Hundreds have served with distinction and honour in all ranks of the Armed Forces and sacrificed their lives on the fields of battle.

Sheriff's vision was to establish a 'free grammar school' for local boys. While this was achieved in the early days, there is no denying that, in its Victorian heyday, Rugby's position as one of the great public schools of England was a significant step from what Sheriff had in mind. The distance Rugby had travelled from the principles of its founder led to the creation in 1878 of a second school, this time bearing Lawrence Sheriff's name.

More recently, it is perhaps the creation of the Arnold Foundation that has helped the School to re-connect more closely with its origins, providing a way for talented young people to enjoy the benefit of a Rugby education regardless of background and means.

Rugby School should honour and celebrate its past, but it should not be a slave to it. Should any Rugby Head, for instance, be bound by the words of a predecessor, however great his influence? Perhaps not, but we should not forget them. Thomas Arnold's famous *hendiatric* aim for Rugby was 'firstly, religious and moral principles; secondly, gentlemanly conduct; thirdly, intellectual ability'.

In reflecting on what Lawrence Sheriff had in mind for his School, and on the views of such educational titans as Arnold, what should be the aspirations of Rugby as it looks forward to its next 450 years?

At Rugby, when we speak of the three Rs we mean 'restlessness, reflection and rigour'. Encouraging a restlessness within our pupils and staff is a desirable pursuit. St Augustine described the primal yearning in each of us in his classic, *The Confessions*: 'Thou hast made us for thyself, O Lord and our hearts are restless until we rest in thee.' This is a theological point but en route to the final rest, we hope to fashion restlessness for the here and now, extending us intellectually, and pointing us to the *magis* – the more and the good. Restlessness means that we are vigilant, dynamic and open to growth, not content to drift in the currents of culture without making ripples. Rigour is integral to such restlessness, as we seek the greater good, the deeper reflection.

Our duty goes beyond imparting knowledge and coaching children to pass exams. It lies instead in helping them to use the potential they have been given wisely, adventurously, kindly and carefully, as they navigate a path through a world that will almost certainly change more in the next fifty years than it has in the past 450. The ability to recognise both the rights and needs of one's neighbour or the wider community and to acknowledge that they are as real as one's own is an essential characteristic of every Rugbeian.

We are not a school of privilege but a school of obligation. Our goals are to foster academic excellence, to nurture individual talents, and to equip our boys and girls with the tools to maximise their individual learning. Critical thinking, memory skills, goal setting and the use of new technology are blended with reflection, self-awareness and stillness. And through service we aim to form young people who can contribute intelligently and effectively to the welfare of society.

Arnold's *hendiatris* represents a breadth of purpose that today's target driven educational context is in danger of forgetting. Arnold recognised a modern concern - that education should address the formation of character, going beyond an understanding of learning as simply the acquisition of knowledge. He equated this with wisdom, which in Aristotelian terms would be called practical reason. The Ancient Greeks, as always, have a good word for this - *eudaimonia*: well-being flowing from each individual so that they make the most of their talents and abilities. In other words, the whole person is the whole point. The Rugby ethos, which we shall continue to uphold, provides the reassurance of a complete education: mind, body and spirit.

2014

2015

School pupils took part in the opening and closing ceremonies of the Rugby World Cup which was hosted by England. Hero of the 2003 World Cup team, Jonny Wilkinson and HRH Prince Harry also visited the School to be filmed as part of the opening ceremony film.

AT THE FOREFRONT – LUCINDA HOLMES

This wonderful book is a perfect illustration that the whole is greater than the sum of its parts; in other words, the success of Rugby School over 450 years has depended on its various components working together to develop the excellence of the institution.

Four of the themes of this book which covers Rugby's 450-year history are governance, Head Masters, pupils and buildings. Each has made its own indelible contribution and worked together to shape and make the Rugby School that we know today.

It is this shared determination to stand by the traditions and ethos of the School alongside the resolve to be at the forefront of teaching and learning which continues to guide us into our future.

From the first steps taken by Lawrence Sheriff in 1567 through to the opportunities and challenges faced by today's Governing Body, governance has provided the foundations on which the School has been able to stand for over four and a half centuries.

The most important responsibility of the Governing Body as the guardian of the School and custodian of its ethos, is of course the selection and appointment of the Head Master. The choice of Head is fundamental to the success of the School, and Rugby has had a remarkable gallery of Head Masters down the centuries – Thomas Arnold arguably set enduring principles and demonstrated to those who followed how it should be done.

Our Head Masters have sought excellence in all things and their staff work under their leadership and guidance to deliver it. If Head Masters are responsible for nurturing and fanning the flames of their pupils' talents, then ours have done their job well.

The roll call of those who have left Rugby to make their own mark on the world – boys and girls, from Britain and overseas – is long and distinguished.

Politics, academia, law, the Armed Services, medicine, the arts, business, technology, sport and science are among the many fields in which Rugbeians have played an important part and made a lasting impression.

We will never forget either the enormous sacrifice of the hundreds of Rugbeians who gave their lives serving their country, particularly during the 20th century's two World Wars.

Rugby is fortunate that so many of its central buildings, from the rebuilt School House at the heart of the School, to its Butterfield-designed near neighbours, are so striking and distinctive.

Many schools have buildings older or grander than Rugby but there are few vistas to rival the broad sweep of The Close and our multi-coloured Chapel standing with quiet, assured confidence in the background.

Nor can many schools match some of the more recent additions to the School campus with the state-of-the art Modern Languages building and the evolving Collingwood Centre.

This book has made our own Rugby School story all the more interesting by being set in the context of world history and it is astonishing to consider the development of the School alongside the momentous episodes and changes witnessed by the past centuries.

The pace of world change has increased and will apparently continue to increase and Rugbeians leaving the School in 2017 must be prepared not only to embrace that change but to develop and stimulate it as they enter the global marketplace.

Our own history shows that those who have had the privilege of a Rugby education have been given the tools required to achieve and prosper. At the heart of a 'whole person' Rugbeian education is the fundamental belief that respect and tolerance of others is key to flourishing and making a difference in the world.

Lawrence Sheriff could never have imagined in 1567 that his bequest to found a school would result in the Rugby School that we know today.

What his school will look like in 2467 AD, 450 years from now, is anyone's guess. But my hope is that Rugby School will continue to be at the forefront of the teaching and learning of young men and women from every background, and that Rugbeians will still be playing their full part on the world – or possibly interplanetary – stage.

Our collective thanks to everyone who has contributed to the glorious compilation of this history book.

Lucinda Holmes (D 78-80)
Chair of the Governing Body
November 2016

2016.

2016 Theresa May 🇬🇧

RUGBY SCHOOL 'FIRSTS'…

Apart from inventing the game of rugby football itself, Rugby School can lay claim to a wide range of other 'firsts'…

The Town's first fire engine… in 1780
The first to have boarding houses run by Masters… in 1829
The first to have its own gymnastics equipment… as ensured by Dr Arnold in 1835
The first science curriculum offered by a school… Natural Philosophy in 1849
The first Mission created by a public School… a Rugby Mission in India in 1848. The School's Rugby Clubs Missions in Notting Dale founded in 1889, and later Birmingham, were again the first of their kind.
The first to have its own art museum… in 1878, established in the TRR following Head Master Jex-Blake's hope that *"leisure hours would then be given by many boys to a delightful form of culture, often too little thought of at home or school"*.

The founding of the Rugby School Electric Lighting Company Ltd… in 1892 which meant that both the School and the Town had their own electricity supply.
The first game of rugby… in 1823.
The first to produce the written code of the game, the first to establish official games kit and the first to introduce Caps.
The first to create Australian Rules Football… through Thomas Wentworth Wills (Bradley).
The first to produce captains of both England and South Africa rugby teams.
The first to introduce a cross country run, the Crick, established in 1838 and said to be the oldest run of its kind in the world.

'from ELIZABETH to ELIZABETH': THE 450th ANNIVERSARY

As this book goes to print, the School is preparing to celebrate its 450th anniversary....450 years since Lawrence Sheriff left his bequest to fund a school in Rugby in 1567.

There are many ways to celebrate such a milestone and it is easy to remember the many firsts, the global achievements and the brilliant philosophy of our most famous Head Master, Dr Thomas Arnold. What really interested us were the key characteristics that make up Rugby School's DNA today.

So we began by asking all Rugbeians what they felt we should be doing to celebrate this anniversary... and we received 380 ideas! We then grouped them together under seven key headings:

Our Founder... Our History... Our Commitment to the Community... Our Global Reach... Our Sporting Heritage... Our Christian Faith and **Our Charitable Ethos**.

A programme of events and activities was then created to recognise and celebrate these headings and, when taken together, they reflect who we are.

OUR FOUNDER

It was Rugby-born Lawrence Sheriff's founding bequest in 1567 that sowed the seed of what was to become one of the world's top co-educational public schools. He had originally planned to leave a larger sum to found a school but reduced the amount to just £50. However, he later added eight acres of pasture land in Conduit Close to the bequest which was to become one of the capital's most cosmopolitan shopping hubs, Lambs Conduit and Rugby Streets in Bloomsbury. Some of this land has also since been bequeathed to Great Ormond Street Hospital.

We will celebrate this shrewd investment on our 'London Estate Day' on Friday, April 28, 2017, when the streets' traders will join together with Rugbeians and parents, bringing together many of those who have benefited from this bequest.

OUR HISTORY

The School's history will be brought to life through this anniversary book, *from Elizabeth to Elizabeth*. Featuring events at the School and in the wider world at the time, this book will appeal to avid historians and anyone with a connection to the School. It will demonstrate that for the past 450 years, the point of Rugby School has been to develop the character, personality and ability of the whole person.

From this book, we will also create an exciting, fun and informative 450th exhibition to be installed in the Collingwood Centre throughout 2017. As a walk through history, starting with Queen Elizabeth I through to Queen Elizabeth II, this exhibition will act as an educational experience for schools and visitors to the School.

OUR COMMITMENT TO THE COMMUNITY

Another essential part of our DNA is the School's commitment to the community. This will be marked on our Community Day to be held at the School on Wednesday, September 27, as a culmination of a year's fundraising by staff and pupils on behalf of the Bradby Club in Rugby. The Club, originally started in 1919 as a youth club for boys at a loose end, has since become a valuable service for young people in Rugby today.

It is planned that a new set of gates into The Close by School Field will be officially opened on this day too, to complement the Queen's Gates which were opened by Her Majesty to celebrate the School's 400th anniversary.

OUR GLOBAL REACH

Rugby School has been a global launch-pad for hundreds of pupils and, in return, hundreds of students choose to leave their own country and study here. We currently educate pupils from more than 30 different countries while our alumni, parents and staff number around 18,000 worldwide. To bring this incredible and far-flung community together, there will be a Global Day on 24 June culminating with a Gala 450th ball on The Close.

We are also organising 'The Global Pass'. A rugby ball will leave The Close on January 9 and will then be passed 450 times from Rugbeian to Rugbeian as it makes its way around the world. The ball will have a tracker unit installed so that its whereabouts can be checked via GPS at any time. It will return to The Close on the Community Day, September 27.

OUR SPORTING HERITAGE

One essential part of our DNA is our sporting heritage. From starting the game of rugby itself, inventing the game of Rugby Fives and involvement in the founding of the Modern Olympic Games and the London Marathon, there's plenty to celebrate!

The highlight for sport during 2017 will be the International Schools Rugby Sevens Tournament on March 24 and 25 when teams from Canada, Japan, Australia, New Zealand and South Africa will fly in to play on the famed Close along with all four home nations. There will also be an Inter-Schools Hockey Festival on October 1 along with events organised by the Old Rugbeian Sports Societies.

OUR **CHRISTIAN FAITH**

Members of the Rugby family flourish in a supportive Christian community. We believe a well-balanced individual needs a sense of spiritual awareness along with academic achievement and physical ability. The experience of holiness, an understanding of right and wrong, and respect for the worth of each human being create the invisible glue that holds our community together. To reaffirm these values and their importance over past years, today and into the future, Rugby School's Christian faith will be reflected at a Thanksgiving Celebration in Coventry Cathedral on 26 November 2017.

Peter Berners-Price (St 56-61)
Chair of the 450th Anniversary Committee

2016

2017 Donald Trump

OUR CHARITABLE ETHOS

Our charitable status at Rugby has been dependent on public benefit since 1601. In support of our long-term commitment to widening access to a Rugby School education, we offer scholarships and bursaries, provide financial support for the Lawrence Sheriff School, engage in community partnerships and organise fundraising activities for charities.

A tangible example of our charitable ethos has been the creation of the Arnold Foundation, which enables motivated young people from some of this country's most deprived communities to benefit from a boarding education. In recognition of the School's anniversary celebrations, all members of the Rugbeian community have been invited to include the Arnold Foundation in their will as an acknowledgement of our founder's original legacy.

450TH ANNIVERSARY
THE 2017 TIMELINE

In 2017, we are recognising the 450th anniversary of the founding of Rugby School. This anniversary gives us a wonderful opportunity to reinforce Rugby's position as a world leader in independent education and we hope that what we are planning for 2017 will engage the interest and support of all Rugbeians, staff and parents, worldwide. These special events will take place in addition to the regular programme of annual events organised by the School, the Rugbeian Society and the Arnold Foundation.

For visitors to the School throughout the year, an exhibition entitled *from Elizabeth to Elizabeth* will be installed in the Collingwood Centre based on images and text from the 450th Anniversary book as a dramatic visualisation of the School's history and alumni achievements. More mobile 'pop-up' versions will support smaller events during the year, both in the UK and overseas.

2017

Monday 9 January
THE OFFICIAL LAUNCH OF RUGBY 2017 will take place at the School in front of invited guests from Rugby Town, the world of Rugby Football, distinguished Rugbeians and the press. It will include the formal opening of the **450th Exhibition: *'from Elizabeth to Elizabeth'*.** The passing of a Gilbert rugby ball 450 times between Rugbeians globally will also start on its world journey from The Close.

Tuesday 21 March
A CITY DINNER hosted by the Lord Chief Justice, Lord Thomas (W 61-65), will be held at Middle Temple.

Friday 24 and Saturday 25 March
AN INTERNATIONAL SCHOOLS RUGBY SEVENS TOURNAMENT on The Close with invited teams from Canada, Japan, Australia, New Zealand and South Africa, as well as England, Ireland, Scotland and Wales.

Friday 28 April
The **RUGBY ESTATE DAY** when we can celebrate the bequest of Lawrence Sheriff in Lambs Conduit Street and Rugby Street in London.

Sunday 30 April
The **RUGBEIAN SOCIETY VS THE SCHOOL SPORTS DAY** where teams will compete at Netball, Rackets, Fives, Squash, Tennis and Sailing.

Saturday 24 June
The **GLOBAL EVENT DAY** connecting the Rugbeian community across the world. Events will be organised in Rugby, London, Dubai, New York, Hong Kong and Sydney to première a new film documentary about the School, and in Rugby, this will be followed by the **GALA 450TH BALL** on The Close.

Sunday 26 November
A **THANKSGIVING CELEBRATION** to end the 450th anniversary year is being planned in Coventry Cathedral.

Wednesday 27 September
A **COMMUNITY DAY** that will bring staff and pupils together in a day of fun and fundraising activity further to celebrate the School's charitable ethos and service to the community.

Sunday 1 October
An **INTER-SCHOOLS HOCKEY FESTIVAL** inviting teams from both the UK and overseas.

If you are interested in becoming involved in our anniversary celebrations through patronage, please contact Denise Osborne, Events Manager, on 01788 556121 or via email at do@rugbyschool.net

www.rugbyschool.co.uk/450th

These dates may be subject to change.

PATRONAGE

Through the generosity of our Patrons, we will be able to realise our ambitious plans for the 450th Anniversary, which will make it a very special year for the School. We have pleasure in recording their names for posterity…

FOUNDING PATRONS

Alexander and Susan Anton (Sh 73-77)
Peter Bennett-Jones CBE (Governor)
Peter and Brenda Berners-Price (St 56-61: Past President of the Rugbeian Society and Governor 02-06)
Mark and Sally Burton (SF 68-72)
John Chiene (SF 50-55)
John Collis (SF 74-76)
Giles Currie (K 47-52)
James William de Penning (SH 96-01)
Justine Mary de Penning (RB 00-05)
Sir Ewen Fergusson (SH 45-51: Governor 1984-2002, Chairman of the Governing Body from 1995)

Michael Fowle CBE (St 53-58: Governor 1988-2009, Chairman of the Governing Body from 2002)
Robert C. Hingley (SF 73-77: Governor from 2007, Deputy Chairman from 2012)
Lucinda Holmes (D 78-80: Governor from 2006, Chairman of the Governing Body from 2014)
Clifford Lam (Sh 88-93)
David Leathers (St 56-60)
Christopher P. Lees-Jones (W 49-54)
Simon C. Lees-Jones (K 79-84)
W Richard Lees-Jones (W 47-51)
William G. R. Lees-Jones (W 78-82)
George C. Magnus OBE (Sh 49-54)

John J. S. Marston MBE (Tu 49-53)
Simon R. T. Penniston (C 65-70: President of the Rugbeian Society and Governor 14-16)
Jeremy and Sally Rowlands (Parents)
Anthony Slingsby (St 57-61)
Julian G. Stanford (T 45-51)
Robert Swannell (Tu 64-68; Governor 2004-2014, Chairman of the Governing Body from 2009)
Alan Warner (Tu 63-68)
Ben Wilmot-Sitwell (M 09-14)
Jake Wilmot-Sitwell (M 04-09)
Luke Wilmot-Sitwell (M 06-11)

PATRONS

Mark Abrol (SF 77-82)
John P. Allen (Staff: 64-03)
Richard Saxton Appleby (M 54-59)
Jane Atkins (B 81-83)
Dr John Avery Jones CBE (SF 53-59)
Guy Ayling (W 84-89)
Nicholas Bacon (SF 77-81)
Robert L. Barclay (SF 61-65)
David B. Barraclough (B 48-53)
Allan Benn (T 42-47)
John H. Bennett (K 49-53)
Michael Benson (W 43-47)
Andrew Berners-Price (St 83-88)
Nicholas Berners-Price (St 85-90)
Michael Blair QC (SF 54-59)
Martin H. Bloomer (M 68-72)
Richard Bowes (C 45-50)
Peter M. Brown (K 48-52)
Clive J. Browning (SH 51-55)
Nigel Walter Buchanan (SH 47-52)
Martin Bunting (K 47-52)
Richard J. Carter (T 80-85)
Charles Clarke (SH 82-87)
Roger Howard Butler Clough (K 61-65)
Dr Gerald Christopher Coles (T 52-57)
Mark Adrian Cotton (C 89-94)
David Coubrough (St 68-73)
Angus Crichton-Miller (SF 53-58)
Alex Crombie (M 87-92)
M. M. Cruickshank of Auchreoch (St 47-51)
David E. Cutforth (SH 37-41)
Hugh Llewelyn Davies (St 55-60)
Tim Day (T 83-88)
David M. Dell CB (St 44-49)
Jonathan Dodgson Carr (M 52-57)
Peter Dow (B 50-51)
John Duke (C 78-82)
Antonio Echavarria (K 02-07)
Lucia Echavarria (G 04-09)

Alan Elliot (SF 50-55)
Stuart Errington (B 43-47)
Dr Dick Esslemont (W 55-59)
Ian Ferris (Sh 40-44)
Michael Fetherston-Dilke (B 62-66)
A William fforde (SH 70-74)
Robin Fletcher (K 79-84)
Simon France (St 45-50)
David H. Francis (W 51-55)
P. Noël Gerrard CBE (W 43-48)
Robert Gibson (C 72-76)
Blaise Guerrand-Hermes (SF 96-97)
Richard W. Haldane MBE (W 60-65)
Dr. Robert Hancock (SH 57-62)
The Rt Hon Sir Jeremy Hanley KCMG (K 59-63)
The Rev Canon Giles Harcourt (Tu 50-55)
Roger Harrison (K 46-52)
Peter J. W. Henderson (SF 65-70)
Ian F. Hoggarth (St 56-61)
John Hooper (B 48-52)
Michael Houdret (St 55-60)
The Earl Howe (Tu 64-69)
John Howkins (SF 59-63)
Jack Inglis (C 74-79)
Michael W. Innes (St + K 38-43)
David J. L. Innes (St 36-41)
John W. Jackson (Tu 43-47)
Adam Jeevanjee (W 10-15)
Jeremy Jevons (K 73-78)
Nigel Johnson-Hill (St 60-65)
Dr Philip Ioan Ellis Jones (T 58-63)
Major General Andrew Keeling CB CBE (Tu 56-61)
Peter Knight (T 48-52)
Georgina Krone (née Wynniatt-Husey) (Cr 87-89)
Martin P. Lee-Warner (C 57-61)
Jonathan Leslie (St 64-69)
Christoff Lewis (Tu 71-76)
Kenneth Loong (Sh 81-84)
Robert Lyons (K 56-60)

Robert Macvicar (W 71-73)
T. David Maxwell (SH 58-63)
Tim Mercer (Mercer Design)
Paul Milner (M 71-75)
Mike E. Morton (Sh 41-46)
Commander Jeremy Nash OBE (SF 34-37)
Dai Newington (SH 74-79)
Tirapongse Pangsrivongse (Tu 69-72)
Mark Pattinson (M 44-49)
John M. Plumb (St 59-63)
Eric Poyser (B 37-42)
Dr. Perry Edward Putnam (SH 43-48)
Dr. George E. T. Raine (B 48-52)
John M. Raisman CBE (SH 44-47)
Alan David Bedford Reid (St 60-64)
Michael C. Roberts (SH 50-55)
Anthony Mark Leslie Roberts (B 67-71)
David Sanger (SF 79-83)
Martin A. S. Simons (T 70-75)
Duncan and Alex Skailes (W 79-83)
Dr John P. Sproston (T 57-62)
Micky R. Steele-Bodger (Tu 39-44)
Berkeley Stewart (St 58-63)
David Sturrock (SH 56-61)
David A. Tanqueray (M 52-57)
David Theodore Thompson (K 54-59)
Henry R. Thompson (K 17-21, in memoriam)
John Twallin (K 46-51)
Chris P. Tyler (B 75-79)
Paul Viney (St 63-68)
Richard Warner (W 64-69)
The Rev Mervyn R. A. Wilson (SH 47-52)
John M. Wilson (T 47-52)
Stuart Andrew Wilson (W 81-86)
Sir Nicholas Winterton DL (St 51-56)
Isabel Wolff (Cr 76-78)
Roderick John Woodhead (K 53-58)
Paul Yates (W 70-75)

BOOK SUBSCRIBERS

We are also very grateful to the following pre-publication subscribers to our Anniversary book, from Elizabeth to Elizabeth, and have pleasure in recording their names for posterity to add to the history of Rugby School…

Mark Abrol (SF 77-82)	Damian Bell (SH 81-86)	John A. H. Butters (SH 52-56)
Andrew D. F. Acheson (SH 76-81)	Erica Bell (St 96-98)	Jonathan Buttery (K 72-76)
Murtaza Akbarally (C 86-91)	Martin Bell (B 80-85)	Edward N Cahill (W 96-01)
Jonathan L. W. Alden (T 74-79)	Michael Bell (SH 80-85)	Dom Cahill (W 13-18)
Celeste Grace Eva Allen (RB 15-20)	Cosmo Bellamy (Sh 14-19)	Jamie A.D. Cameron (Sh 97-02)
Felix G. Z. Allen (K 12-17)	Michael Stewart Benson (W 43-47)	S M Cammack (St 82-84)
John P. Allen (Staff 64-03)	David Berkeley (M 58-62)	C. M. R. Campbell (SF 54-59)
Tara Altamimi (St 16-18)	Andrew Berners-Price (St 83-87)	Alexander Nicholas Candlish (Sh 12-17)
Alexander Anton (Sh 73-77)	Nicholas Berners-Price (St 85-90)	Thomas Charles Candlish (Sh 14-19)
Harrison Anton (Sh 09-14)	Peter Berners-Price (St 56-61)	Tom Capewell-Salisbury (T 14-19)
Sydney Anton (B 16-21)	James Biles (K 14-19)	Paddy Powell-Capper (K 16-21)
Richard Appleby (M 54-59)	T. G. B. Birbeck (SH 91-96)	David Capron (T 59-64)
Ayuko Katie Aram (St 16-18)	John A. Blackford (Tu 49-54)	Luisa Carballo (G 17-22)
Richard Archer (W 56-61)	Michael Blair QC (SF 54-59)	Stuart F. Carnegie (B 61-65)
Henry W. Arculus (K 87-92)	Sir Michael Blake, Bt (SF 57-61)	C. R. Carr (St 44-49)
James E. G. Arculus (K 83-88)	Martin H. Bloomer (M 68-72)	Graham D Q Carr (M 52-57)
Robin G. Arculus (K 49-54)	Peter Boardman (C 55-59)	Hattie Carr (St 16-18)
Jessie Armbrister (Ma + S 09-16)	Dr Chris Bolter (T 60-65)	Jonathan D. Carr (M 52-57)
Simon John Armitage (SF 93-98)	P. Graham H. Bolton (M 63-67)	Jonty Carr (C 11-16)
Anthony John Nevill Arthur (C 45-50)	Raquel B. M. Bolton (Tu 01-06)	Mark Carr (C 77-82)
Charles Vincent Arthur (K 66-71)	T. G. Booth (B 51-55)	Alexander Carter (M 13-18)
Robert Arthur (SH 13-18)	Maia Bouchier (G 12-17)	Christina Carter (RB 91-93)
Zoë Ashby (B 13-18)	Christopher Bourne (M 48-53)	Richard J. Carter (T 80-85)
Peter Ashcroft (M 56-60)	Christopher Tristram Alexander	Martin James Carvell (W 94-99)
Richard Assheton (SF 07-12)	Mclaren Bourne (C 14-19)	Charles Carver (SH 74-79)
William Francis Assheton (Tu 70-75)	William James Augustus Mclaren Bourne (C 11-16)	Poppy Carver (B 12-17)
Jane Atkins (née Magill) (B 81-83)	Dick Bowes (C 45-50)	Samuel Carver (SH 04-09)
Mahmoud Atta (C 15-20)	S Michael A Boyd (Tu 39-40)	Tobias Carver (SH 07-12)
Genevieve Jagdeep Kaur Aulakh (S 11-16)	Benjamin Bradshaw (M 13-18)	Simon James Castello (SH 50-54)
Zachary Ajeet Singh Aulakh (T 04-09)	Henry Bradshaw (M 11-16)	Chris Cecil-Wright (Sh 84-87)
James Avery (Tu 88-93)	Nicholas D. R. Bradshaw (Sh 55-59)	Harry T. Chapman (SH 16-21)
Mark Avery (Tu 91-93)	Tam Bream (W 85-90)	Ollie F. Chapman (SF 16-21)
Nicholas Patrick Sewell Bacon (SF 77-81)	Peter Edward Bright (St 51-56)	David Charlton (St 76-81)
Rohan Singh Badial (Ma + T 16-23)	Katherine Annette Broad (B 10-15)	William Alexandre Louis Chaumet (K 14-19)
Nopadon Baholyodhin (SF 80-85)	Maxwell John Broad (Sh 14-19)	Anthony Cheshire (T 82-87)
Cecily Bain (St 12-14)	Daniel Pontoppidan Broby (C 78-82)	Talitha Georgiana Lloyd Chichester (St 15-17)
David Bain (St 66-71)	Cassandra Alexis Brogie (B 94-99)	Adnan Choudhury (SH 04-09)
David Ascroft Clutton Baker (SH 59-64)	Jason Edward Brogie (SH 92-97)	Laura Clark (B 15-20)
Luke Baldock (T 16-18)	C. G. D. Brook (St 53-58)	Charles Clarke (SH 82-87)
Tom Baldock (T 10-12)	W. A. D. Brook (St 14-17)	James Clarke (SH 79-84)
Richard Ballantine (B 66-70)	Jason Brown (M 84-88)	Jess Clarke (Tu 11-16)
Abisola Barber (St 08-10)	Peter Brown (SH 45-51)	Rosie Clarke (Tu 13-18)
Robert L Barclay (SF 61-65)	James A. J. Brumwell (Tu 79-81)	Freddie Clayton (W 15-20)
C. R. Barker-Bennett (K 49-53)	John C. H. Brumwell (Tu 48-53)	John Clegg (Tu 53-57)
Nicholas Barraclough (SF 80-85)	Richard W. A. Brumwell (Tu 83-88)	Richard Clegg (SF 76-80)
Pia Barratt (S 96-01)	Hannah E Bruneau (RB 13-17)	J. G. Cleverly (B 47-52)
Florence Catherine Barshall (G 16-20)	Max A W Bruneau (SH 15-19)	Gail Cockburn (B 93-95)
Dr. C. A. Barson (T 46-51)	Lochie C N Bruneau (SH 17-21)	Michael R. Cockerton (Tu 61-65)
Arkadiy Baskaev (Sh 13-18)	Auda-Mai Morgane Bryan (G 05-07)	Jack Cohane (SH 15-20)
Inna Baskaeva (B 16-21)	Andrew Buchanan (Sh 65-70)	Stella Miranda Cohen (Tu 14-19)
A. J. Bateson (C + Tu 38-43)	Timothy Michael Buckingham (C 90-95)	Georgina Colbourne (Ma + S 08-15)
Dinti Wakefield Batstone (D 88-90)	Maelon Rorke Buckland (Ma + T 14-21)	Isabelle Colbourne (Ma + S 15-22)
N. E. Bayman (Sh 54-59)	Peter Bullett (Staff)	Nicholas Colbourne (Ma + T 09-16)
Josh Beal (T 15-20)	Martin Bunting (K 47-52)	Peter Colbourne (T 15-20)
Tom Beal (T 12-17)	Alice Burbidge (RB 15-19)	Dr Gerald Coles (T 52-57)
Edward William Beard (M 12-17)	David R B Burn (SH 60-65)	Peter Colville (SF 52-57)
Patrick Beddows (B 74-79)	Jennifer Burton (Tu 05-10)	Eric Andrei Constantinescu (C 13-18)
Charlie Beere (Sh 09-14)	Mark Burton (SF 68-72)	Marc Alexandru Constantinescu (C 16-21)
Emilia Beere (Tu 13-18)	Oliver Burton (SF 02-07)	Ashley Coombes (Tu 81-86)
Jack Beere (Sh 11-16)	Timothy Burton (SF 01-06)	Jane Coombes (D 81-83)
Charlotte Bell (S 16-18)	Justin Busarakamwong (SH 90-93)	Mark Adrian Cotton (C 89-94)

Nicholas John Cotton	(Sh 79-84)	Lucia Echavarria (G 09-14)	H. Gessler (SH 48-52)

Nicholas John Cotton (Sh 79-84)
Stuart Cotton (SH 83-88)
David Coubrough (St 68-73)
George Alfred Coward (C 12-17)
Emma Clare Cowley (RB 94-99)
HM Lord-Lieutenant of Warwickshire
   T B Cox (Governing Body 2014-Present)
J. M. Crawhall (Tu 51-56)
Robert Stephen Craxton (T 62-66)
Angus Crichton-Miller (SF 53-58)
Mr & Mrs D Crockford
Anthony Croker Poole (SF 50-54)
Alex Crombie (M 87-92)
Neil R. Crombie (M 89-94)
Harry Cross (C 09-14)
Jack Cross (C 16-21)
Martin Melvin Cruickshank (St 74-79)
David Cutforth (SH 37-41)
Harriet IK Cuthbert (Tu 15-20)
Robert Cutler (St 67-71)
Leo James Dakin (Ma 16-19)
Harry Darby (K 15-20)
Mia Darby (S 17-22)
Gavin Darlington (B 62-67)
Elinor Dautlich (née Booth) (D 82-84)
Dr William Davidson (T 58-63)
Claire Davidson (Ma + D 97-04)
Tom Davidson (SF 97-02)
Ben Davies (SF 89-94)
Hope Davies (D 14-18)
Jonathan Davies (Sh 79-84)
Tom Davies-Pope (T 15-20)
Giles Davis (C 85-89)
Harrison Davis (C 16-21)
Alice Day (Ma + S 13-20)
Edward Day (T 86-91)
James Day (Ma + T 15-22)
Tim Day (T 83-88)
Guy de Boursac (B 59-63)
Chauncey De Los Santos (Sh 13-18)
James William de Penning (SH 96-01)
Justine Mary de Penning (RB 00-05)
Anna de Pourtales (G 14-19)
Michael De St Croix (W 43-46)
Maria Deery (S 12-17)
Jonathan Denison-Cross (SH 58-63)
Jacob Louis Denness (T 15-20)
O. G. Dereham (B 52-56)
Patrick and Alison Derham (Head Master 02-14)
Karl Kyriakos Bernhard Desselberger (SF 16-21)
Sam Gwynn Dewhurst (SF 82-86)
A E J Diamond (B 42-47)
Anthony R. Dobell (M 62-66)
Myles R. R. Dobell (W 00-05)
Richard P. R. Dobell (W 98-03)
Peter Dow (B 50-51)
Michael J D'Oyly (M 45-48)
N. J. Drake (SH 47-52)
D. W. Draper (T 50-54)
John Drysdale (Tu 62-67)
William George Russell Dudley (SF 16-21)
Holly Duke (S 14-19)
Lauren Duke (S 16-21)
Roderick Charles Duval (SF 64-69)
Antonio Echavarria (K 07-12)

Lucia Echavarria (G 09-14)
John Edge (K 59-63)
James Edmiston (M 57-61)
A.W.C.Edwards (Sh 59-63)
Thea Edwards (D 15-20)
C. J. Edwards (Housemaster M 99-05)
Nicole Egan (S 15-20)
Alan Christopher Elliot (SF 50-55)
David Phillimore-Grenfell Elliot (SF 32-37)
Graeme Arthur Elliot (SF 55-60)
Ian Clinton Elliot (SF 55-60)
Richard Ellis (M 97-02)
Edward Elmhirst (SH 13-18)
Titus English (SH 05-10)
Stuart Errington CBE DL (B 43-47)
Dr Dick Esslemont (W 55-59)
W.A. Esslemont (W 52-56)
Peter William George Evans (C 62-66)
Sue Evans (Cr + St 79-81)
Giles Everist (St 79-83)
Jonathan Patrick Feltrum Fagan (SH 12-17)
Harriet Rachel Feltrum Fagan (B 14-19)
Donald J. Fairclough (B 53-58)
George Knight Erskine Fairholme (SH 34-38)
Hugh Falconer (M 14-19)
Jack Falconer (SF 13-18)
Jeanie Falconer (Tu 16-21)
P. S. Farmer (K 49-53)
Archie George Bruce Farquharson (SH 13-18)
Rory Charles Bruce Farquharson (SH 11-16)
Thomas John Farren (M 13-18)
Mathieu Farren Verjus (M 17-22)
Charles S. Faulkner II (C 53-54)
Jeremy Fawcett (SH 84-89)
Hans Fechner (SF 16-21)
Richard Fechner (SF 87-87)
J. J. Fenwick (C 45-50)
Ian Ferris (Sh 40-44)
William fforde (SH 70-74)
Felix Fitch (SH 85-90)
Charles Flax (SF 13-18)
Robin Fletcher (K 79-84)
A. R. Fontes (SH 47-52)
Olivia Eugenie Flowers (Tu 08-13)
Nicholas Shien Wei Fong (K 15-17)
His Honour Giles Forrester (SH 53-58)
George Forsdyke (C 14-19)
Peter Forster (T 57-62)
Claire Jia Tsin Fossick (D 14-19)
Jack Kit Fossick (K 15-20)
Kit Fothergill (M 14-19)
Tilly Fothergill (B 15-17)
John McLean Fox (T 47-52)
Angelica Beau Fry (S 14-19)
Nathan James Fuentes Grant (Ma + T 14-21)
Dr Samuel KS Fung (C 78-82)
R. M. Furber (T 54-59)
Max Gamburg (M 13-18)
Alastair Gamble (W 88-92)
James Gamble (W 97-02)
James A. Gardener (Sh 15-20)
William R. Gardener (M 14-19)
Robert Garforth-Bles (SF 62-67)
Robert Hugh Stoten Geary (C 12-17)
P. N. Gerrard (W 43-48)

H. Gessler (SH 48-52)
Thomas St. John Harvey Gibbs (Ma + T 14-21)
John D. Gilbert (T 57-62)
Professor Bruce Gilbert (T 55-60)
Robert Gilchrist (Sh 46-51)
Ewen Gilmour (C 67-70)
Felix Gladstone (SH 13-18)
India Gladstone (G 04-09)
Jack Gladstone (SH 02-07)
Kinvara Gladstone (G 10-13)
Tara Gladstone (RB 06-11)
Xanthe Gladstone (G 08-13)
Amelia Rose May Glenn (St 16-18)
Grace Ellen Scarlet Glenn (St 14-16)
Holly Emma Gowen (S 13-18)
James Thomas Trevor Gowen (T 15-20)
Emily Gower (Ma + S 10-17)
William Gower (Ma + T 13-20)
Patrick Grady (W 15-20)
James C. Graham (Tu 89-94)
Paul M. Graham (Tu 90-95)
Nigel Gray (T 58-63)
Emily Green (D 13-18)
J. T. J. Green (Sh 81-86)
L. R. Green
Oliver Green (Sh 15-20)
Peter Green (Head Master 2014-Present)
P. A. R. Greenstreet (St 45-50)
Angus J ST G Gribbon (SH 65-69)
Eleanor Griffin-Smith (S 12-17)
Dylan J. W. Griffith (W 16-21)
Richard J. Grillo (SH 58-62)
Blaise Guerrand-Hermes (SF 96-97)
Brigadier A. B. D. Gurdon CBE DL (SF 44-49)
Henry Hugh Gurney (Sh 16-21)
D. Guthrie (T 41-46)
Ben Habib (M 79-84)
Adam J. P. Hackett (St 63-68)
Robert John Hadman (C 59-64)
Richard W. Haldane MBE (W 60-65)
Stephen Hall (C 60-65)
Stephen H Hall (Sh 46-51)
Donald Hamilton (Sh 59-64)
Molly Hammond (G 12-17)
Oscar Hammond (C 12-14)
Peter Hammond (C 15-20)
Neil and Lara Hampton (Staff 2001-Present)
Mouse Hamwee (B 16-21)
Patrick C. J. Hannan (M 11-16)
Iona Emily Hanson (St 15-17)
Lottie Harbottle (Tu 12-17)
Canon Giles Harcourt (Tu 50-55)
Thomas Hardman (SH 12-17)
William Hardman (SH 15-20)
Robin Hardwick (W 15-20)
Thomas Hardwick (W 15-17)
William Austin Hardwick (T 56-61)
Theo Hargreaves (SF 43-47)
D R W Harrison (K 46-52)
Revd. Doreen Harrison
Freya Harrison (B 14-19)
Sir Michael Harrison Bt JP (B 49-53)
R. J. M. Harrison (K 39-44)
Wesley Hartwell
Mohammad Fariz Hashim (B 87-89)

- 256 -

Jess Hastings	(RB 05-10)	George Jackson	(Sh 13-18)
Ollie Hastings	(SH 11-16)	Ian Robert Hart Jackson	(B 76-80)
Ben Hatton	(M 10-15)	Marcus H Jackson	(Sh 81-86)
Dan Hatton	(M 15-20)	Mark Lucian Jackson	(C 64-69)
Wills Hatton	(M 12-17)	Matt Jackson	(Sh 11-16)
Louis Alastair George Hatton	(Sh 15-20)	Adam Rahul Valliapeedikayil Jacob	(K 12-17)
Jordan Robert Thomas Hayward	(T 15-20)	Amy Tara Jacob	(St 11-13)
Nathan Jonathan Hazzan	(Sh 11-13)	Maya Sian Jacob	(St 04-06)
Sebastian Jonathan Hazzan	(Sh 15-20)	Tom Jaffrey	(M 05-07)
Malcolm Headley	(T 78-82)	Shahrukh Jafree	(B 89-91)
Revd. Alistair Heagerty	(K 55-60)	D. L. James	(Staff 67-72)
Alistair Helliwell	(T 77-78)	Harvey James-Bull	(C 15-20)
Toby Henderson	(SF 15-20)	Kamarul Jamil	(M 92-94)
John E. G. Hendry	(B 63-68)	Simon Jefferson	(M 71-76)
Clair Geoffrey Thomas Herbert	(T 50-55)	Katie-Jane Jermine	(B 95-97)
Edward John Watkin Hess	(SF 76-80)	Sophie Jermine	(B 94-96)
Emily Charlotte Flora Hess	(B 05-10)	Jeremy P. Jevons	(K 73-78)
John Peter Hess	(SF 47-52)	H.E. Johnson	(SF 69-74)
Nathaniel Charles Arthur Hess	(SF 09-14)	Leo Johnson	(T 14-19)
William Frederick George Hess	(SF 03-08)	Michael Johnson	(T 11-16)
D. W. Heys	(C 61-65)	Morgan Johnson	(SH 97-99)
J. R. Antony Hirst	(Sh 50-54)	Nigel Johnson	(W 48-52)
Rosa Hirtzel	(RB 10-13)	Mark Johnson-Hill	(St 80-85)
Olivia Hoareau	(St 13-15)	Nigel Johnson-Hill	(St 60-65)
Bartholomew Hobson	(SH 14-19)	Gareth Jones	(T 98-03)
Michael S Hockey MBBS FRCEM	(T 63-67)	Dr Philip Ioan Ellis Jones	(T 58-63)
Richard Hodder-Williams	(SH 56-61)	Eric Malcolm Mande Kabamba	(W 16-21)
Fergus Nathaniel Hodgson	(C 16-18)	Burhan Kamal	(W 89-94)
S. Louise Holland (née Hartill)	(D 78-80)	Harjeev Kandhari	(SH 87-92)
Walter W Holland	(T 42-47)	Jay Manharlal Kantaria	(M 89-94)
Chloe Holmes	(B 04-09)	Kamalesh Himatlal Kantaria	(M 82-86)
Henry Holmes	(SH 09-14)	Monica Sharma Kapoor	(Cr 90-92)
Imogen Holmes	(Tu 11-16)	Zakhar Kazantsev	(K 16-21)
Lucinda Holmes	(D 78-80)	Major General Andrew M. Keeling CB CBE	(Tu 56-61)
Peter Holmes	(SH 41-46)	Peter Kember	(Tu 79-82)
Will Holmes	(K 06-11)	Simon Kember	(Tu 77-81)
John Hooper	(B 48-52)	Edward J. R. Kendell	(W 12-17)
James William Holt	(SF 15-17)	Harry C. P. Kendell	(W 12-17)
Georgina Homer	(Ma + S 97-04)	Eleanor Kennedy	(RB 13-18)
Edmund Hon	(C 84-88)	Martin John Kenrick	(M 53-58)
Rashid Hoosenally	(St 84-89)	Peter Kent	(St 76-81)
Lucy Hoosenally (née Hughes)	(D 88-90)	Adam Kenworthy-Fahy	(Ma 16-22)
The Rev M Hopkins	(T 89-94)	Clive Rowland Kerner	(M 75-79)
Natalie Jayne Houlston	(Tu 12-17)	Thomas Michael Kerry	(M 15-17)
Adam Huckle	(Sh 94-99)	Harry Kesterton	(W 12-17)
Alan Huckle	(Sh 62-64)	Jack Kesterton	(W 09-14)
Neil James Hudson	(Sh 69-73)	Captain A.S.H.Kettle CB. RN	(T 38-42)
Annabel Hudleston	(RB 00-04)	Oluwaloseyi Khalidson	(K 15-20)
Marcus Hunter	(SH 09-14)	John King W	(49-52)
Olivia Hunter		P. C. Knight	(T 48-52)
Rory Hunter	(SH 11-16)	Alex Korotkov	(SF 13-18)
Rupert Hunter	(SH 74-79)	Jasper Kwesi Kraamer	(C 15-20)
Geoffrey Huntingford	(T 66-71)	William N. C. Krarup	(B 74-78)
Christian James Hutchinson	(T 16-21)	Kartik Kumra	(W 16-18)
James R. Ingleby	(Tu 59-63)	Tom Lachelin	(SH 50-54)
John M. Ingleby	(Tu 55-59)	Michael CK Lai	(Tu 83-85)
Tom C. Ingleby	(Tu 60-64)	Sofia Maria Laine	(G 15-20)
Alastair Inglis	(W 55-60)	Jocelyn A. Laing (née Stokhuyzen)	(S 96-01)
Jack Inglis	(C 74-79)	Stewart C. K. Laing	(SH 96-01)
David Ingram	(B 53-58)	Stuart Laing	(St 61-66)
Anna Ivanov	(S 15-20)	M. J. H. Lamberty	(Tu 60-65)
Sophia Ivanov	(S 15-20)	Kate Angharad Lamont	(D 96-01)
Alice Jackson	(G 16-21)	James Robert William Douglas Langham	(T 16-21)
Archie Jackson	(Sh 16-21)	George Langran	(Sh 14-19)
David Jackson	(T 75-79)	Choedoke Laosirichon (Ton)	(C 97-02)

David Latham	(SF 51-56)
Colin Latimer	(St 61-66)
Gavin Launder	(C 76-81)
Helen Lawson	(Staff 12-15)
Jeremy Lawson	(B 79-83)
Alexander Lawson-May	(M 10-15)
Captain Alan James Burnett Laybourne RN	(Sh 47-52)
Professor John Lazarus	(C 55-59)
Jack Lea Jones	(Sh 14-19)
Christopher Leathers	(B 55-59)
Martin P. Lee-Warner	(C 57-61)
Alicia Leech	(St 15-17)
David Lees	(K 50-54)
Hugh Campbell Leggat	(SH 54-58)
M. F. B. Leslie	(St 59-63)
Ian Frederick Lettsom	(M 07-12)
Sophie Levin	(RB 11-16)
Georgia Levin	(RB 14-19)
G. C. Lindop	(T 31-36)
J. L. Lindop	(T 28-32)
R. H. Lindop	(T 24-27)
Richard J Lindsay	(St 49-54)
Sean Lindsay	(St 81-86)
Charlotte Rose Lister	(St 16-18)
Mark Lloyd	(Tu 85-90)
R. H. Lloyd	(Tu 47-51)
Jeff Lo	(M 03-05)
Lucia Longfield (née Duff)	(D 01-06)
Kenneth Loong	(Sh 81-84)
Meg Lowe (née Newton)	(RB 89-91)
Brian Luker	(T 47-53)
Henry Robert James Lushington	(T 15-20)
Oliver William John Lushington	(T 13-18)
Thomas Benjamin Michell Luttman-Johnson	(M 16-21)
Andrew Lyndon-Skeggs	(St 63-67)
Patrick Lyons	(K 90-95)
Robert Lyons	(K 56-60)
Simon Machell	(SF 77-81)
Henry G W MacInnes	(M 92-97)
Miles MacInnes	(M 60-65)
Ian Mackenzie	(St 48-52)
Patrick Mackie	(W 51-56)
Peter T. W. Mackie	(St 76-79)
Zoë E. Mackie	(D 14-19)
Robert MacVicar	(W 71-73)
His Honour Bertram Maddocks	(Sh 45-50)
Eshan Madhvani	(K 16-21)
Caitlin Lucy Maguire	(Tu 16-21)
Louis Thomas Malin	(K 15-20)
Annabel Mangan	(S 15-20)
William Manners	(SH 12-17)
Holly Mansell	(RB 12-17)
Issy Mansell	(Tu 10-15)
Jess Mansell	(RB 07-12)
Alice Marchand	(B 16-18)
Eliza Marlow	(G 16-21)
Edward John Alexander Marquis	(W 63-68)
Alastair Marr	(C 58-63)
Elliott Marshall	(M 13-18)
Lucas Marshall	(W 16-21)
N. B. D. Marshall	(B 48-53)
Dennis Stanley Martin	(T 46-51)
Alex Masefield	(C 15-20)
Jessica Mason	(Tu 08-13)
Dr Richard C. St.H. Mason	(W 84-88)

Raphael Paul Varghese Mathews	(T 16-21)	Alastair Newton	(M 91-96)	Robert Prior	(C 81-86)
George Mathieson	(St 54-59)	Ian and Fiona Newton	(Housemaster Cr 76-92)	Harry Pryce	(SF 16-21)
David Maxwell	(SH 58-63)	Katie Newton	(S 16-21)	Roger William Purssell	(C 58-62)
William Murray McColl	(W 42-46)	Catriona Ng	(G 14-19)	John Raisman CBE	(SH 44-47)
Colin Andrew McCosh	(Tu 69-74)	Julian Ng	(W 12-17)	Douglas Ralston	(T 15-20)
Finlay D. W. McCreath	(SF 15-17)	Ronald Ng	(SH 94-99)	Fraser Ralston	(T 12-17)
Libby McCullough	(S 16-21)	Alysia Vivienne Nimmo	(S 14-19)	Robert David Richard Ray	(Staff 78-09)
Aiden Sinan McGuirk	(Ma + T 10-17)	The Hon F. R. Noel-Paton	(St 52-57)	Alan Rayden	(T 53-58)
Myles Patrick McKay	(T 11-16)	Lancelot Nomura	(Tu + W 00-05)	Dr. Auberon Redfearn	(B 48-52)
Orla Maria McKay	(S 14-19)	Dato' Ainuddin Noordin	(SF 73-77)	B. A. Reed	(St 45-49)
Ronan Noel McKay	(T 15-20)	Annabelle Norton	(St 15-17)	B ST G A Reed CBE MC DL	(St 45-49)
Clio McKibbin	(Tu 13-18)	Charlotte Norton	(St 15-17)	Alice Rees	(RB 14-19)
Mick McKibbin	(Sh 14-19)	Isabelle Norton	(S 17-22)	Alice Lydia Rees	(B 12-17)
Sean McKibbin	(Sh 16-21)	Lydia Norton	(RB 11-16)	Amy Alison Rees	(St 06-08)
D. S. McMullen	(SF 58-63)	Sophie Norton	(S 14-19)	Simon Regan	(Sh 84-89)
R. P. McMullen MBE	(SF 23-27)	Chidaro Nyirenda	(B 16-21)	Alan Reid	(St 60-64)
Harry McNee	(C 16-21)	Lunijka Nyirenda	(B 14-19)	Caroline Reid	(S 90-92)
Charles F. J. McQuilkin	(SH 10-15)	Zenga Nyirenda	(B 12-17)	Robert Barclay Seymour Reid	(T 76-81)
Hannah Meades	(RB 99-04)	Robert O'Farrell	(T 71-76)	Susannah Reid	(S 92-94)
Miranda Meades	(RB 02-07)	George Harry O'Keefe	(C 14-19)	Lily Reynolds	(St 16-18)
Alexander James Byrom Mee	(SF 03-08)	Akachi Onyia	(W 14-19)	Bernadette Marie Reynolds	(S 16-18)
Sarah Elizabeth Mee	(D 01-06)	Marion Orgill	(Staff 01-11)	Harriet Ellena Sumpter-Reynolds	(Ma + S 10-17)
Gerry Meek	(Staff 75-91)	Lucinda Orr	(B 95-00)	Lawrence Joseph Reynolds	(T 14-19)
Peter Middlemas	(SH 88-93)	Dave Orrock	(C 94-99)	Roger Richardson	(SH 45-50)
Alicia Middleton	(Tu 13-18)	Morgan Oruche	(M 16-21)	Lauren Rigby	(St 16-18)
Freddie Middleton	(SH 15-20)	Denise Ruth Osborne	(Staff 16-17)	Andrew Robb	(Tu 56-60)
M. D. Miller	(SH 41-45)	Alexander Pagendam	(SF 14-19)	Alexander Morgan Roberts	(T 14-19)
Richard J Miller	(SH 81-86)	Isobel Pagendam	(Ma + S 08-15)	Michael Roberts OBE	(SH 50-55)
Alice Miller	(D 13-18)	Stefan Palade	(T 15-20)	Mark Roberts	(B 67-71)
James Miller	(Sh 16-21)	Christopher Palmer	(K 08-13)	Fiona Robertson	(D 14-16)
David Milligan	(Sh 73-78)	Sophie Palmer	(D 11-16)	Gordon Ross Robertson	(Sh 44-48)
Lucinda A. S. Millner	(RB 97-02)	Nicholas Panitza	(Tu 76-77)	Alexander Francis Robinson	(SH 15-20)
Nick Mills	(C 03-08)	Major General M.R. Varoros Paribatra	(W 73-78)	Bethan Louise Robinson	(B 14-19)
Alexander Milner	(SH 17-22)	Alexander Parker	(W 15-20)	Ed Robinson	(SF 12-17)
Harry Max Milner	(SH 18-23)	Alice Parker	(RB 11-16)	Major Monty Robinson	(T 43-47)
Paul Milner	(M 71-75)	Edward Parker	(W 13-18)	Andrew E Robson	(SF 75-80)
S. H. Milward	(T 62-67)	Dilan Patel	(M 14-19)	Vincent Rogers	(M 14-19)
Catherine Joy Minards	(Ma + S 13-20)	Mark Pattinson	(M 44-49)	J. M. Roisman CBE	(SH 44-47)
Arun Mistry	(Ma + T 12-19)	Michael and Elizabeth Pattinson	(Staff 69-01)	Edward Romer-Lee	(K 87-92)
Flora Mitchell	(Tu 16-21)	Nicholas Pawson	(Sh 65-70)	George Romain	(K 11-16)
Gideon Kalebe Miti		Alice Payne	(G 13-18)	Tommaso Rombelli	(Sh 16-21)
Bijan Modjtahedi	(W 77-80)	Neil Lewin Payne	(M 57-61)	D. Michael Rose	(M 48-52)
Abigail Monteith	(Ma 15-17)	Steve Peacock	(T 70-74)	Flossie Rosser	(G 13-18)
John Montgomery	(SH 44-49)	Alastair Pei	(W 14-19)	Rugbeian Society	
James Moore	(K 17-22)	Anthea Pei	(D 16-21)	Helena Russell	(B 15-20)
David Lloyd Morris	(B 77-81)	John Peirson	(Housemaster W 65-77)	Richard Rutherford	(B 83-88)
Michael Lloyd Morris	(B 75-79)	S. R. T. Penniston	(C 65-70)	Alain Sabga	(M 98-03)
Philip E. Morris	(SH 45-50)	Sophia Perronet Miller	(G 13-18)	Nuri Sadeek	(W 16-18)
Stewart Morris	(M 92-97)	Victoria Perronet Miller	(G 15-20)	Jane Sale (née Helliwell)	(Cr 78-80)
Michael Ernest Morton	(Sh 41-46)	Charles Pertwee	(Sh 83-88)	James Sargant	(SF 49-53)
Abraham A T Mosley	(C 16-21)	Robin Phayre	(SH 63-68)	Nicholas Saunders	(C 14-19)
Joseph William Dixon Moss	(K 16-21)	Oscar Phillips	(M 16-21)	Sam Saunders	(C 13-18)
Tinius Figenschau Mosvold	(Sh 16-21)	Michael Pierson	(Tu 36-40)	Thomas Saunders	(SF 14-16)
Joy Mukerji	(SH 74-76)	Andrew S. D. Pierssene	(M 43-48)	Alan Sayles	(T 46-51)
Georgie Munnings	(D 15-20)	Andrew M. Pitt	(St 65-70)	Colin Scott	(M 63-68)
Karen Munnings (née White)	(D + Sh 78-80)	Rory Pond	(M 12-17)	Peter Scott Graham MA CA	(M 50-54)
Kitty Munnings	(D 11-16)	Doug Ponsonby	(M 11-16)	Lucy Seidler	(Tu 15-20)
Lautaro Agustin Musiani-Perez	(Sh 13-15)	Ned Ponsonby	(M 15-20)	Fouad Shakhshir	(K 76-78)
Omar Mustapha	(C 89-91)	Tilly Ponsonby	(RB 13-18)	Imogen Sharkey	(D 16-21)
Commander Jeremy Nash OBE DSC	(SF 34-37)	Dr. Robin Edward Poulton	(C 65-69)	Philip Sharkey	(M 15-20)
J. O. Nettleton	(Tu 40-44)	Eric Poyser	(B 37-42)	Charles Shaw	(M 52-56)
B Newbound		John James Prescott	(SF 57-61)	Dr. Michael M. Shaw	(T 62-67)
Dai Newington	(SH 74-79)	Simon Price	(M 87-92)	Miles Shaw	(T 13-19)
Alexander Newman	(SH 87-90)	Sophie C. A. Price	(St 14-16)	George David Cecil Shaw	(M 48-53)
Adam Newton	(T 14-19)	Johnny Pridmore	(T 54-58)	George William Richard Shaw	(M 81-86)

Samuel Benjamin Barnaby Shaw (M 84-89)	Professor C. J. Sykes (SF 60-64)	Tim Watts (St 66-71)
Tim Sheldon (Sh 79-83)	Michael Symington (SF 43-48)	Saskia Weir (G 10-15)
Andrew Shepheard (T 77-81)	Edward Tabor (SF 11-16)	Theo Weir (SH 12-17)
Nathaniel Sheppard (T 16-18)	Hugo Tailby-Faulkes (K 12-17)	Jonathan M. Weiss (K 13-17)
Toranosuke Shimada (Sh 12-17)	Imogen Tailby-Faulkes (D 10-15)	Charles Peter Welch (Sh 75-80)
Maximilian T R Shippey (Sh 16-21)	Madeline Tailby-Faulkes (B 17-22)	Dennis Yung Kuang Wen (SH 75-78)
James Henry David Sibley (M 12-17)	Natasha Tailby-Faulkes (B 15-20)	Patrick Yung Chih Wen (Sh 73-75)
Clementine Silverwood (Tu 16-21)	Marco Tam (C 94-99)	Stephen Yung Kwan Wen (SH 75-77)
James Simpson (SF 87-92)	Mahiro Tanaka (Tu 14-19)	Bella Wesson (20-25)
Walter Simpson (SF 61-66)	Supalert Tarmallpark (SF 79-83)	Philip Anthony West (T 57-62)
Jamie Sinclair (W 73-77)	Oguz Emir Tataroglu (C 15-20)	Magnus Wheatley (Sh 88-90)
Ben Skailes (C 12-17)	Nigel Philip Seth Taylor (Sh 62-67)	C. D. White (T 47-51)
Duncan Skailes (W 79-83)	Max Oliver Taylor (M 16-21)	Freddie Whitelaw (W 14-19)
Ollie Skailes (C 09-14)	George Ernest Taylor (T 16-21)	George Whitelaw (W 17-22)
Toby Skailes (C 07-12)	Mr & Mrs O Taylor	P. J. M. Whiteman (SH 50-55)
D. M. B. Skinner (K 55-60)	Sarah Taylor (Ma + S 97-04)	David Wigley (B 59-64)
Jeremy John Skinner (K 50-55)	Jonathan Teare (Sh 60-64)	Charlie Wilkinson (SH 70 -74)
Skye Emily Slatcher (Ma 16-23)	Bede Henry Charles Teeton (Ma 16-23)	Rod T. Willard (C 53-57)
Peter James Sleight (T 63-68)	Ian N. Tegner C.A. (C 47-51)	Jonathan Willetts (W 09-11)
James Stanley Slemeck (C 16-21)	Martin Ignatius Teo (SH 13-17)	Eliza Williams (G 13-18)
Anna Sloan (RB 16-21)	David Theodore Thompson FRCS FRCR (K 54-59)	Eve Williams (G 11-16)
Matt Sloan (SF 83-88)	A. E. L. Thomson (SF 14-19)	Guy Michael Williams (SF 13-18)
Tom Sloan (SF 15-19)	Caoimhe Tara Lily Tobin (B 16-21)	John Bruce Alexander Williams (W 50-55)
Dr. Alan Smith (W 42-47)	Conor Tobin (SF 15-20)	Mark B. Williams (Tu 90-95)
Helena M F Smith (St 95-97)	Sean Tobin (SF 15-20)	Michele Carol-Ann Williams (D 92-94)
Peter J. Smith (C 57-62)	G. R. C. Todd (C 46-51)	Rhiannon Williams (Ma + S 97-04)
Peter Strother Smith (SF 60-64)	Brett G. Tollman (SF 76-79)	James Williams-Bulkeley (W 84-89)
Sebastian James Edward Somervail (SH 12-17)	Edward Towne (M 60-65)	Hugh Williamson (Tu 60-65)
Harry Sparke (T 16-21)	Ed Trelinski (Staff 2009-Present)	J. M. Wilson (T 47-53)
Christopher Edward Spencer (C 93-98)	Commander AB Trentham (SF 59-64)	Revd. M. R. A. Wilson (SH 47-52)
Nicholas Spencer (C 91-96)	David W. Trimble (St 52-58)	Beno Wiltshire (SF 15-20)
Mary Spenser-Higgs (Staff 11-16)	Clemmie Trott (G 17-22)	Ed Wiltshire (SF 11-16)
Marlon Spiers (Sh 15-20)	Ludo Trott (M 13-18)	Matthew Windett (St 83-85)
David Spottiswoode (St 64-69)	Richard Noy Trounson (SH 64-69)	Michael Anthony Wingate-Saul (SF 51-56)
Laurence Andrew Springall (T 16-21)	Paul Tumim (M 77-81)	Alex Winter (SF 11-16)
S. II. W. Spurrier (C 54-59)	D. G. Turnbull (SH 35-40)	Sir Nicholas Winterton DL (St 51-56)
A. T. Stanford (T 48-53)	Isobel Turner (RB 14-19)	Robert 'Bob' Winterton (St 74-79)
J. G. Stanford (T 45-51)	John Twallin (K 46-51)	Isabel Wolff (Cr 76-78)
J. R. Stanford (T 44-49)	Rose Tweddle (G 05-07)	Matthew Wong (Sh 96-00)
Alexander Stasinski (T 14-17)	Nick Tyler (B 77-81)	Robert Wood (SH 16-21)
Duncan Steele-Bodger (Tu 75-79)	Keita Umetani (C 13-18)	Timothy Wood (B 77-81)
Guy Steele-Bodger (Tu 74-78)	Yuta Umetani (C 16-21)	John M. Woodall (W 46-50)
Micky Steele-Bodger (Tu 39-44)	D. A. Urquhart (K 65-70)	Christopher Woodd-Walker (Sh 49-54)
Arabella Stephenson (St 15-17)	R. P. Vacher (St 81-86)	C. Martin Woodhead (SH 60-65)
Patrick Stephenson (W 47-52)	T. A. B. Vacher (St 83-88)	Daisy Woodley (Tu 14-19)
Berkeley Stewart (St 58-63)	Robert Vallings (Sh 57-61)	Emma Woods (née Packer) (S 83-85)
Margaux Steyaert (G 07-12)	Benjamin van Laar (T 10-15)	Gemma Woodward (RB 88-90)
Manon Steyaert (G 09-14)	Ellie van Laar (S 14-19)	Georgina Charlotte Woodward (S 15-20)
Sir James Stirling (B 44-49)	Jonathan C. Vaudrey (SF 61-66)	Dilly Woolliams (St 16-18)
Graham Stokhuyzen (T 87-92)	Joseph Vaudrey (SF 70-75)	Charlie Wreford-Brown (Sh 63-66)
Wiet A. Stokhuyzen (T 85-90)	Will Vaughan (SH 16-21)	Chris Wreford-Brown (Sh 59-63)
Angus Strachan (Sh 16-21)	Paul Viney (St 63-68)	Samuel Wright (K 13-18)
Sir Hew Strachan (K 63-67)	Lily von Möll (B 15-20)	Christopher Wright (Sh 10-15)
I. G. C. Stratton (Tu 52-56)	Freddie Walker (SF 12-17)	Lauren Wright (Tu 13 -18)
Duncan Stuart CMG (M 47-53)	Seb Walker (SF 12- 15)	Skye Tianyi Wu (G 17-22)
James Stuart (M 78-83)	Charles Walker (SF 70 -75)	Angharad Imogen Wylie (Ma + S 12-19)
Patricia Stuart (St 81-83)	David Wallace (K 66-71)	Elen Elizabeth Wylie (Ma + S 13-20)
Ella Sturley (S 12-17)	Gary Waller (B 59-63)	Christopher Robson Corbin Xavier (W 15-20)
David P. Sturrock T.D W.S (SH 56-61)	Brian Walton (Former Staff)	Jethro Chung Hei Yang (W 16-21)
Michael Suddaby (K 12-17)	David Walton (Tu 59-63)	Jeffrey Yang (K 78-83)
Lucy Suddaby (St 08-10)	Luke Wandless (W 15-20)	Jeremy Yong Hao (Sh 03-07)
Mohamad Zubayr Careem Sulaiman (SH 61-65)	Major General Robert Ward (SH 49-53)	Nicholas Youell (K 62-67)
Robert Swannell (Tu 64-68)	Alan and Sue Warner (Tu 63-68)	Jessica Young (S 14-19)
Georgia Sweeting (St 16-18)	Professor John A. H. Wass (M 61-65)	Olena Yudina (St 16-18)
Alastair Sword (B 78-83)	Alexander Watson (SF 16-21)	Ivan Zhevago (M 12-17)

PARTNERS

We would also wish to record our sincere appreciation for those commercial organisations who will also be supporting our 450th Anniversary year…

As Principal Partners…

DHL is the leading global brand in the logistics industry. With about 340,000 employees in more than 220 countries and territories worldwide, DHL connects people and businesses securely and reliably, enabling global trade flows. With specialised solutions for growth markets and industries, a proven commitment to corporate responsibility and an unrivalled presence in developing markets, DHL is decisively positioned as "The logistics company for the world". DHL was Official Logistics Partner of Rugby World Cup 2015 and currently partners with the World Rugby Sevens Series and Aviva Premiership side Harlequins.

Quilter Cheviot has built a strong reputation over several hundred years as a respected firm of investment managers. Quilter Cheviot focuses on structuring and managing bespoke portfolios for private clients, professional intermediaries, charities, trusts and pension funds. Throughout our history, our standards and values have remained consistent. Our impartial approach, high standards in personal service, drive to build and preserve the wealth of our clients and belief in the importance of a robust investment and underlying processes have remained unchanged.

Chartwells is the leading provider of contract catering and support services to the education sector in the UK. At Chartwells, we take our responsibility of catering for today's children and young adults seriously. We know it's not just the food on the plate that is important but a real understanding of health and nutrition too. Our simple set of commitments - Eat, Learn, Live - helps us to educate young people about how to have a happy, safe and healthy lifestyle while contributing to a sustainable world.

As Individual Event Partners…

Farebrother is an established Practice of commercial, retail and leisure Real Estate advisers and Chartered Surveyors. Working across Central London and the UK, Farebrother provides a full range of services, including Asset Management, Investment, Leasing, Development and Professional advice to a range of landlord and occupier clients. We are proud to support The Governing Body of Rugby School on their 450th year celebrations. A fantastic achievement and we look forward to being part of the festivities to mark such a landmark occasion.

De Boer is market leader in the rental of fully fitted temporary locations for large events and commercial applications. De Boer was founded in 1924 and is headquartered in Alkmaar, The Netherlands. De Boer now has offices in the Netherlands, Germany, Belgium, the UK, France, Spain, Sweden, Qatar and Abu Dhabi. It is also represented in the United States.

450th ANNIVERSARY: COMMITTEE MEMBERS

We are very grateful to all those Committee members who have very kindly given their time and thought to the planning of the School's 450th Anniversary year…

Tracey Ahmet	Rugbeian Society Executive Assistant
John Allen	Past Staff
Tristan Baker	(Tu 92-97)
Peter Berners-Price	(St 56-61, Chairman, 450th Anniversary)
Edward Boddington	(K 78-83)
Simon Brown	Director of Sport
Andrew Chessell	Artistic Director
Charles Clarke	(SH 82-87)
David Clews	(K 76-80)
Tim Cox	HM Lord-Lieutenant of Warwickshire
Tim Day	Teacher (Classics), (T 83-88)
Mindy Dhanda	Teacher (Chemistry)
Jake Elmhirst	(B 81-85)
Michael Fowle CBE	(St 53-58)
Brenda Green	Teacher (English)
Peter Green	Head Master
Neil Gutteridge	Assistant Head (Co-Curricular)
Katie Harries	(St 00-02)
Matthew Hodder-Williams	(SH 88-93)
Lucinda Holmes	(D 78-80, Chairman, Governing Body)
Amanda Hunter	Head of Marketing
Helen Jackson	Parent
Gareth Lloyd-Jones	(M 80-84, President Elect, Rugbeian Society)
Rusty MacLean	Archivist (Teacher)
Toby Marsh	(SH 88-93)
Tim Mercer	Director, Mercer Design
Denise Osborne	Events Manager, 450th Anniversary
Simon Penniston	(C 65-70, President, Rugbeian Society)
Richard Poole	Commercial Manager
Michael Powell	Teacher (Cricket)
Gabrielle Pütter	(B 04-09)
Sally Rosser	Deputy Head (Pastoral)
Tracey Skinner	Manager, School Shop
Heather Smith	(St 02-04)
Jonathan Smith	Teacher (Modern Languages)
Anthony Thomas	Chair of Governors, Lawrence Sheriff School
Becky Ukleja	(G 06-11)
Kerry Wilson	Director of Development

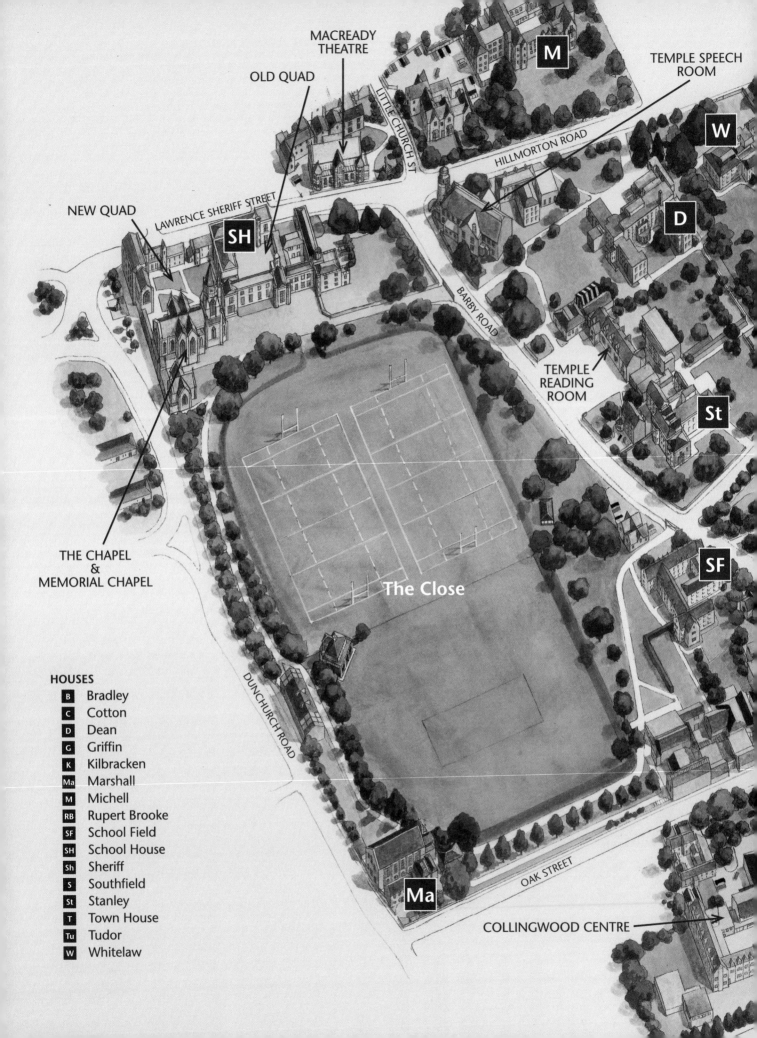

MACREADY
THEATRE

OLD QUAD

M

TEMPLE SPEECH
ROOM

W

LITTLE CHURCH ST

HILLMORTON ROAD

D

NEW QUAD

LAWRENCE SHERIFF STREET

SH

BARBY ROAD

TEMPLE
READING
ROOM

St

The Close

SF

THE CHAPEL
&
MEMORIAL CHAPEL

DUNCHURCH ROAD

HOUSES

B	Bradley
C	Cotton
D	Dean
G	Griffin
K	Kilbracken
Ma	Marshall
M	Michell
RB	Rupert Brooke
SF	School Field
SH	School House
Sh	Sheriff
S	Southfield
St	Stanley
T	Town House
Tu	Tudor
W	Whitelaw

Ma

OAK STREET

COLLINGWOOD CENTRE